THIS
BELONGS
TO

# Gifts & Crafts from the Garden

# Gifts & Crafts from the Garden

## Over 100 Easy-to-Make Projects

### Maggie Oster

Rodale Press, Emmaus, Pennsylvania

For my parents,
who have taught me so much
about gardening
and crafts,
but most of all
about giving.

Printed in the United States of America on recycled paper containing a high percentage of de-inked fiber.

Book Design by Linda Jacopetti

Illustrations by Frank Fretz

Photos Styled by Kay Lichthardt and Marianne G. Laubach

We would like to thank the kind people whose homes added grace and charm to our photographs: artists Don and Pauline Campanelli of Warren County, New Jersey; Althea Yuracka of Allentown, Pennsylvania; and John and Bernice Emmett.

**Library of Congress Cataloging-in-Publication Data**

Oster, Maggie.
     Gifts and crafts from the garden : over 100
        easy-to-make projects / Maggie Oster.
            p.      cm.
     Bibliography: p.
     Includes index.
     ISBN 0-87857-775-0
     1. Fiberwork.    2. Dried flower arrangement.
        3. Handicraft.    I. Title.
     TT873.O77    1988
     745.92 – dc19                         88-14845
                                             CIP

2   4   6   8   10   9   7   5   3   1   hardcover

# Contents

**Acknowledgments** . . . . . . . . . . . . . . . . . . . . . . . . . . . . . . . . . . . . . . . . . .   vi

**Introduction.** Crafts from the Garden . . . . . . . . . . . . . . . . . . . . . . . . . .   vii

**Chapter 1.** Crafts from Dried Flowers, Herbs, and Grasses  . . . . . . . . . .   1

**Chapter 2.** Crafts from Pressed Flowers  . . . . . . . . . . . . . . . . . . . . . . .   68

**Chapter 3.** Potpourri and Related Crafts  . . . . . . . . . . . . . . . . . . . . . .   81

**Chapter 4.** Beauty Basics  . . . . . . . . . . . . . . . . . . . . . . . . . . . . . . . . . .   97

**Chapter 5.** Crafts from the Landscape  . . . . . . . . . . . . . . . . . . . . . . . .   112

**Chapter 6.** Crafts from Corn and Wheat  . . . . . . . . . . . . . . . . . . . . . .   135

**Chapter 7.** Crafts from Fruit and Vegetables  . . . . . . . . . . . . . . . . . . .   148

**Appendixes: 1.** Tying the Perfect Bow  . . . . . . . . . . . . . . . . . . . . . . .   165

**2.** Supplies and Tools  . . . . . . . . . . . . . . . . . . . . . . . . . . . . .   166

**3.** Dress Pattern for Apple Doll  . . . . . . . . . . . . . . . . . . .   168

**4.** Sources  . . . . . . . . . . . . . . . . . . . . . . . . . . . . . . . . . . . .   169

**Bibliography** . . . . . . . . . . . . . . . . . . . . . . . . . . . . . . . . . . . . . . . . . . . . .   172

**Index** . . . . . . . . . . . . . . . . . . . . . . . . . . . . . . . . . . . . . . . . . . . . . . . . . . .   176

# Acknowledgments

Although writing may be a solitary occupation, putting a book like this together requires a cast of thousands. Many people have played roles, both large and small, in the years that this one has been in process. I am deeply indebted and grateful to those who have contributed in so many ways.

First, I want to thank the people at Rodale who encouraged, nudged, and supported me: Anne Halpin, for starting me on this project; Michael Lafavore, for seeing me through the writing stage; and Ellen Cohen, for her grace, patience, diplomacy, and editorial skills in guiding it to fruition.

I am also indebted to the craftspeople who have been my inspiration and sources of ideas, techniques, and many of the illustrated projects: Mary Jane Taylor of Cornfield's in Corydon, Indiana, for taking a chance on me and letting me photograph many of her crafts for the initial presentation, and for her and her daughter Jeni's exquisite hat, basket, and wreath designs with dried flowers; Wendy Cooper of the Posy Bowl in Corydon, Indiana, for her style and creativity, and for her skeletonized leaf arrangement, basket with dried flowers, and glycerinized magnolia leaf wreath; Peggy Leake of Cottage Gardens in Louisville, Kentucky, for her generosity and her elaborate dried flower wreath and cone tree designs; Heidi Clift of On the Wind in Mountain View, Missouri, for the delightfully trimmed garlic braid design; Lynne Gream of New Albany, Indiana, for her long-enduring friendship, for showing me the great fun of spontaneity with crafts, and for her vegetable printing designs; Maybelle Collins of Georgetown, Indiana, for sharing her knowledge and skill of cornshuck seating; Davy Dabney of the Herb Greenhouse in Louisville, Kentucky, for coming through in the eleventh hour with some hard-to-find supplies; the members of the Kentuckiana Unit of the Herb Society of America, for their incredible individual and collective talent and support; the people who made crafts that were deleted from this book – hopefully we'll have a chance to use them in the future; and Lucille and George Oster, for their sense of adventure, for being willing not only to do the crafts they already knew how to make but new ones as well, and for untold hours of every possible type of assistance.

Finally, I want to thank the many friends, near and far, who have kept me and my life together: the ones who finished the house and surroundings, and who kept the faith, the farm, office, and garden in order, the tears dried, and the laughter coming. A special thanks to Ilze Meijers, Ron King, and last, but very certainly not least, Peter Watson.

# Introduction
# Crafts from the Garden

The house in which I spent my first six years was a large, old, rambling place with lots of nooks and crannies that were perfect for a child with a love of fantasy. My favorite place was an offset of the living room with a little desk and chair hidden behind the sofa. Here was the place where construction paper, paints, crayons, glue, leaves, flowers, and butterfly wings first came together. I spent many delightful hours creating cards, pictures, covered boxes, and other objects that preschoolers are likely to do, especially preschoolers with doting, creative mothers.

When I was about five years old, my mother was a 4-H craft leader. Her basketmaking workshops had me enthralled. After each basketry session, I'd try my hand at weaving baskets under her direction. Later, in grade school, pupils who completed their work quickly and correctly could use their spare time decorating bulletin boards and doing craft projects. One such project was making a doll-size log cabin complete with a loft, tiny twig ladder, cornshuck mattress, miniature quilt, and other furnishings. Another project involved making puppets and a theatre, then putting on a show.

Through the years, my interest in gardening and crafts has followed a steady but circuitous path. By age ten, I was very involved with cooking and table settings. This spurred my interest in flower arranging; several years later came corsage making. Cornshuck and dried apple dolls, gourd bird feeders, pine and pinecone wreaths, Indian corn door swags, vegetable block printing, unicorn plant birds, yule log candle holders, and sachets all hold special attachment in my memory from my "growing up" years.

Because I had been exposed to vegetable and flower gardening since early childhood, it seemed only natural to become a horticulture student in college. During my undergraduate years, I was able to work at a local flower shop to supplement my college allowance. Needless to say, it was also an invaluable learning experience. In graduate school, I did yard work to augment the income from my fellowship. In addition, I wrote a weekly column on gardening for the local newspaper.

Since college I have lived in a variety of places, sometimes with lots of room, more often with very little. At present I have about the best space for craft work that I've ever had. My basement laundry/furnace/utility area is finished with vinyl tile flooring, drywall, paneled ceiling, recessed lighting, wood cabinets, and a large sink. In the adjacent hallway are long open shelves for books and storage.

The basement comes out at ground level, so the window over the sink looks out on a woodland setting and planters filled with flowers. This sink area is handy because it makes water and cleanup space readily accessible. The cabinets offer lots of storage space and a long work surface.

Having a work area like this allows me to leave out craft projects that are incomplete without their being in the way of other tasks. The storage is great, not only for supplies but also for completed projects. I try to keep a variety of completed crafts on hand to use as bread-and-butter, special occasion, and thank-you gifts, as well as remembrances to friends.

To learn new crafts and new materials and techniques, I attend a lot of craft fairs, visit craft and gift shops, participate in workshops, and talk with other people who love handicrafts. Magazines, books, and catalogs also offer endless new ideas.

Since you're already looking at this book, you most likely have an inherent interest in crafts. But perhaps you've never really thought about the many roles that crafts can take in people's lives. Obviously, they are a form of recreation. Crafts offer a creative use of our leisure time, and a way to relax, have fun, and relieve stress. They offer a break from strictly mental work, and an outlet for frazzled nerves or excess energy.

By doing something constructive, we make our lives seem more worthwhile. There is also a therapeutic value to crafts; they have long been used to hasten the recovery of the sick and injured. Acquiring craft knowledge is a lot like the old adage about riding a bicycle; once learned, skills can be shelved and brought out again years later.

Crafts and children go hand-in-hand. While they're having a great time playing, they'll also be learning patience, perseverance, self-control, manual dexterity, judgment, resourcefulness, creative expression, originality, and the ability to see possibilities.

Many crafts offer not only a historical link with the past but also an opportunity for different generations to play together. Working on craft projects with other people offers us a chance to develop new friendships and enrich old ones. Further, many of the crafts we make are genuinely useful in our homes and gardens for personal use as well as for gifts.

The benefits of gardening and crafts in my life run much deeper than the obvious tangibles of income and career. Being able to do the flowers for a friend's wedding, making dried bouquets and arrangements for churches, giving homemade potpourri or wreaths as presents – all this has a value that can't be measured in dollars and cents. Over the years, my involvement in gardening and crafts has instilled in me a sense of self-confidence and has been an outlet for my creativity. Sharing both the skills learned and the end products of my efforts is a very personal way of saying to people that I love and care about them.

Although I was very fortunate in having the "growing up" environment that I did, I firmly believe that each person has the ability to be creative, and that our creativity needs to be exercised just as our muscles do. Creativity is not the exclusive province of the painter, pianist, or author. Virtually anyone is capable of having an original thought and expressing it. Sometimes all that is needed is to have our adult fears banished by allowing ourselves to be as free as a child once more.

That's not to say that you'll necessarily be highly skilled at everything you try to do. Remember that the outcome is less important than the process. The experience of using a medium, whether it is dried flowers or watercolors, and investing one's own feelings and ideas into it helps an individual gain confidence about the decisions involved in personal expression. In addition, it allows a person to develop visual perception, observational powers, and an understanding of what is beautiful or special about the environment.

In this book I have included the methods necessary to complete each project satisfactorily. Directions are often open-ended, so that you can let your imagination fly while adding your own personal touch to projects. Because there are so many variables of size, shape, form, and texture in nature, the end product will always be distinctive.

This format allows the book to be used by a wide range of people. A plaster of paris leaf imprint is a Bible-school project in a child's hand, or an abstract relief in the hands of a skilled potter or jeweler.

In tandem with these thoughts, I repeatedly encourage you to experiment throughout this book. Experimentation is how we learn and grow. If you're not happy with the way a project turned out one time, try again. Flex that imagination!

Finally, never forget that beauty ultimately is in the eyes of the beholder, and that gifts should be given and received from the heart.

# Chapter 1
# Crafts from Dried Flowers, Herbs, and Grasses

## Materials and Methods

Drying flowers and herbs to use in arrangements and as decorations on anything from wreaths to hats, jars, baskets, and lampshades is a satisfying way to capture the essence of the garden for your enjoyment indoors year-round. Having a variety of dried plant material available makes it easy to put together gifts for the holidays or for that last-minute occasion. No matter how you use them, dried flowers and herbs combine their lasting quality with all the magical beauty of fresh flowers and herbs.

The goal in drying flowers and herbs is to remove the moisture quickly in order to maintain the form and color as closely as possible to their garden-fresh state. There are three basic methods used to accomplish this: drying plants in warm, gently moving, dry air with no light; removing the moisture by means of a desiccant; and removing the moisture in a microwave oven. Each method has advantages and disadvantages. Experiment with different flowers, methods, and drying times.

You can collect plant material starting with the earliest jonquil and tulip in spring, through the full panoply of summer, then harvesting fall's vibrantly colored offerings. Even winter can yield interesting items: bare or berried branches, pods, and the flowers of hellebore, witch hazel, and snowdrop. Because a certain amount of the material will not dry as perfectly as you want or will be damaged in storage, collect and dry twice as much as you think you'll need.

When picking flowers and other plant material, choose the most perfect specimens possible, as even the smallest flaw will seem magnified by drying. Pick flowers at various stages of development, from buds to almost fully opened. They will open further as they dry. Never pick flowers that have already been in bloom for several days. Gather foliage at the peak of the growing season.

Whichever drying method you will be using, always pick plant material when it is thoroughly dry but not wilted from the hot sun. Late morning is usually best. Try to gather material when you will be able to continue the drying procedure immediately. If it must be delayed, put the flowers or foliage in a bucket of lukewarm water and set in a cool, dark place.

Many factors affect how the leaves and flowers will dry. You will find that flower color will often change as follows: reds and purples darken or turn blue; yellows and greens fade; white turns cream or beige; rust turns brown; flowers grown in the shade or picked past their prime turn brown; oranges

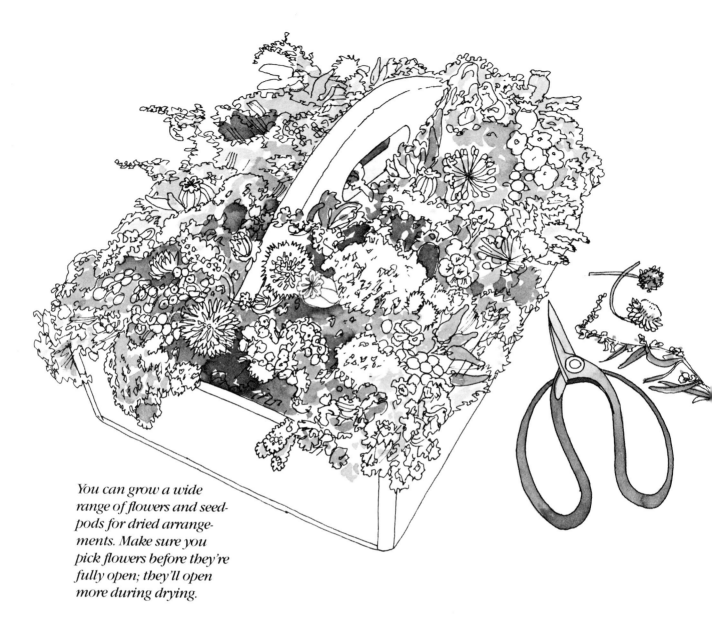

*You can grow a wide range of flowers and seed-pods for dried arrangements. Make sure you pick flowers before they're fully open; they'll open more during drying.*

sometimes turn red ('Tropicana' roses dry to a wonderful red); blues, oranges, and pinks generally retain their color best.

## Air Drying

Removing the moisture from plants in warm, dark, dry, gently moving air is the simplest and cheapest method of drying. It also requires the least equipment and space. An attic is the classic location, but a large closet, unused room, garden shed, garage, or similar space will also work, provided the requirements are met. A fan, dehumidifier, or heater may be necessary.

Air drying works well with plant materials that tend to dry naturally and retain their form, such as the "everlasting" flowers, grasses, weeds, reeds, pods, seed heads, grains, cones, lichens, and mosses. Long spiky flowers that are actually a lot of small flowers on short stems also dry well by this method; these include blue salvia, delphinium, larkspur, goldenrod, and monkshood.

Flowers with large, many-petaled heads, and flowers containing a lot of moisture, such as marigolds, zinnias, tulips, and lilies, do not air-dry well. Use a desiccant like silica gel with them, as described on page 4.

2

Most plant material can be air-dried by hanging upside down in bunches. You don't want to make the bunches too big, or the flowers may mold or crush each other; usually about six to ten stems to a bunch is right. Make sure the stems and flowers are totally free of water drops. Remove the foliage from the stems of flowers unless you want to leave it. Wrap a rubber band at least twice around the stems about 2 inches from the stem ends. Rubber bands are preferable to string or twist-ties, because the bands will tighten as the stems dry and shrink.

Attach the bundles directly to clothes hangers by putting the stems behind the hanger and pulling the second rubber band loop forward, up, and over the hanger and the stems. Bunches can also be hung by making S-shaped hooks out of 3-inch lengths of #9-gauge wire. Hang the bunches by the rubber band on one end of the hook and place the other end of the hook on a nail, over a pipe, or on a dowel or rod.

Depending on the plant, the weather conditions before and after gathering, and the drying conditions, the time required to dry plant material will usually vary from less than a week to as much as three weeks or more. Material is thoroughly dry when the stems snap readily.

There are certain flowers and plants that dry with better form if they aren't hung upside down. You'll also want to dry some flowers and plants right side up in order to have some material with gracefully curving stems. Tall, cylindrical containers, such as wide-mouthed jars, coffee cans, and cracker or pasta tins, work well for this type of drying. Consider this method for baby's breath, globe thistle, Chinese lanterns, poppy seed heads, grains, and grasses.

Still other plants and flowers should be dried right side up in a container with ½ inch of water. Plants that do best with this method include hydrangea, heather, floss flower, bells-of-Ireland, yarrow, alliums, and grasses. Pick the material just as it begins to dry naturally on the plant.

Round, flat flowers will be most attractive if they are dried by placing the stems through a screen, such as ¼-inch hardware cloth. The stems hang loose below, and the flowers are supported face-up by the screen. Use this method with fennel, dill, Queen Anne's lace, wild carrot, and edelweiss.

Many of the everlastings will dry almost completely while still on the plant, but the best quality is obtained if they are picked in the bud. They will finish opening as they dry and be less likely to shatter.

Some of the everlastings have weak stems when they dry, especially strawflowers, so the stem should be removed prior to drying and replaced with a wire "stem." Dry some without stems on a screen to glue directly onto items as decorations.

To make wire stems, cut the plant stem off ½ inch below the flower and insert a length of #22-gauge floral wire up through the remaining plant stem and center of the flower and out the top. Make a small "hairpin" hook in the wire above the flower and gently pull it back down through, but not entirely out of, the flower. The flower and stem will shrink and dry tightly around the wire. Tape the wire stem with floral tape by stretching the tape as you wrap it around the wire. Use this method with globe amaranth, strawflower, rose-everlasting, and immortelle.

Many of the seed heads and pods, grasses, and grains of fall practically dry themselves. Gather and loosely bunch these upside down or upright in containers, as you prefer.

Air-dried flowers and plants can be stored where they were dried, or placed loosely in shoe or suit boxes lined with tissue paper. Place tissue paper between layers, and never make so many layers that the material is crushed; I recommend only two or three layers. Seal the box with masking tape and label with the name of the plant, date, and color. A few mothballs may be added to repel moths and rodents. To prevent shattering, lightly coat dried flowers and grasses with hair spray, clear plastic craft spray, or clear lacquer spray. Store the boxes in a dry location.

# Desiccant Drying

Certain substances have a high affinity for water and readily absorb moisture. Placing flowers in one of these substances serves to draw out the moisture and preserve them. The advantage of these materials is that they retain flowers' color and shape better than air drying. The disadvantages are that they must be purchased and stored; they sometimes cake and stick to or damage the petals; and the flowers may reabsorb moisture from the air after they are arranged, causing them to droop.

Books from the early 1600s report the use of sand for drying flowers. Fine, well-cleaned sand is still useful today for drying heavier flowers like dahlias or peonies; follow the same procedure as described for the silica gel below.

Another effective material is a mixture of one part fine, clean sand or white cornmeal combined with two parts borax. Adding 3 tablespoons of uniodized salt per quart aids color retention in flowers. Although inexpensive, this mixture is the one most apt to cake, stick, or damage flowers. Flowers in any of these materials will take one to two weeks to dry.

Several decades ago, a commercially used material called silica gel became available for preserving flowers. Resembling white sand, silica gel has a number of advantages as a dessicant. It can absorb up to 40 percent of its weight in water; it is lightweight, so it won't damage delicate flowers; it acts quickly so flowers dry in two to several days, with superior color and form; and it is least likely to cake, stick, or damage petals.

Interspersed among the fine white crystals of silica gel are blue crystals of cobalt chloride, which act as moisture indicators. When they turn light blue, pink, or white, the silica gel has absorbed the maximum amount of water and must be reactivated. This is accomplished by reheating it in a shallow, ovenproof pan in a 250° F oven for several hours, or in a microwave oven on high for two to five minutes or until the crystals turn bright blue. Store in airtight containers until ready to use.

Sold under various brand names, silica gel is available from mailorder craft supply companies as well as many local hobby and craft stores, garden centers, and florists. Start off by purchasing 5 to 10 pounds. Offsetting the initial expense of silica gel is the fact that, through reactivation, it can be used over and over indefinitely.

When drying with silica gel, you will also need airtight containers, such as tin cake boxes or plastic food-storage containers. A shoe box and masking tape can also be used. Floral wire in a range of gauges from #20 to #26, the stretchy type of ½-inch-wide green floral tape, and wire cutters are also necessary.

Gather unblemished flowers in various stages of development when they are completely dry. Cut the stems 1 or 2 inches long. Select a wire that seems not quite heavy enough to support the flower, cut it into a 6-inch piece, and insert it either straight up into the base (calyx) of the flower on blooms like daisies or pansies, or crosswise through the heavier bases on flowers like roses. If inserted into the calyx, bend the wire down at a right angle so it takes up less room in the box; if crosswise, leave straight until drying is completed, then bend the two sides down so they are parallel. After the flowers are dry and you are ready to arrange them, put a piece of wire that has been bent in half alongside the wire already in the flower. Wrap the wire stem with floral tape, twirling the stem and spiraling and stretching the tape as you work.

To begin drying flowers, spread a ½- to 1-inch layer of silica gel on the bottom of your drying container. For daisy-type flowers, make a little mound of the gel and place the flower face down. Flowers with many petals like roses and marigolds should be placed face up. Lay long spiky flowers, such as larkspur or snapdragons, sideways, with upside-down Vs of cardboard supporting the stems every couple of inches. Lay fern fronds and leaves flat. They can be stacked with several inches of silica gel between layers. Allow at least several inches of silica gel between each flower, and place only one kind of flower in each container.

*Don't limit yourself to flowers when you make dried wreaths. Foliage like the bay leaves and artemisia shown here add textures that contrast to that of the blooms.*

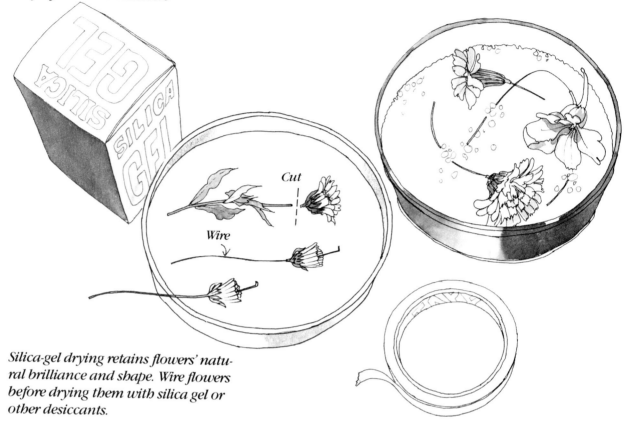

*Silica-gel drying retains flowers' natural brilliance and shape. Wire flowers before drying them with silica gel or other desiccants.*

When all of the flowers are in place, carefully cover each flower with silica gel by letting it flow either by the tablespoonful down the sides of the container or in a thin, fine stream from your fist or through your fingers. Make sure the flowers retain their natural shape. Cover the flowers with ½ to 1 inch of silica gel. Use a flat toothpick, if necessary, to help the gel trickle into crevices.

Seal the container and label with the date and contents. Check the contents in two or three days by gently tilting the container until a few petals are exposed. Touch them with your fingertips; if they are crisp and papery, then the flowers are dry. Carefully pour the silica gel into another container until each flower is removed. Use a soft makeup brush or camel's hair artist's brush to remove any silica gel that may cling to the petals. If petals were not perfectly dry before being preserved, they will be transparent where the moisture was.

Put a drop of clear household cement or other clear-drying glue at the center and base of the flower to prevent shattering. Spray with a dull-finish clear plastic craft sealer or hair spray to further protect the flower from humidity.

Flowers with a heavy base under the blossom may not be thoroughly dry through the center when the petals are dry. Since staying in the silica gel too long can overdry and shrivel the petals, the flowers should be removed and the base alone inserted into an open container of silica gel for a few days.

Flowers dried in silica gel will reabsorb moisture from the air. They should not be used in arrangements or decorations until the weather is not humid or the furnace is turned on, or else they should be used in a home with air conditioning. To store until ready to use, place the flowers upright in an airtight container with dry sand or silica gel in the bottom, or stick the wires into a block of polystyrene in the bottom of the container.

# Microwave Drying

The microwave oven has taken flower and plant drying even further into the realm of immediate gratification. Several days or weeks of drying time is reduced to several minutes. Everlastings and foliage can be dried quite simply, and other flowers can be dried in silica gel in the microwave.

Other than preserving leaves in glycerine (see Glycerinized Leaves, page 126), it has always been difficult to preserve foliage satisfactorily. With the microwave oven, both green and fall-colored leaves are readily dried. Simply put one or several inside a paper napkin, with two layers of napkin above and below, or inside a piece of folded paper towel, with one layer above and one below. Set a microwave-proof cup or glass on top to keep the leaves from curling. Cook on high for two minutes. Check; if leaves are dry and crisp, then they are done. If almost dry, then let them sit out overnight. If they're still damp, cook them another minute or so. If the leaves are too dry, try again with new leaves and halve the cooking time.

To dry everlastings in a microwave, put flowers inside a paper napkin or towel as above. Dry for two minutes on high as a test. Alter the time as seems appropriate.

Combining the microwave and silica gel gives the freshest-looking, most colorful flowers possible by any method. With this technique, you can accumulate a great many flowers while they are at their peak in a short period of time. Another advantage is that less total silica gel is needed.

It is best to dry only one flower at a time. Use relatively small, heat-proof containers such as glass measuring cups, custard cups, or microwave cook-and-serve dishes. Choose a container that is 3 inches taller than the flower to be dried.

In a separate dish, preheat the silica gel for one minute. Put a ½- to 1-inch layer in the bottom of your drying container. Place the flower inside, either facing up or down, as with regular silica gel drying. Fill in around the flower, covering it with at least ½ inch of the gel. There should be 2 inches of space from the surface of the gel to the top of the container.

A large, many-petaled flower like a rose should be cooked on high for about two minutes; rotate every 30 seconds or use a rotating rack. After the cooking is completed, let it stand for 20 to 30 minutes. Gently pour off the silica gel. If the flower is beige, it may have been cooked too long, past its prime, or low in water. Try cutting the cooking time in half.

Wire and tape the flowers as previously described. Store for future use or use immediately.

# Arranging Dried Flowers

Flower arranging is a contemplative, relaxing craft that can provide "the great escape" in your life. Exploring its avenues can give you boundless satisfaction. Just about anyone can arrange flowers. These flower arrangements will make celebrations and holidays as well as everyday events seem very special indeed. Special equipment and supplies are not essential, and the few items that are helpful are inexpensive.

What goes into a flower arrangement is practically limitless, also. Just about anything that grows in the garden as well as in the wild has probably been used in some arrangement, somewhere, by someone. You don't even have to use flowers! It's very easy to have a wonderful assortment of materials to work with practically year-round.

## Equipment

The items that are helpful in gathering and arranging are probably already around the house; what isn't can be purchased from a hardware or discount department store. To facilitate making flower arrangements, keep all the equipment together in a cabinet or closet.

**Bucket** – To put plant material in when gathering in the garden; use a standard 3-gallon pail or a smaller empty bucket from peanut butter, paint, or ready-mix plaster.

**Pruning shears** – For cutting woody stems; use either the anvil or scissors type; oil and sharpen periodically.

**Scissors** – For cutting softer stems; use the special short-bladed florist type or standard stainless steel household scissors.

**Sharp, long-bladed knife** – For cutting large blocks of floral foam into smaller pieces.

**Wire cutters** – Also known as side cutters; for cutting wires when elongating stems or making corsages.

## Containers

When containers are mentioned, one's first reaction is to think "vase." But, quite literally, just about any container can hold a flower arrangement. The most important factor to consider is that the container does not take away from the flowers. Simplicity is the key word. When collecting containers, begin with basic geometric shapes in neutral or subdued colors with very little decoration.

As you select a container for a flower arrangement, consider the size, shape, form, color, and texture of the flowers in relationship to the container, the setting, and the occasion.

Experiment and be bold. Use your imagination. Don't overlook anything, be it baskets, gourds, soup cans, pitchers, brass pots, teacups, or whatever strikes your fancy.

## Mechanics

Flower-arranging devices and materials that help to hold flower or foliage stems in a certain position are called mechanics. Informal arrangements can often be made without these, but using them opens up all manner of design possibilities.

Many of these items are available at florists or craft stores. There are also mailorder suppliers (see Sources on page 169).

**Pinholders** – Essentially, a pinholder is a small, heavy metal base with sharp, closely spaced metal pins sticking straight out of it. A good one will last several lifetimes. Different sizes and shapes are available. Some are permanently attached to a small water-holding receptacle. Looking like some item left over from a dungeon, pinholders are the favorite of those who do Japanese-style arrangements or like to use shallow containers. Many people also feel that pinholders offer the most precise placement in arranging, while floral-foam fans strongly disagree.

**Waterproof floral clay** – Looking like modeling clay and sold in rectangular blocks or flat coils, this clay is used to anchor the pinholder to the container. To use, make sure the clay, pinholder, and container are quite dry. With both palms, make a ¼-inch-diameter rope long enough to go around the pinholder at least once. Place the rope on the perimeter of the bottom of the pinholder, then press firmly onto the bottom of the container, twisting slightly.

**Wire netting** – Most often chickenwire is used, although special wire holders are available. One way to use chickenwire is to crumple a piece and stuff it into the container. Another way is to stretch a piece over the top of the container and attach it securely with waterproof floral tape.

**Waterproof floral tape** – Similar to adhesive tape but green or clear, this tape is used to anchor wire netting and floral foam to containers. It can also be used by itself: make a grid over the mouth of the container by spacing the strips ½ inch apart. Stems are inserted in these spaces.

**Floral foam** – This lightweight, fine-celled material is sold in blocks, cylinders, and in ready-made containers. Do not confuse floral foam with polystyrene. Use a knife to cut the foam so that a piece will fit snugly in your container. If your container is shallow and you think the foam may be topheavy when filled with flowers and might tip out, criss-cross two pieces of waterproof floral tape across the top of the foam and down onto the container. One of the greatest advantages of this foam is that the top of it can extend beyond the top of the container, allowing flower and foliage stems to be angled downward. Don't try to reuse floral foam. New stems will not be the same diameter or length, so they won't be held securely.

**Pebbles, marbles, gravel, shells, and sand** – These can be either collected or bought. They are an easy means of holding a few stems secure in a container or for camouflaging other mechanics.

**Floral tape** – This is a thin, stretchy ½-inch-wide tape that is most readily available in green, brown, and white. It is used to wrap the floral wire that reinforces natural stems or to make artificial stems for boutonnieres, corsages, and dried-flower arrangements.

**Floral wire** – Usually green in color and available in a variety of gauges, floral wire is sold either in 18-inch lengths or on reels, called paddle wire. Floral wire is used to reinforce stems or to make artificial stems for boutonnieres, corsages, and dried-flower arrangements.

## Styling Principles

For flowers to be more than a few stems in a glass, certain principles of design must come into play. Whatever the style or shape of your arrangement, consider the elements of balance, rhythm, scale, and color.

A balanced arrangement is one that seems secure and stable. To consider balance, draw an imaginary line down through the middle of the arrangement from top to bottom. An arrangement that has equal materials on each side is considered symmetrical, or formal. An asymmetrical, or informal, arrangement will not have the same items on each side, but it will still seem in balance.

**Balance** is achieved by maneuvering such factors as color (darker colors appear heavier), shape (a round flower holds your attention while spiky ones lead it away), texture (fine texture seems lighter), and size (larger items are heavier). To achieve a balanced, stable effect, put the heavier-looking flowers toward the center and lower part of the arrangement.

**Rhythm** is the way that your eyes are led from one aspect of an arrangement to another. The goal is to have the eyes first attracted to the focal point, then carried throughout the entire arrangement. This is achieved by repeating the shapes of materials in the arrangement, by putting the larger and darker elements toward the center and base and the smaller, lighter ones toward the edges, and by the continuous flow of the line in the arrangement through the use of branches and stems.

**Scale** is the size relationship of the various elements in the arrangement. Good scale means that the proportions of each element are pleasing and supportive of the others, with none dominating. You should also consider the size of the container relative to the arrangement; the basic guideline is that the arrangement should be one and a half times as high or as wide as the container. Also, consider the size of the arrangement relative to where it will be placed.

**Color** affects balance, rhythm, and scale. But it also conveys certain moods and feelings. Consider not only the colors within the arrangement, but also those of the container and setting combined with the flowers' colors.

To use and combine colors, study the color wheel based on the three primary colors – red, yellow, and blue. All other colors are obtained by mixing these in various proportions. The three main colors directly between the primary colors are called the intermediate colors; they are green, orange, and purple.

A one-color scheme uses different values and intensities of one color. A complementary color scheme uses colors that lie directly opposite each other on the color chart. A double-complementary color scheme uses two directly adjacent colors and their complements, such as blue, green, red, and orange. A split complementary color scheme is a combination of a primary or intermediate color with the colors on either side of its complement, such as blue with orange and purple. A triad is formed with the colors that an equilateral triangle forms on the color wheel.

## The Shape of Things

It is helpful to decide what shape the arrangement is going to take before beginning to make it. Some shapes have become standards, but they are definitely not the only options. It is also possible to use one shape in many different forms.

The most common shape is the round, or globe, form. The triangle shape includes the symmetrical A-shape, upside-down T-shape, and asymmetrical L-shape. Low, broad horizontal arrangements are useful for centerpieces on dining tables. A vertical arrangement is tall and narrow. Finally, there are the gracefully curving S-, crescent-, and circle-shaped arrangements. These arrangements are described and illustrated beginning on page 12. But why not try a cube-shaped arrangement in a square dish? Anything is possible!

## The Basic Steps

Before beginning a flower arrangement, consider where it is to be placed, what it is to be used for, and the plant material you have available. Then select the container and put the mechanics in place.

Now you're actually ready to start placing the flowers and foliage. First, establish the shape by building the framework with linear materials such as branches and long, thin leaves and stems of flowers like delphiniums. Next, add the fuller, rounder elements to create the focal point. Finally, use filler material like baby's breath and fern fronds to camouflage the mechanics and to connect the other elements.

Beauty in a flower arrangement does not depend on complexity, costliness, or rarity. Rather, it is the careful selection and placement of the flowers, foliage, and container in conjunction with where it is displayed. As such, flower arranging draws on our senses and develops our ability to see and express that which is pleasing and satisfying to us.

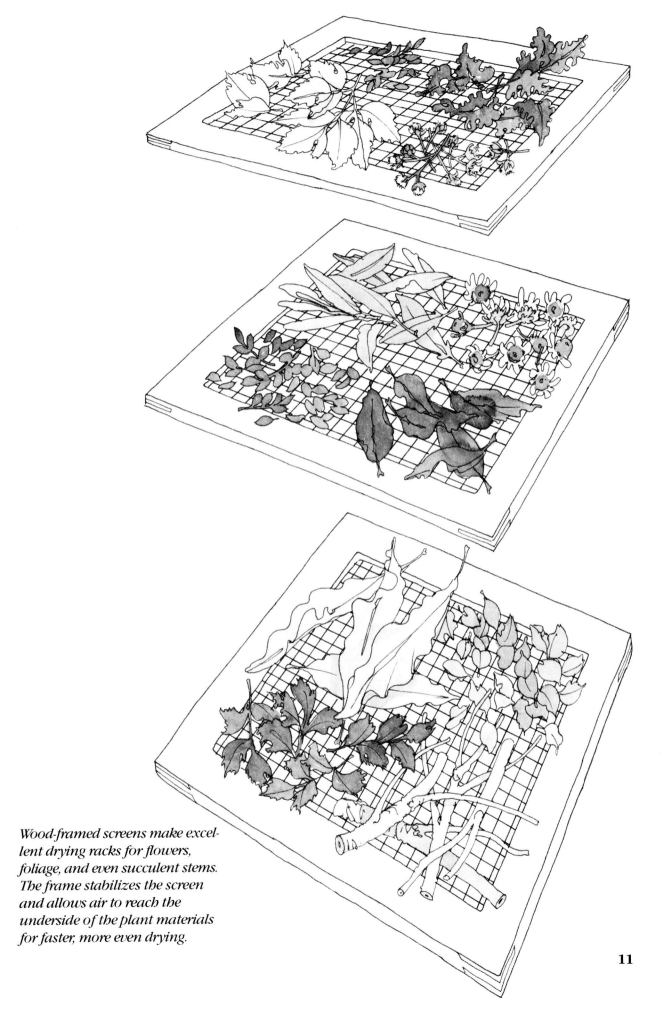

*Wood-framed screens make excellent drying racks for flowers, foliage, and even succulent stems. The frame stabilizes the screen and allows air to reach the underside of the plant materials for faster, more even drying.*

**11**

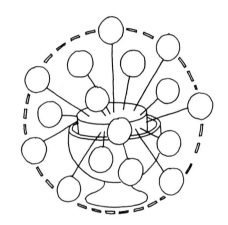

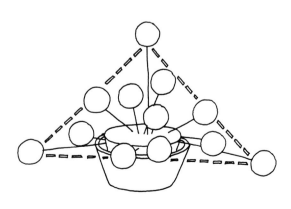

# *Eight Flower Arrangements*

## Round Arrangement

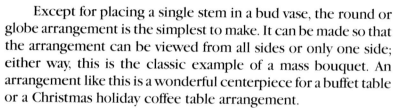

Except for placing a single stem in a bud vase, the round or globe arrangement is the simplest to make. It can be made so that the arrangement can be viewed from all sides or only one side; either way, this is the classic example of a mass bouquet. An arrangement like this is a wonderful centerpiece for a buffet table or a Christmas holiday coffee table arrangement.

My favorite container for this type of arrangement is a twig basket with a plastic 16-ounce deli cup holding the flowers. The cup is hidden by placing dried Spanish moss between it and the basket. The flower arranging aid I use is a modified pinholder that looks like dented hairpins rather than straight pins, but a regular pinholder or floral foam would work equally well. Try other baskets as well as more sophisticated containers.

To make a round arrangement, form the basic outline with linear material, such as snapdragons, stock, or blue salvia. Although the stems won't necessarily all be the same length, the overall appearance will give that effect.

Next, fill in the outline with round flowers, which may be all of one color or type or several different kinds. Have these at varying stages of development to add interest. Some of the best materials that are readily grown in the garden include zinnias, marigolds, annual dahlias, cosmos, and calendula. Some stems can be shorter than others, but no flower should project beyond the outline.

Finally, add the filler material, such as baby's breath, to soften the transition between the linear and round materials.

## Triangular Arrangement

The triangular-shaped mass arrangement is another very popular design, and just about as easy as the round type. For this design, the tallest point is established with linear material, such as fern fronds, gladiolus flowers or leaves, or snapdragons. Form the two base points with slightly shorter materials. Fill in the area between these three extremes of the triangle with slightly shorter linear material.

With the shape now formed, add the round, darker-colored flowers in the center. Add buds of the same flower at other points in the arrangement, as well as other flowers. Finally, add filler material.

Roses at various stages of development, from buds to fullblown, are the classic flowers to use in an arrangement like this. A vase on a short pedestal complements the elegance of the roses. Ferns, baby's breath, and spiky iris leaves complete the composition and hide the floral foam, if that is what you're using.

Using floral foam that extends 1 inch above the rim of the container allows some of the plant material to be angled downward, since the stems can actually be pointed up rather than down.

Many different kinds of containers and plant materials lend themselves to this design. For an open effect, the arrangement can be composed of just a few twisting branches and a perfect large flower, such as a lily or orchid, instead of a mass of flowers.

# L-Shaped Arrangement

Think of the L as a right-handed triangle, and you'll realize how easy this arrangement is. Usually an L-shaped arrangement has strong linear elements such as very spiky foliage, branches, or flower stems. Contorted branches like corkscrew willow are another favorite choice.

Use a low, shallow container with a pinholder or floral foam for mechanics. Besides the linear plant material, you will also want an assortment of round flowers and filler.

Start the arrangement by placing a tall, vertical stem in the container; next, add the horizontal arm of the design at a 90-degree angle. Flank both the vertical and horizontal pieces with several shorter linear stems. Add several large round flowers at the base of the L, with at least one facing forward and the others facing vertically and horizontally. Fill in between the linear pieces and the round flowers with smaller flowers and foliage.

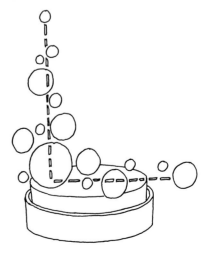

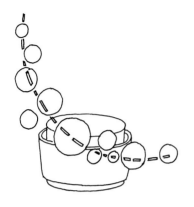

# Crescent Arrangement

A crescent-shaped arrangement is actually an L-shape with a rounded corner. A traditional way to use this design is to have either a single crescent arrangement or a pair on the mantel.

A tall, deep, narrow container can be used as well as a low, shallow one. For the mechanics, or flower-arranging aid, use marbles, floral foam, or a pinholder in a tall vase, and a pinholder or floral foam in a shallow container.

Start the crescent arrangement using a stem with a naturally strong curve, and insert it into the mechanics slightly to the left or right of center. Using linear plant materials, flank each side of this piece with approximately five more stems of progressively shorter lengths, following the established curve. Next, select another stem with a slight curve, and place it so that it originates horizontally from the base. Use shorter pieces to flank each side of it as you work back toward the center of the arrangement. Use round flowers to add fullness at the center base of the arrangement. Fill in both directions with smaller and finer plant material.

# Horizontal Arrangement

Most often constructed in a low bowl, a horizontal arrangement is ideal for a dining table centerpiece, as diners can readily see and talk with one another without obstructions. It's actually a low triangle mass arrangement.

Floral foam is usually the best choice for mechanics, as it allows low, downward-facing placement of plant material. An oval gravy boat, soup tureen, or other dish makes an appropriate container, but there are lots of other possibilites.

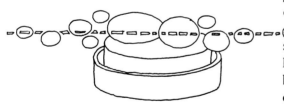

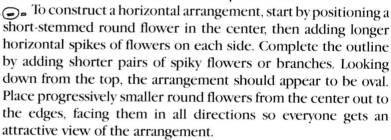 To construct a horizontal arrangement, start by positioning a short-stemmed round flower in the center, then adding longer horizontal spikes of flowers on each side. Complete the outline by adding shorter pairs of spiky flowers or branches. Looking down from the top, the arrangement should appear to be oval. Place progressively smaller round flowers from the center out to the edges, facing them in all directions so everyone gets an attractive view of the arrangement.

Zinnias, calendulas, gerberas, Queen Anne's lace, poppies, anemones, and chrysanthemums are all excellent round flowers. Some spiky flowers to feature are blue sage, lavender, snapdragons, monkshood, mullein, lamb's ears, and bells-of-Ireland. This arrangement would also lend itself well to pine and mums or carnations at Christmas; make wire stems for small silver or gold ornaments to add a bit of glitz.

# Contemporary
# Vertical Arrangement

A flower arrangement needn't be large or elaborate to be striking. This very dramatic contemporary vertical arrangement is composed of several round flowers and leaves, plus a few linear branches or spikes of flowers in an angular, stemmed cocktail glass. Change the whole look by using a depression-glass or cut-crystal compote or stemmed goblet.

There are plenty of round flowers that will work for this arrangement, including zinnias, chrysanthemums, daisies, tuberous begonias, dahlias, asters, lilies, and cosmos. Corkscrew willow branches and flower stems of delphinium, southernwood, nicotiana, veronica, penstemon, tritoma, and salvia are possibilities for the linear material.

For mechanics, anchor a small round pinholder with waterproof clay and surround with polished pebbles. For added flexibility in arranging, spear a small piece of floral foam to the pinholder. Put in one tall linear piece, then two shorter linear pieces angling to each side at the base. Add about three more in between. Put in one large flower at the center base facing forward, then a smaller one pointing up. Fill in with several large leaves to cover the mechanics.

# Traditional Vertical Arrangement

Tall, deep containers for flowers can include a slender bud vase, larger unfinished or glazed pottery, or sparkling crystal. A bud-vase arrangement is very easily done with two or three fern fronds, a single perfect rose or other flower, and perhaps a bit of baby's breath.

Larger containers require only a bit more effort. Sand, pebbles, or marbles, as well as pinholders or floral foam, work well as mechanics, or flower-arranging aids.

A wealth of plant material with a vertical effect is available in the garden, fields, and roadsides. Consider bellflower, grasses, ixia, nerine, long-stemmed roses, tulips, acidanthera, astilbe, plumed celosia, blackberry lily, brodiaea, gladiolus, pineapple lily, hosta, liatris, lupine, cardinal flower, and solomon's seal. Don't overlook the branches of trees and shrubs, too.

To make a vertical arrangement in a tall, deep vase, start with one tall, spike-shaped flower, bud, or leaf. On each side put progressively shorter spikes to form a tapering outline. The flowers and foliage can become rounder and fuller near the base of the arrangement.

# Hogarth Arrangement

Shaped in an S-curve, this style of arranging is named after the eighteenth-century English artist, William Hogarth. He incorporated this S-curve, or "line of beauty," based on the nape of a woman's neck, into many of his works. Essentially the arrangement is made with a gentle curve going in one direction above the container and in the reverse direction below it.

Often made into rather formal, elegant, and sometimes stuffy arrangements, the same concept used in a different way creates a jubilant tribute to the autumn harvest season and holidays. Cut the lid off a pumpkin just as if you were going to make a jack-o-lantern. For mechanics, using floral foam that is 1 or 2 inches taller than the liner is easiest, but marbles, sand, or a pinholder can also be used.

Bittersweet is the vine of the season, but perhaps you'll have other berried or bare branches to establish the flowing lines of the Hogarth curve. The top and bottom halves are essentially mirror images of each other. Use the bittersweet or other material to establish the main line, then place progressively shorter linear elements on either side of the main line, forming the top and bottom halves. Fill the center with large, round flowers, and connect them with the linear elements by filling in with smaller, lighter flowers and foliage.

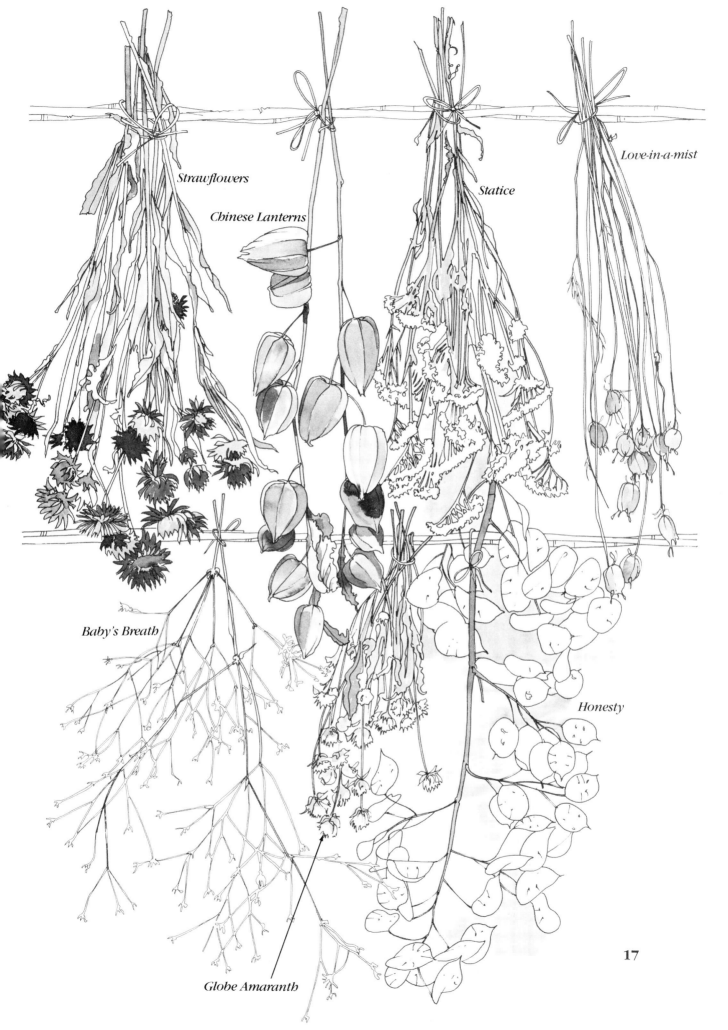

*Strawflowers*

*Chinese Lanterns*

*Statice*

*Love-in-a-mist*

*Baby's Breath*

*Honesty*

*Globe Amaranth*

17

# Dried Flower and Herb Arrangement

## MATERIALS

**Container**
**Floral foam**
**Paring knife**
**Rubber cement, hot glue gun**
 **with clear glue sticks, white**
 **craft glue, or sticky floral tape,**
 **depending on the container**
 **(see Step 1, below)**
**#22-gauge floral wire**
**Dried Spanish moss or dried**
 **sheet moss**
**Green floral tape**
**Scissors**
**Wire cutters**
**Wired wooden floral picks**
**Assortment of dried plant**
 **materials**
**Clear plastic craft spray sealer**

1. Prepare the container by cutting a block of dry floral foam to fit snugly in the container with an inch extending above the rim. Firmly attach the foam to the container, using one of the following methods: rubber cement with glass and china; clear hot glue or white craft glue with baskets and wooden or metal containers. Alternatively, the foam may be anchored with strips of the sticky tape going from rim to rim of the container in at least two directions.

2. Make small "hairpins" out of floral wire. Spread a layer of Spanish or sheet moss over the foam and attach with the wire pins.

3. If your plant material has short stems (or none at all), you can still use it by making wire stems. There are several ways to do this. One is to

Arranging flowers and herbs, whether fresh or dried, is a lot like learning to swim. At first it's intimidating, but once mastered, not only will it seem easy but you'll always be able to do it. Hopefully, too, it will bring joy to your life as well as the people with whom you share.

Arrangements can be as simple or as complex as you desire. The range of plant material that can be dried and used is awesome, as are the possibilities of the shape, size, style, and color of arrangements. Just follow your imagination and instincts.

The basic principles of fresh flower arranging also apply to arranging dried plant materials. Instead of being short-lived, however, the arrangement will last anywhere from months to years.

You can choose from a wide range of containers, since you don't have to worry about their holding water. The container you select should blend with the style, color, and size of the arrangement you have in mind.

As discussed earlier in this chapter, the shape of the arrangement can be rounded, oval, triangular, a crescent, an L, or an S. Any of these may also be diagonal, horizontal, or vertical. A small rounded arrangement is a good one to begin with, as is a one-sided triangular arrangement. Once you feel comfortable making these, don't be afraid to try something more complicated.

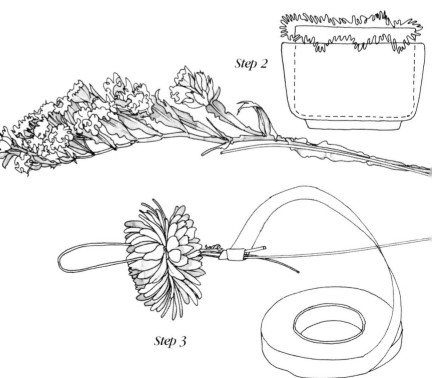

*Step 2*

*Step 3*

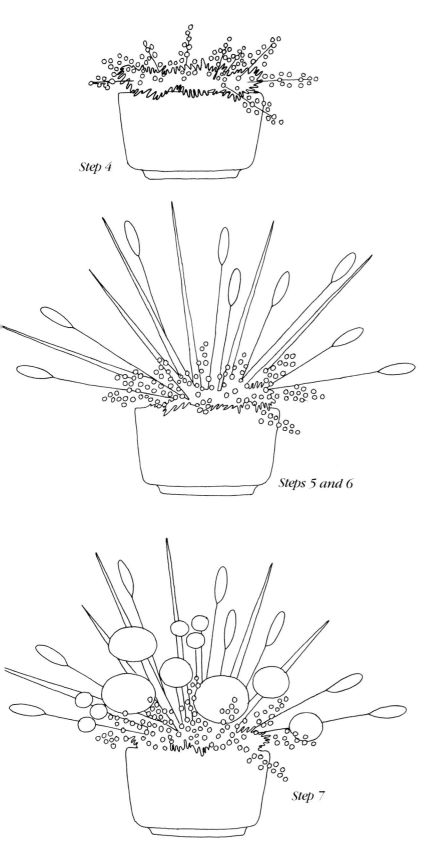

*Step 4*

*Steps 5 and 6*

*Step 7*

take a length of floral wire and bend it in half; place this alongside the existing stem of a sprig such as German statice, and wrap with floral tape, twirling and stretching it as you work. For strawflowers and similar flowers, insert the wire through the center of the flower from the base, make a 1-inch "hairpin" and gently pull it back into the flower until hidden; then tape the stem by twirling and stretching it as above. You can also wire plant material to wooden picks.

4. Begin your arrangement by outlining the design with "filler" materials such as German statice, baby's breath, or any light, airy material. Put some sprigs around the lower edge and others in a more vertical position to establish the height of the arrangement. The tallest piece in an arrangement should be 2½ times the height or width of the container. Except for the topmost piece, stems are usually inserted at an angle.

5. Next, add slightly heavier material, such as pastel statice, plumed celosia, and goldenrod. Place the material at different depths.

6. Add spiky material, such as dried grasses, Victoria sage, and delphinium next. Let it extend 1 or 2 inches beyond the filler material.

7. Finally, add the larger, darker-colored flowers, such as cockscomb, zinnia, and roses, spacing them more or less evenly around the arrangement.

8. Step back and evaluate your arrangement. Add or remove as you see fit, or push and pull as necessary. When satisfied, spray the arrangement with the sealer to prevent it from absorbing moisture.

# Nosegays

## MATERIALS

**Scissors**
**One central flower with a 4- to 6-inch stem**
**Other flowers, herbs, and leaves, as desired, with 4- to 6-inch stems**
**Rubber bands, string, or #26-gauge covered wire**
**6-inch-diameter paper doily or lace-trimmed nosegay holder (available at craft shops)**
**Floral tape (optional)**
**⅜-inch-wide ribbon, enough as desired to make bows and streamers**

1. Holding the central flower in one hand, begin surrounding it with other flowers, herbs and leaves. Use the rubber bands, string, or covered wire to help you hold the stems together or wrap them in paper.

2. When the arrangement satisfies you, cut an X in the center of the doily, or use the holder to surround the flowers and herbs.

3. Add ribbon streamers and bows, if desired.

Meant to be carried in the hand, the nosegay, posey or posie bouquet, tussy-mussy, tussie-mussie, tuzzy mussy, tussiemusie, tutty, turry, or tussemose is a round cluster of flowers. Usually there is one conspicuous central flower encircled with smaller or finer-textured flowers and herbs. Foliage and ribbons as well as lace, if desired, complete this delicate and charming artifact so often associated with the Victorian era and the language of flowers.

Actually, the term appears in one of its spellings in an early English-Latin dictionary in general use by 1440. The term "tussy-mussy" first appeared in the Oxford Dictionary in 1585. Herbalist John Parkinson mentioned tussy-mussies in 1629 in *Paradisus Terrestris*. During this span of time, nosegays were basically just simple clusters of herbs recommended by physicians as a means of warding off diseases and counteracting foul-smelling air.

The change in orientation of nosegays to elaborate bearers of messages is usually credited to the descriptions published by an eighteenth-century English poet named Lady Mary Wortley Montague. During a visit to Constantinople, she learned of the amorous messages Turkish women sent via flowers, the heritage of which can be traced to Persia, China, Assyria, and Egypt. Over the next century or so, a great variety of floral dictionaries were published, the best-known being Kate Greenaway's *Language of Flowers*. In today's fast-paced world filled with blaring messages of all sorts, it's rather fun to take the time to use more subtle communication forms, so I've included a list of popular flowers and herbs with their meanings.

Today, nosegays can still be made to convey a sentiment, or just be made as beautiful and fragrant gifts for all manner of holidays and celebrations. Consider them for birthdays, Valentine's Day, Mother's Day, Christmas, anniversaries, bridal or baby showers, christenings, and promotions. They are also a lovely way to thank a hostess, set a luncheon table, or cheer a shut-in. One of the most romantic uses of a nosegay and the language of flowers is in a bridal bouquet.

There really are no restrictions on what can be used in a nosegay. Whatever dried flowers, herbs, and foliage are available will work. Or you can make a nosegay of fresh flowers, let it dry, and keep it as a lasting remembrance on a dresser, table, or bookcase. Why not make a pair and use them as curtain tiebacks? Dry a fresh-flower nosegay either upright or hanging upside down in a dark, dry, well-ventilated spot. To best retain the shape and color of the flowers, remove the lace and ribbons and cover the entire arrangement with silica gel; let it dry for about two weeks before removing.

## SAMPLER OF FLOWER AND HERB MEANINGS

**Angelica** – inspiration
**Basil** – hatred, love, good wishes
**Bay leaf** – I change but in death
**Borage** – bluntness, courage
**Burnet** – a merry heart
**Calendula** – joy, remembrance, happiness
**Caraway** – faithfulness
**Carnation, red** – alas for my heart
**Carnation, striped** – refusal
**Carnation, yellow** – disdain
**Chamomile** – energy in adversity, may your wishes come true, humility, patience
**Clover, red** – industry
**Columbine** – folly
**Coriander** – concealed merit
**Cornflower** – single blessedness
**Daisy** – innocence
**Dandelion** – oracle
**Dock** – patience
**Fennel** – worthy of all praise
**Forget-me-not** – true love
**Foxglove** – insincerity
**Geranium, nutmeg** – an unexpected meeting
**Geranium, rose** – preference
**Goldenrod** – precaution, encouragement
**Heliotrope** – devotion
**Hibiscus** – delicate beauty
**Honeysuckle** – generosity
**Hops** – injustice
**Hyacinth, blue** – jealousy
**Hyssop** – cleanliness, sacrifice
**Ivy** – fidelity
**Lavender** – distrust, cleanliness, luck, devotion
**Lemon balm** – sympathy
**Lily-of-the-valley** – purity
**Marjoram** – blushes, joy, happiness
**Mint** – virtue, love, passion
**Mugwort** – happiness
**Myrtle** – love, passion
**Narcissus** – self-love
**Nasturtium** – patriotism
**Pansy** – happy thoughts
**Parsley** – festivity
**Pennyroyal** – flee away
**Peppermint** – warmth of feeling
**Pink** – boldness, fascination
**Rose** – love
**Rose, damask** – brilliant complexion
**Rosebud, red** – pure and lovely
**Rosebud, white** – girlhood and a heart ignorant of love
**Rosemary** – remembrance, fidelity, loyalty

**Rue** – disdain, sorrow, repentance, virginity, virtue, vision, good health, long life
**Saffron crocus** – mirth
**Sage** – domestic virtue or esteem, long life, good health, wisdom
**Salvia, blue** – I think of you
**Sorrel** – affection
**Southernwood** – jest, banter, constancy, perseverance
**Spearmint** – warmth of sentiment
**Speedwell** – female fidelity
**Sunflower** – haughtiness
**Sweet alyssum** – worth beyond beauty
**Sweet woodruff** – be cheerful and rejoice in life
**Tansy** – I declare war against you, immortality
**Thyme** – activity, happiness, courage, bravery, strength
**Violet, sweet** – modesty
**Wormwood** – absence, bitterness
**Yarrow** – war
**Zinnia** – thoughts of absent friends

*Assembling a nosegay: Wrap the stems in paper or tie them, then slide them through a doily and add ribbon.*

## MATERIALS

**Straw hat**
**Assortment of dried plant materials**
**Scissors**
**Hot glue gun with clear glue sticks, or white craft or household glue**
**Ribbon for a bow and/or streamers (see Tying the Perfect Bow, page 165); optional**
**Pregathered lace (optional)**
**Clear plastic craft spray sealer**

1. The most widely used method of trimming a hat is to begin by encircling it with a base of filler material such as German statice or baby's breath. Cut sprigs 2 to 2½ inches long and glue, working around the hat in one direction. Leave a space for the bow, if desired.
2. Next, add other dried flowers and herbs, tucking them in and gluing them to the filler.
3. Finally, glue on the bow. Make a simple bow of 1- or 1¼-inch-wide ribbon, or make a multiple-loop bow with ribbon of several different widths. If desired, pregathered lace can be glued down first.
4. When completed, spray the hat with clear plastic craft sealer to keep the plant material from absorbing moisture or shattering.

**NOTE:** The method described above can be used to trim all manner of objects with dried flowers and herbs, such as a brass hunting horn, an old-fashioned slate used as a message board, wreaths, wheat dolls, twig wall hangings or doll cradles, an old fiddle, ad infinitum. I am reminded of a quote from Pogo: "We are faced with insurmountable opportunities."

# Hat Trimmed with Dried Flowers and Herbs

Revive a bygone era in a most romantic way by trimming a broad-brimmed straw hat with dried flowers and herbs. Hang the hat on a door or wall in a bedroom, bathroom, or hallway. You could also place it on a table, hang it on a bedpost, or display it on an antique hat stand. Of course, you can wear it, too!

Decorating a hat is very easy. If you don't have enough dried material to completely encircle the hat, simply surrounding the bow with flowers will be enough to make a stylish composition.

Experiment with different materials and color combinations. Trim a hat with pods, berries, and grasses for the fall, or with cones and holly for the holidays.

# Lamp Shade

A delicate lamp shade trimmed with an assortment of dried flowers is perfect on a dressing table outfitted with Victorian linens, hand-blown and cut crystal perfume bottles, and a silver hairbrush and mirror. It would also be charming in a guest bathroom, on a table in an entrance hall, or as an accent in a kitchen.

## MATERIALS

**Lamp shade**
**Scissors**
**Hot glue gun with clear glue sticks, or white craft or household glue**
**Dried Spanish moss or German statice**
**Assorted dried flowers**

1. Doing a small section at a time, dot a 1-inch-wide strip of the edge of the lamp shade with glue and attach a clump of moss. Or put some glue on a short piece of statice and attach to the edge of the shade. This forms the base of your design.
2. Select dried flowers and attach with glue to the moss or statice. Continue adding an assortment of both small and large flowers until your design is complete.

## MATERIALS

**Basket**
**Assortment of dried plant materials**
**Scissors**
**Hot glue gun with clear glue sticks, or white craft or household glue**
**Ribbon bow (see Tying the Perfect Bow, page 165); optional**
**Lace (optional)**
**Clear plastic craft spray sealer**

1. Begin decorating the basket by trimming the edges and as much of the handle as desired with filler material, such as German statice or baby's breath. Cut sprigs about 2 inches long and glue to the basket, working in one direction and overlapping the pieces so the stems don't show.
2. Next, add whatever other dried materials you want, nestling them in the filler and attaching with glue.
3. Finally, if desired, make a bow and attach with glue. Tuck the long streamers in among the flowers. The bow pictured uses ribbon that is ⅛-, ¼-, and ½-inch wide. Half-inch-wide lace could be substituted if desired.
4. When completed, spray the basket with clear plastic craft sealer to keep the plant material from absorbing moisture or shattering.

**NOTE:** The grapevine basket pictured can be made readily by soaking grapevines in warm water, then shaping them into a circle, or "wreath," about 4 inches tall and 2 inches thick. Intertwine several pieces, bend into a U-shape, and insert on each side for a handle. For the bottom, insert two sticks one way, then two at right angles, tucking them into the "wreath." Another way to use a grapevine basket is to fill it in with small pots of geraniums or other flowers as a centerpiece for a table or decoration for the deck.

Most of the time I prefer objects – be they antiques, crafts, or just "finds" – that have a function. Occasionally, though, it's fun just to be frivolous. These dried flower- and herb-trimmed baskets are just such objects. Yet their beauty is a kind of function in itself.

Actually, they *can* be used to hold things, if treated gently. I have seen trimmed baskets filled with special homemade foods or beauty preparations given as gifts, or fireside-type baskets used to hold hand towels or table napkins. No doubt you'll find other uses as well.

24

*Fragrant potpourris and pomanders, pressed flower pictures, and a multicolor bouquet invite you to linger awhile in a room awash with flowers and light.*

Carl Doney

**Above:** *Candles, boxes, book-marks, stationery – everyday objects become works of art with a bit of pressed flower magic.*
**Right:** *The most awkward nook or cranny becomes a showplace with an artful arrangement of dried flowers. The graceful bou-quet and striking standard bring this wall niche to life.*

Christie C. Tito

*Victorian beauty at its best: A rosebud wreath, a potpourri-filled sachet and satiny hanger, tiny dried-flower pins, and a heady lavender wand are regal on a mahogany dresser.*

**Above:** *The subtle tints of the potpourri remind us that the beauty of fresh flowers doesn't end when they fade.* **Right:** *Mix and match your crafts for special displays. The sea green dress of the cornshuck doll is nearly identical to the color of the ribbons and flowers of the basket. The doll's natural cornshuck color is a perfect match for the flower-trimmed hat.*

*Celebrate a craft-filled Christmas. Trim a grapevine tree with birds and dried flowers. Decorate holiday ornaments with dried delights.*

*During the holidays deck your home with a traditional yule log and a pinecone wreath.*

*Corn is reborn in this heart-shaped wreath. Dyed cornshucks add flashes of red and catch the earthy tones of the miniature Indian corn that forms the "ribbon" for this wreath.*

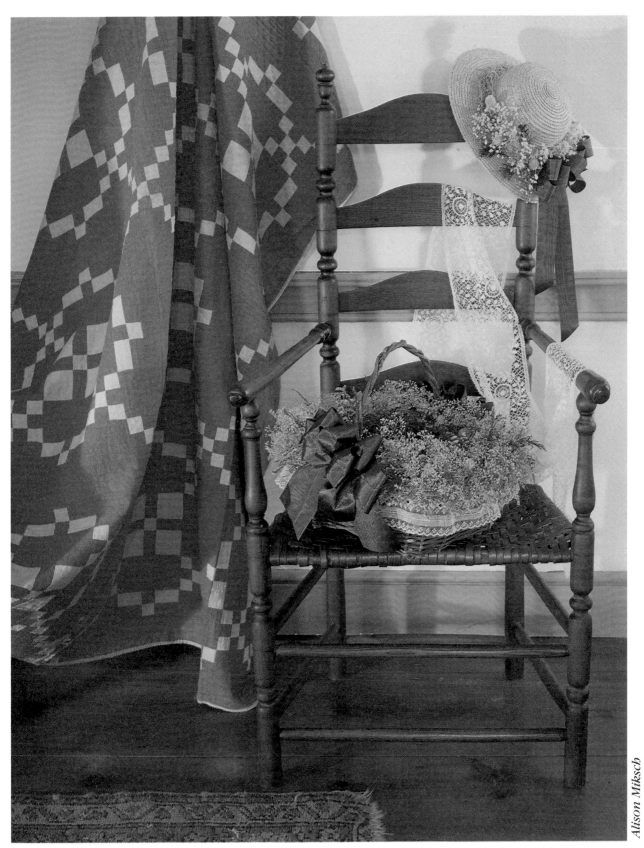

*Dried herbs and flowers, ribbons, and delicate lace adorn a broad-brimmed straw hat and spill out of a country basket.*

**Above:** *A braided trio of red annual statice, German statice and garlic creates a gift as beautiful as it is useful.* **Above right:** *An antique crock filled with eyecatching cherry-red celosia; purple, pink and white globe amaranth; violet and yellow statice; golden tansy; and other dried flowers greets visitors as they step onto the porch.* **Right:** *A Mordiford wheat weaving traditionally brought a good harvest. Now it's a symbol of good luck in the home, which makes it a favorite housewarming gift.*

*Swags and bouquets of homegrown dried flowers are always welcome gifts and perfect arrangements for country settings.*

*A welcoming wreath of dried flowers on green artemisia.*

*A yarrow wreath with its golden warmth for door or drawing room.*

*A dried apple wreath with its candystripe colors.*

37

*A harvest grapevine wreath of fresh vegetables, fruits, and herbs.*

Beauty in a bottle can be yours. Make rich shampoos, soothing creams and jellies, pungent essential oils, heavenly perfumes, and aromatic vinegars. Create new combinations with every bottle and jar.

*Carl Doney*

*To transform a routine chore into a special event, carry a homemade harvest basket to your garden. Fill it with garden-fresh spring flowers and vegetables for a special friend.*

# Silver Spoon Wall Hanging

Whether you inherited yours from Great Aunt Agatha or just had a great day at the flea market, an ornate silver spoon makes an unusual "container" for a dried flower arrangement. Although most appropriate hanging in the dining room or kitchen, you can use it anywhere you want a small, beautiful object. This is also a nostalgic way to use a baby's or child's spoon.

## MATERIALS

**Silver spoon, preferably a soup spoon or tablespoon**
**Clear polyurethane spray (optional)**
**6 to 8 inches of ⅛-inch-wide ribbon**
**Hot glue gun with clear glue sticks, or white craft or household glue**
**Dried Spanish moss**
**Assorted small dried flowers**

1. Polish the spoon and bend the bowl so that it is at a 90-degree angle to the handle. Spray with clear polyurethane varnish, if desired, to prevent tarnishing.
2. If the handle of your spoon is pierced, run ribbon through the holes and tie in a bow, forming a hanger. On other spoons, tie the ribbon in a knot on the backside of the handle at the point where the handle begins to widen; bring the ends up and tie into a bow, forming the hanger.
3. Glue a small clump of Spanish moss to the bowl.
4. Begin gluing dried flowers to the moss. German statice makes a nice background for larger flowers; baby's breath is an airy filler. Rosebuds and other small flowers will look best as a focal point.

## MATERIALS

Scissors
Fresh artemisia, such as worm-
    wood or 'Silver King'
12-inch-tall polystyrene cone
Floral pins
Dried flowers and herbs
Hot glue gun with clear glue
    sticks, or white craft or house-
    hold glue
⅛-inch-wide satin or velvet
    ribbon (2 to 3 yards)
Wired wooden floral picks

1. Cut artemisia into pieces about 5 inches long. Gather several stems together and place about 3 inches from the top of the cone. Secure stems with a floral pin inserted into the cone.
2. Continue adding clumps of artemisia around the cone, overlapping to hide the ends, until the entire cone is covered.
3. Set in a dark, well-ventilated place until dry.
4. Decorate with dried flowers and herbs as you desire, gluing each piece in place.
5. To make ribbon loops, cut a length of ribbon 5 to 7 inches long, make one or more loops, and wrap the wire on the wooden floral pick around them. Insert the pick into the cone.

# Dried Artemisia Christmas Tree

Delicate and fragile-looking, a cone-shaped tree made of any of the silvery-gray artemisias, especially one of the wormwoods, and decorated with all manner of dried flowers and leaves, is one of my favorite ways of capturing summer's glory. I usually make a fresh one each fall, picking the wormwood as it begins to bloom and attaching it with floral pins to a polystyrene cone while still fresh.

After it dries, I select my choicest dried flowers, most often including pastel-pink globe amaranth, hydrangea, and bamboo flowers; money plant and love-in-a-mist seed pods; and lamb's-ear leaves, gluing them on like ornaments. As a final touch, I add ribbon loops and set the tree within a circle of dark, glossy glycerinized magnolia leaves on a silver platter.

Whether you make a tree such as this large or small, or decorate with other colors and kinds of plant material, the effect will be stunning. Use it just for the Christmas holidays or leave out from fall to spring.

Artemisias are the workhorses of the dried flower and herb garden. If you've never grown them before, make 'Silver King' your first. It is the variety most often used by professionals. Don't overlook the other varieties, as each has a special characteristic. Some of the names to look for include southernwood, wormwood, sweet annie, white sage, and mugwort. All of these are perennials except for sweet annie, which is an annual.

In general, artemisias are easy to grow and can thrive even in poor, dry soil. They do need full sun. Artemisias may have silvery gray or green foliage that is finely divided. Harvest the stems just as the plants begin to bloom. If possible, make the tree while the artemisia is still fresh. If you don't have time, hang the stems to dry, then mist with water before working.

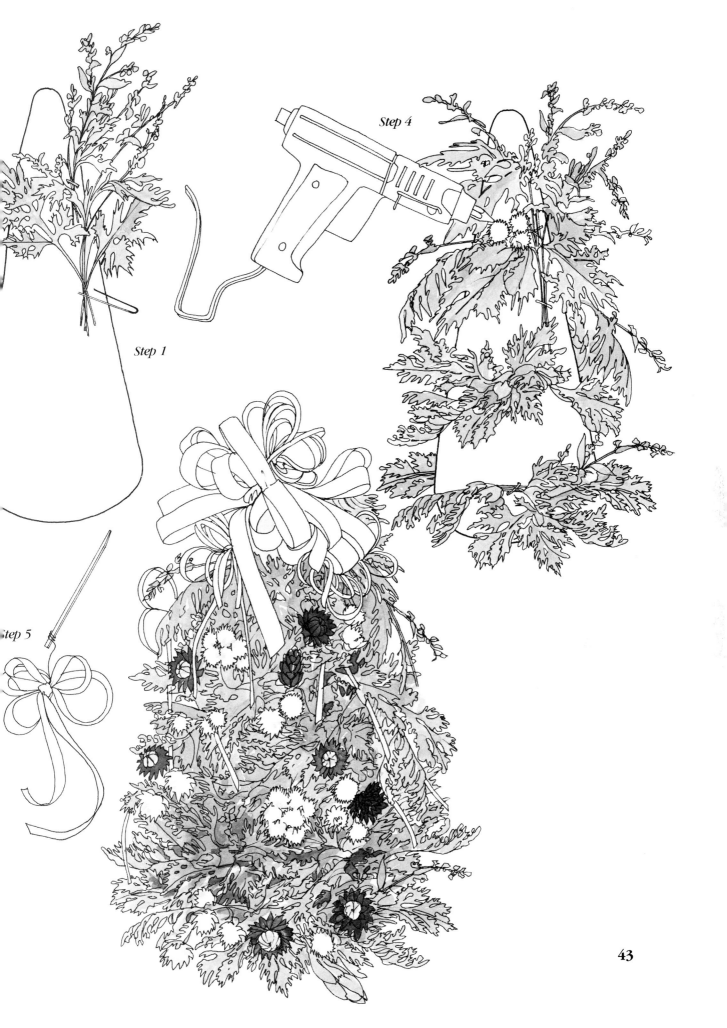

Step 4

Step 1

Step 5

**43**

# *Dried Flower Standard*

The formal French style of gardening, epitomized by the gardens of Versailles, reflects the spirit of the "Age of Reason." Descartes's influence, with his introduction of analytical geometry, was such that logic, order, and control pervaded much of seventeenth-century life. Gardens and plants were considered beautiful only if they were mastered by man. Plants became a strong architectural element in the landscape as they were sheared and took on all manner of geometric shapes.

Although this formality and control is far removed from our lives today, some aspects are still worthy of use in our homes and gardens because of the elegance they contribute. One of the most basic of ornamental shapes is the standard, a horticultural term that refers to a plant trained to a single stem topped with rounded or weeping growth. Roses, fuchsias, verbenas, and lantanas are often trained this way.

Just as the use of standards in the garden lends a dignity and richness to the landscape, so will standards made from dried flowers and herbs give that feeling indoors. Put a single splendid standard at one end of the sideboard or mantel, or a beautifully matched pair at either side of French doors or on a long buffet table. Make a great number of them to use as centerpieces for each table at a bridal shower or wedding luncheon.

Dried flower standards can be used in so many ways because they can be made large or small, trimmed for the various seasons or to fit a particular occasion, put in all manner of containers, and given a variety of looks.

## MATERIALS

**Bowl**
**Plaster of paris**
**Water**
**Clay pot**
**Branch or dowel about 3 times as long as pot diameter and ¼ to ½ inch in diameter, depending on the size of the pot**
**Polystyrene ball, ½ to 1 inch less in diameter than pot**
**Scissors**
**Assortment of dried flowers and herbs**
**Wired wooden floral picks (optional)**
**#22-gauge floral wire (optional)**
**Hot glue gun with clear glue sticks, or white craft or household glue**
**Ribbon (optional)**
**Dried Spanish moss**

1. Using an old bowl or other container, mix a quantity of plaster of paris with just enough water to give it a thick consistency. Mix up enough to have at least 2 to 3 inches in the bottom of the clay pot.
2. Pour the moistened plaster of paris into the pot and insert the dowel in the center. Allow to harden.
3. Insert the top end of the dowel several inches into the polystyrene ball.
4. Use a filler material such as German statice, baby's breath, or hydrangea to loosely cover the ball as a base for your design. Material with strong stems, such as statice, can be directly inserted into the ball; softer-stemmed material, if desired,

like baby's breath will need to be attached to small floral picks or wired with floral wire first. An alternative is to cover the ball with dried Spanish or woodland moss, then glue on other dried materials.

5. Next, attach other dried flowers, leaves, and seedpods to the base material with glue. Small loops of ribbon, if desired, can be added by gluing or wiring to floral picks.

6. Cover the plaster of paris with dried Spanish moss.

# Dried Flower Lapel Pin

## MATERIALS

**Scissors**
**Ruler**
**4 to 5 inches of 1-inch-wide lace**
**Needle**
**Thread**
**Lapel pin base (available from craft and hobby stores)**
**Hot glue gun and clear glue sticks, or white craft or household glue**
**Dried flowers**

1. With needle and thread, gather one edge of the lace tightly around the head of the lapel pin and knot the thread well. Sew the two ends of the lace together so no raw edges show. Add a few final stitches and a bit of glue to secure the lace flat behind the lapel pin head.
2. Glue a dried rosebud or other flower about ½ inch wide in the center. Glue tinier flowers in a circle around it.

People have been adorning themselves with both flowers and jewelry for centuries, so combining the two seems perfectly logical. The dainty beauty of a lapel pin made from dried flowers is far removed from logic, however. Rather, it tends to evoke emotions – perhaps a vague nostalgic fondness for earlier, gentler times, or more specific sweet memories of a garden and a special day.

These tiny nosegays take a minimum of material, time, and effort, yet provide an exquisite bit of adornment for yourself or a friend. Use them as favors at a luncheon or party, or keep several on hand for last-minute gifts or stocking stuffers.

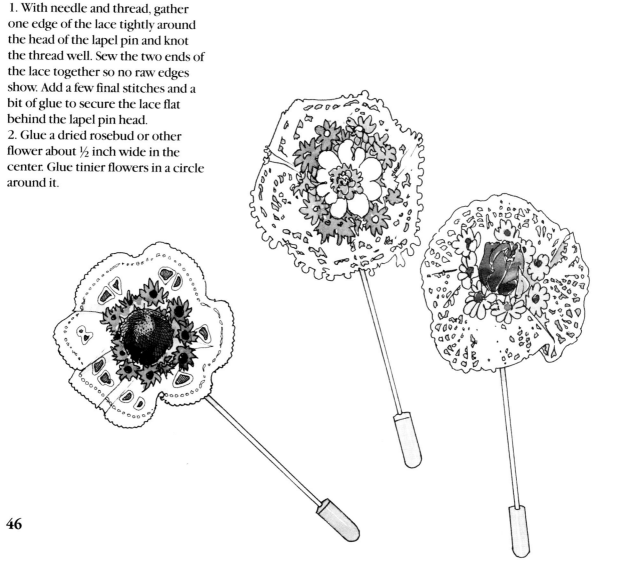

# Mixed Flower Wreath

Elaborately trimmed wreaths with a mixture of dried flowers and herbs (as well as pods, berries, cones, and even glycerinized leaves) are the epitome of the flower-crafter's work, commanding high prices in stores and catalogs. With patience and effort you can create your own masterpiece at much less expense.

If you want to create a large wreath for hanging over a mantel or on a wall, or for laying flat to surround a punch bowl or hurricane-shaded candle, you will need large quantities of a wide variety of dried plant materials. Learn to be observant not only in your garden but also in the fields, woods, and roadsides.

Before gathering wild materials, get permission from the owner of the property and verify that the plants are not endangered species. Some of the wild materials to look for include goldenrod, milkweed, joe-pye weed, wild yarrow, teasel, sumac, curly dock, sweet annie, rabbit tobacco, multiflora rose hips, knotweed, pepper grass, cat's paw, cloud grass, ironweed, thistle, beechnuts, hemlock cones, acorns, and Queen Anne's lace. Feathers from either domestic or wild birds can be used, too.

Before beginning, take an inventory of your materials. Then plan how and where you want to use the wreath, and develop the design accordingly.

## MATERIALS

**Straw wreath base, 12 to 16 inches in diameter**
**Wire cutters**
**#22-gauge floral wire**
**Needle-nose pliers**
**Scissors**
**Assorted dried flowers and herbs**
**Floral pins**
**Wired wooden floral picks**
**Green or brown floral tape**
**Hot glue gun with clear glue sticks, or white craft or household glue**
**Clear plastic craft spray sealer**

1. Make a hanger for the wreath by bending a length of the #22-gauge wire in half, knotting the two ends together, then pulling the knot tight with the pliers. Loop the wire around the wreath, putting one end through the other. Pull it tight on the back side of the wreath.

2. Now, begin covering the wreath with a background material, such as artemisia, baby's breath, statice, goldenrod, or pearly everlasting. To do this, gather three to five stems that are 3 to 5 inches long, and attach them in a cluster to the wreath with a floral pin. Start on the inside of the wreath, working around in one direction, overlapping and covering the stems of the previous cluster. When you get to your starting place, gently lift the first cluster and tuck in the stems of the last. Next, do the front of the wreath, and, finally, the outside edge, following the same procedure.

3. Add accent materials such as flowers, berries, pods, and so forth next. Almost all of these items should be attached in one of two ways. One

**47**

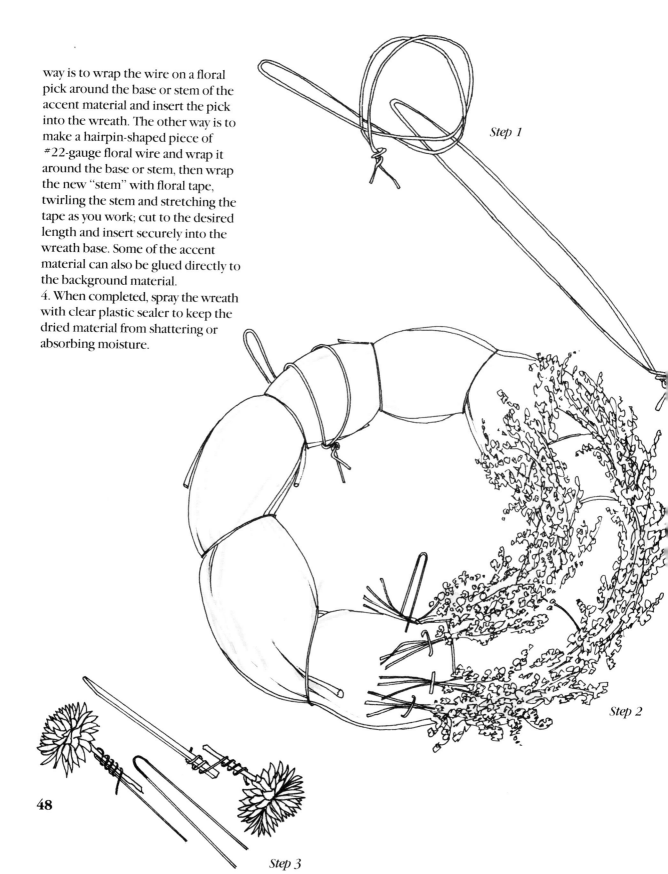

way is to wrap the wire on a floral pick around the base or stem of the accent material and insert the pick into the wreath. The other way is to make a hairpin-shaped piece of #22-gauge floral wire and wrap it around the base or stem, then wrap the new "stem" with floral tape, twirling the stem and stretching the tape as you work; cut to the desired length and insert securely into the wreath base. Some of the accent material can also be glued directly to the background material.

4. When completed, spray the wreath with clear plastic sealer to keep the dried material from shattering or absorbing moisture.

*Step 1*

*Step 2*

*Step 3*

# Everlasting Wreath

The staples of the "everlasting" garden, such as globe amaranth, nigella seedpods, strawflowers, bells-of-Ireland, cockscomb, and annual statice are to my craft projects what butter, olive oil, flour, and honey are to my cooking. Best of all, as long as I keep the weeds at bay, all of these grow with minimal care in the garden, thriving in hot, dry, sunny conditions.

Although they practically grow and dry themselves, there are a couple of tricks to get even more mileage from these everlastings. You can improve the germination of globe amaranth flowers by soaking the seeds for several days before planting. Mice think globe amaranth is the greatest thing since sliced bread, so be sure to store the dried flowers in a mouse-proof container.

Strawflowers will not shatter if they are picked just as they are opening. Another reason for a short life is that moths may lay eggs in them. Freezing the flowers overnight or microwaving them for two minutes on high will eliminate this problem. If microwaving, you must immediately insert floral wire through the center of each flower because they get very hard as they cool.

To keep the pale green color of bells-of-Ireland, cut them when the tiny florets inside the upper bells are fresh, then dry for a day and a half in silica gel. If left on the plant until fall, they turn a lovely silvery gray and can be air-dried by hanging them upside down.

If cockscomb turns an ugly brown for you, try this tip from Betty Wiita in *Dried Flowers for All Seasons* (Van Nostrand Reinhold Company, 1982). She suggests picking the blooms at noon when the sun has dried the dew. Then place the flower stems in a container of water set in a dark, cool place for three days. The flowers will droop, allowing moisture inside to evaporate. Now, hang each stem separately upside down in a warm, dry, well-ventilated place for about ten days.

Like globe amaranth, annual statice is slow to germinate. When buying seed, look for companies that hull the seed, which makes germination quicker and more uniform. Also, give the newer 'Art Shades' seed mixtures a try; these include such colors

## MATERIALS

**Round or heart-shaped poly-styrene wreath base, 6 to 10 inches in diameter**
**Enough dried Spanish moss or dried sheet moss to cover wreath base**
**Hot glue gun with clear glue sticks**
**Scissors**
**Ribbon**
**Dried everlastings**
**Assortment of other dried flowers and herbs (optional)**
**Lace (optional)**
**Clear plastic craft spray sealer**

1. To conceal the wreath base, cover it with pieces of either of the dried mosses, attaching them with clear hot glue.
2. Tie a ribbon at the top of the wreath, then tie the ends together to make a loop for a hanger.
3. Trim the stems from the everlastings. If using bells-of-Ireland, separate the individual bells from the stems. For cockscomb, break or cut the heads into smaller pieces.
4. Starting on the inside of the wreath, begin gluing the flowers to the wreath. Place them as close together as possible until all the front portions are covered.
5. Trim the wreath with ribbon, lace, or other dried materials, if desired. For example, surround the outside of the wreath with pregathered lace glued to the back of the wreath, or glue other dried flowers and leaves plus a ribbon on the wreath.
6. When completed, spray with clear plastic craft sealer.

**49**

as fawn, pink, mauve, apricot, and yellow. The more traditional colors are white, rose, lavender, and blue-purple. To dry, gather when the flowers are fully developed and showing maximum color. Secure bunches with a rubber band and suspend them upside down in a warm, dry, dark place until dry.

Although any of these flowers, as well as lesser-known everlastings like acroclinium, starflower, and xeranthemum, are useful in just about any capacity when making wreaths, arrangements, or other projects, they're especially satisfying when you let them take center stage in a wreath such as the one pictured.

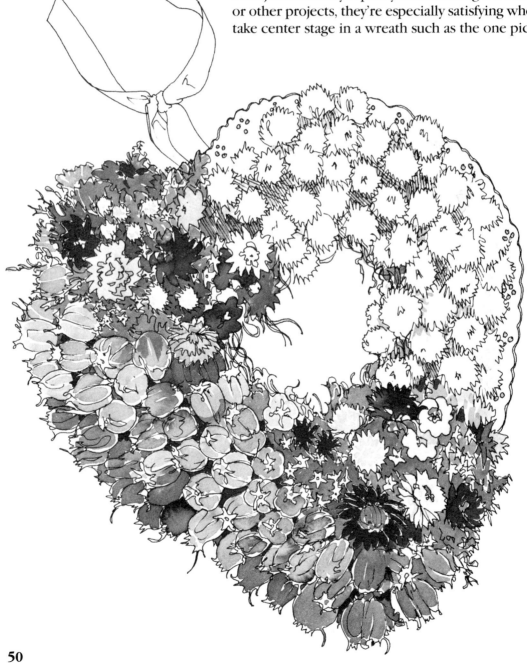

# *Small Herb Wreaths*

For those times when the world wearies and the plain and simple seems most appealing, I like to walk among my herbs, savoring the various scents. These are peaceful times, when I am most able to relax. Heading out the door, I usually grab the pruning shears kept in a basket there. This allows me to idly trim plants as I sort through the day's hassles.

In about five minutes' time, with almost no equipment, I can have a wreath of tangerine-scented southernwood, blue-flowered hyssop, or pungent pennyroyal. Brought into the house and hung or laid about, they scent the air delightfully. Within days, they will be dry and ready for trimming, then giving away.

Some of the other herbs that make simple wreaths are the mints, the thymes, the culinary sages, marjoram, oregano, 'Silver King' artemisia, and mugwort. Experiment with others. Leave them plain or trim with small dried flowers, berries, or hemlock cones, and maybe even a bow.

## MATERIALS

**10 to 15 herb branches, each about 12 to 15 inches long, for a 6-inch-diameter round wreath**
**Scissors or pruning shears**
**Fine paddle wire or nylon fishing line (optional)**
**Assorted dried plant materials (optional)**
**Hot glue gun with clear glue sticks, or white craft or household glue (optional)**
**Ribbon bow (optional)**

1. Make a circle of one stem, overlapping the ends in the palm of your hand. Take another stem and twist it around the first one, tucking in the ends. Repeat, slightly staggering where you start, but still holding in one hand while you use the other to add each new stem. After adding four or five stems, the wreath should be fairly stable. Continue twisting stems around the wreath and tucking in the ends until you have the thickness you want. Remember that the stems and leaves will shrink as they dry.
2. Wrap with fine wire or nylon line and tie off the ends, if you want. Trim as desired.

# *Yarrow Wreath*

## MATERIALS

**12-inch or larger straw or polystyrene wreath base**
**Dried sheet moss and floral pins (if using a polystyrene wreath)**
**Hot glue gun with clear glue sticks**
**Wire cutters**
**#22-gauge floral wire**
**Needle-nose pliers**
**Scissors**
**About 100 dried yarrow blossoms**
**Assortment of other dried flowers, herbs, cones, and pods (optional)**
**Ribbon (optional)**
**Wired wooden floral picks (optional)**
**Clear polyurethane varnish (optional)**
**Clear plastic craft spray sealer**

1. If using a polystyrene wreath base, cover it with pieces of dried sheet moss. Attach the pieces with glue.
2. Make a hanger for either wreath by bending a length of the #22-gauge floral wire in half, knotting the two ends together, then pulling the knot tight with the pliers. Loop the wire around the wreath, putting one end of the wire through the other. Pull it tight on the back side of the wreath.
3. Cut the stems from all yarrow heads, leaving an inch or less. Starting on the inside of the wreath, begin gluing the heads to the wreath, overlapping them slightly.
4. Continue until you have as much of the wreath covered as desired. Try to stagger the heads slightly as you work so they do not end up appearing in rows.

In selecting low-maintenance perennials for the garden, certain varieties of yarrow (*Achillea* species and hybrids) are among the top choices. Once established, they survive in spite of neglect, poor soil, heat, cold, and drought. What they won't be able to withstand is rich or moist soil or shade. Insects and diseases tend to ignore them.

These yarrows bloom for several weeks in June and July; if you faithfully remove all the flower heads, they will often bloom again. Since the flowers are excellent both in fresh and dried arrangements, this should be an easy task.

All of the varieties have flattened, saucer-shaped flowers in shades of white, rose, red, yellow, apricot, and gold. Plant height will vary from 2 to 4 feet, depending on the variety. The gray-green foliage is finely dissected and fernlike with a rich, pungent scent; be sure to press some for trimming pressed-flower projects.

The fernleaf yarrows (*Achillea taygetea* and *A. filipendulina*) are my favorite species, and 'Gold Plate', 'Coronation Gold', and 'Moonshine' are the varieties I prefer for wreaths.

Yarrow will dry naturally on the plant, but may be damaged by rain or turn brown. It's better to pick the flowers just as they become fully open, then tie them in loose bunches, securing with a rubber band, and hang upside down in a dark, well-ventilated place for drying.

Because they are so easy to grow and dry and are also very beautiful, the golden yarrows are a staple for driedflower crafts. If you have plenty, however, you should try covering an entire wreath with them. Alternatively, cover two-thirds of the wreath with yarrow and the remainder with glistening brown pods, cones, and seed heads. Either way, the effect is spectacular, especially in a room with a blazing fireplace or against a dark wall.

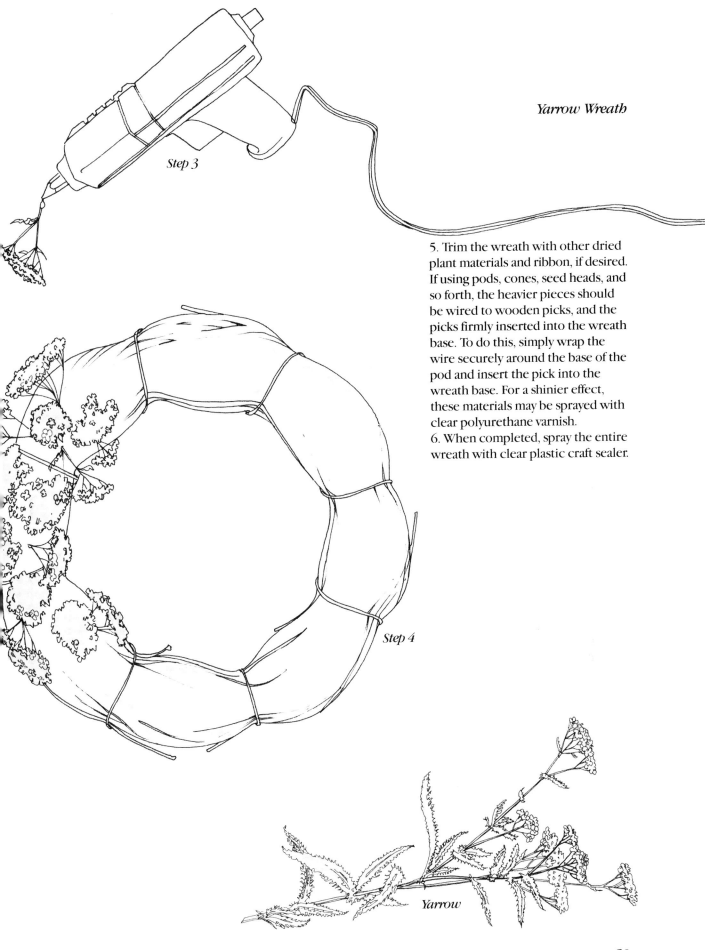

*Yarrow Wreath*

Step 3

5. Trim the wreath with other dried plant materials and ribbon, if desired. If using pods, cones, seed heads, and so forth, the heavier pieces should be wired to wooden picks, and the picks firmly inserted into the wreath base. To do this, simply wrap the wire securely around the base of the pod and insert the pick into the wreath base. For a shinier effect, these materials may be sprayed with clear polyurethane varnish.
6. When completed, spray the entire wreath with clear plastic craft sealer.

Step 4

*Yarrow*

# Hydrangea Wreath

## MATERIALS

**12-inch round straw wreath**
**Wire cutters**
**#22-gauge floral wire**
**Needle-nose pliers**
**Scissors**
**Dried hydrangea heads**
**Floral pins**
**Dried flowers (optional)**
**Hot glue gun with clear glue
sticks, or white craft or house-
hold glue**

1. Make a hanger for the wreath by bending a length of the #22-gauge floral wire in half, knotting the two ends together, then pulling the knot tight with the pliers. Loop the wire around the wreath, putting one end of the wire through the other. Pull it tight on the back side of the wreath.
2. With the scissors, trim off all but about ½ inch of the main stem below the flower head. If the flower cluster is small, put several together. Attach to the wreath with a floral pin.
3. Attach flowers around the wreath, first doing the inside of the wreath, then the outside, and finally the top.
4. Trim with dried flowers, if desired, using glue.

Of the approximately two dozen species of hydrangea shrubs and vines native to the Americas and Asia, the old-fashioned hills-of-snow hydrangea holds a fond place in many people's hearts. It has been a favorite garden plant since its discovery in a gorge near Yellow Springs, Ohio, sometime before the turn of the century. The masses of snow-white blooms borne in June and July add a welcome feeling of coolness to the garden.

The large, rounded clusters of flowers also make a significant addition to the dried flower larder. You can let them dry naturally on the plant, or cut stems for bouquets to dry indoors. Either way, the white flowers will turn a pale tan or green color. The related 'Peegee' hydrangea has a more pointed flower head that dries to a pinkish-gold color. Either one is useful in dried arrangements, wreaths, swags, and so forth. I save even the smallest bits and use them in miniature nosegays and similar projects. Press some of the individual flowers for using in pressedflower projects.

When you have an especially abundant supply of the flowers, this rather spectacular wreath is the perfect project. A hydrangea wreath is unusual enough to stand on its own, but the subtle colors are a perfect foil for other dried flowers, so it's difficult to resist adding some.

# Dried Flower and Herb Swags

Giving directions for swags is a little like having recipes for omelets or stir-fries – a bit superfluous once you know how. So for those of you who've never made a swag, basically all that is involved is taking a handful of "stuff" and tying it with a ribbon. Obviously, however, just as there are omelets and *omelets!* so, too, swags can be made very special.

The first consideration is what to use. My local herb society chapter has quite a reputation for the "weed" swags they sell at a craft fair. Teasel, dock, grasses, bittersweet, and other wild materials are cleverly combined. Kitchen swags might be composed of various culinary herbs. Swags of cultivated grasses, either of just one type or a collection, are another possibility.

Next, there are essentially three ways to make swags. Most are made with the bunch of plant material hung upside down, just as they air-dry. Grasses with drooping heads look best if the stems are tied in the middle and the cluster is displayed upright. A more elaborate swag is made by combining two bunches with the stems meeting in the middle.

## MATERIALS

**Dried plant material with long stems, such as dock, milkweed, money plant, grasses, iris pods, statice**
**#22-gauge floral wire**
**Ribbon bow (see Tying the Perfect Bow, page 165)**

1. Gather as many stems together as you want and arrange as desired.
2. Wrap the wire tightly around the ends of the stems.
3. Tie on the bow.

# *Lavender Sticks*

## MATERIALS

Scissors
13, 15, 17, or 19 lavender flowers
  with stems 10 to 15 inches
  long
String
4 feet of ¼-inch-wide satin ribbon

1. Pick fresh lavender flower stems when the lower flowers are open and strip off the leaves.
2. With an odd number of stems, as suggested above, gather the stems together with the lower flowers even. Tie the stems together snugly just below these flowers.
3. Gently bend the stems down one at a time; they should look like the spokes of an umbrella. There will be a break in the stem, but the stem should not break off.
4. Tuck the end of the ribbon in among the flowers. Begin to weave over and under stems, working down the stems until the flowers are enclosed. The first several rows are a bit difficult, so be patient.
5. Wrap the remaining ribbon in a spiral down the stems and secure with a bow. Trim stems evenly at the base.

Any Anglophile worth his or her afternoon tea is most likely also fond of lavender. But then, lavender is among the most favored of scented herbs, whether you know the words to "God Save the Queen" or not. Since the Renaissance, lavender has been widely used and popularized in soaps, perfumes, and potpourris in England, Europe, and the United States.

In the garden, lavender contributes a delicate, ghostly appearance because the foliage is fine-textured and usually gray-green. The foliage as well as the pale violet flowers charge the air on a hot day with their fragrance. A well-grown low hedge or border of lavender is truly a delight to the senses.

There are at least half a dozen species and varieties of lavender readily available, and a number of others less often seen. Many (but not all) are hardy to 0° F. Lavender plants need full sun and a light soil to grow well and maximize the aromatic oils in the plant.

Lavender flowers are lovely to use in fresh arrangements, but their primary purpose is for dried flowers. To dry, pick the flowers just as they begin showing color by cutting at the base of the stem; the oils are most concentrated around noon. By harvesting the flowers, you can often get at least one, if not two, more periods of bloom.

Lavender sticks are made by weaving ribbon in and out of the stems of a bunch of the flowers. Long stems make them easier to work with. The best variety to use is English lavender (*Lavandula angustifolia*) with its 18- to 24-inch stalks. Add these sticks to your bed, bath, and personal linens to give them that unmistakable scent!

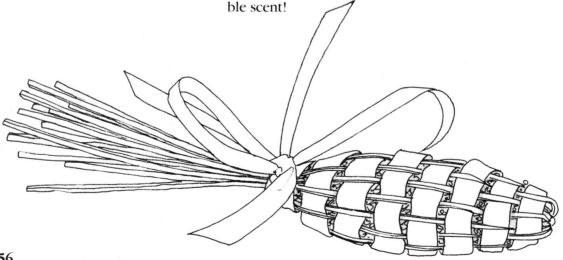

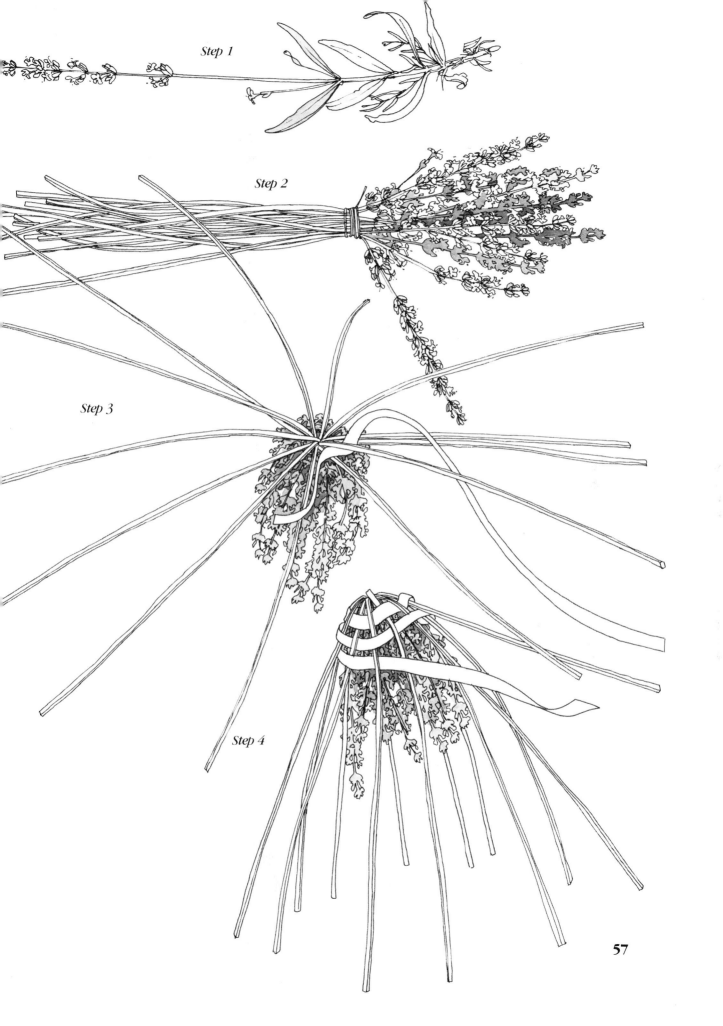

*Step 1*

*Step 2*

*Step 3*

*Step 4*

57

## MATERIALS

Scissors
100 to 125 dried rosebuds
Hot glue gun with clear glue
   sticks, or white craft or household glue
5- or 6-inch polystyrene circular
   or heart-shaped wreath form
   or 3- or 4-inch polystyrene ball
Dried flowers and herbs
Ribbon bow (See Tying the
   Perfect Bow, page 165)

1. Trim the stems flush with the base of the rosebuds.
2. Put a drop of glue on the base and attach to the form. Repeat until the entire surface of the ball or the front of the wreath form is covered.
3. Decorate with other dried flowers and herbs, and a ribbon bow.

# *Rosebud-Covered Wreath or Ornament*

Roses are among the most widely grown and deeply loved of all flowers. Their beauty and fragrance have made them cherished since the time of the ancient Greeks. In fact, it was the Greek poetess Sappho, around 600 B.C., who first called the rose the "queen of flowers." Since then, the cultivation of roses has spread to all corners of the world and become firmly entrenched in our hearts, gardens, and cultures.

There are thousands of rose varieties from which to choose, growing in size from less than 6 inches to well over 6 feet as bushy shrubs. The ones with long, arching canes, called climbers, actually must be tied to supports. Some roses bloom only once a year, while others bloom repeatedly. There are varieties with flowers in just about every color but a true blue. Some kinds have flowers with only 5 petals, while others may have as many as 50 petals.

Although roses are most often planted in formal beds, the tremendous assortment of growth habits, shapes, sizes, colors, and textures makes them a versatile shrub throughout the landscape.

Besides their role in the garden, roses have long been used for their other properties, too. Both the flowers and seedpods, or hips, have been used in culinary, beauty, and medicinal concoctions. The two best-known uses of roses are in perfumery and as cut flowers. Dried rosebuds and petals are a major ingredient in potpourris. One of the most exquisite ways of using rosebuds, if you have a bountiful amount, is to decorate a wreath or ornament form. Not just any rose variety will do for this. The buds should be fairly small and well formed. Pink roses seem to retain their color better than others. The two best varieties are 'Bonica' and 'Cecile Brunner', also known as 'The Sweetheart Rose' (see Sources, page 169).

To dry, pick the buds just as they begin to show color. Spread them on a screen and dry in a dark, well-ventilated place. (If you want to use a drying agent like silica gel, see Dried Flower Materials, Methods, and Techniques, page 1.) Store the dried buds in a single layer in a box until you have enough to cover the form you want.

# *Dried Flowers Under Glass*

Create your very own rarified atmosphere by filling a glass dome with your loveliest dried flowers, foliage, and herbs. These domes with wooden bases will showcase preserved plant materials as if they were precious jewels. Another one of those artful devices inherited from the Victorian era, a dried arrangement under a glass dome is not only beautiful but sensible, because it is protected from curious fingers and dust as well as humidity.

Glass domes can be purchased at import, craft, and jewelry stores in an assortment of sizes. Other glass containers you may want to consider for a similar effect include fishbowls, hurricane candle shades, ginger jars, old-fashioned candy store jars, or any other pieces of decorative glass that seem suitable.

Consider different arrangements for each season, or choose a style or color theme that is particularly appropriate for the occasion or person receiving the glass dome, such as an all-white bouquet for a wedding gift, a pink and blue one for a mother and new baby, or a bouquet of roses for Mother's Day. For an autumn birthday, consider an arrangement of cones, nuts, seedpods, and dried grasses. Just about any plant material is stunning under glass.

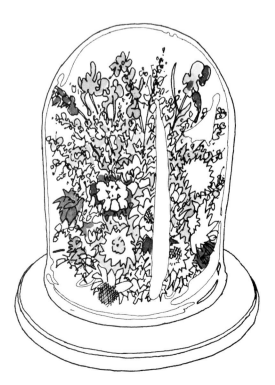

## MATERIALS

**Glass dome with wooden base**
**Round piece of floral foam about 2 inches less in diameter than the inside of the glass cover and 1 to 2 inches thick, depending on the height of the dome**
**Dried Spanish moss or dried sheet moss**
**Hot glue gun and clear glue sticks, or white craft or household glue**
**#22-gauge floral wire**
**Wire cutters**
**Green floral tape**
**Assortment of dried flowers and herbs**
**Clear silicone tub sealer and caulking gun**
**¼-inch-wide velvet ribbon (optional)**

1. Glue the floral foam to the center of the base that came with the glass dome. Cover the foam with some of the moss, attaching with glue or small "hairpins" made from the floral wire.

2. Begin creating your arrangement by inserting the tallest materials towards the back and sides of the design. Keep checking to make sure the dome will fit over the arrangement without touching.

3. Next, add the larger, darker, central flowers toward the lower part of the design. Use smaller flowers as you work toward the top of the arrangement.

4. Fill in around the design with lighter, more airy materials, such as baby's breath. You can use flowers with their natural stems or with stems made from the floral wire and tape. The arrangement can be designed for viewing from just the front or from all sides.

5. When you feel the arrangement is

## Crafts from Dried Flowers

finished, leave it alone for several hours to make sure it is just the way you want. When ready, seal the dome with a thin bead of the clear silicone tub sealer. If desired, trim the point where the dome and base meet with the velvet ribbon glued in place.

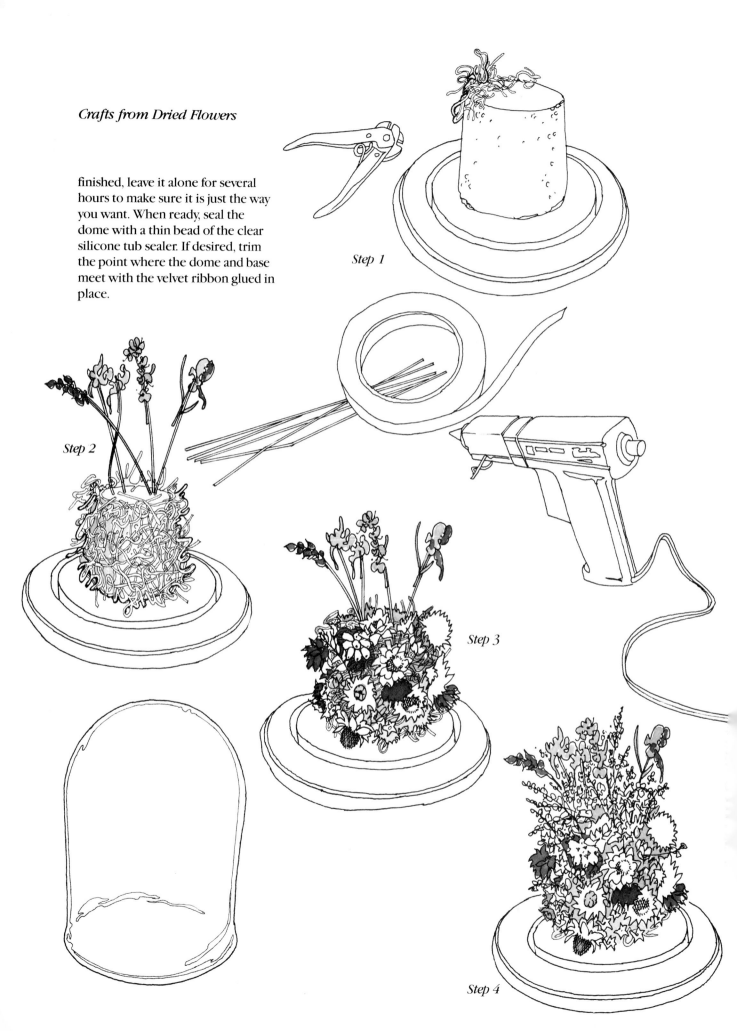

*Step 1*

*Step 2*

*Step 3*

*Step 4*

# Herb-Woven Basket

Through the centuries and civilizations, herbs have inspired gardeners, cooks, healers, and craftspeople. Basket weaving is also rooted in antiquity, yet a fascination with baskets continues today. Combining the two elements is a logical progression.

The amalgamation of fragrance and texture results in a unique and distinctive decorative object that is also useful. For example, when the bun basket illustrated is lined with a linen napkin and filled with hot muffins, the released scent of the mint welcomes guests to your table.

Handmade herb baskets can be interwoven with purchased reed, but why not collect plant materials from your yard or fields? Any of the woody basket materials, such as honeysuckle, wisteria, kudzu, or willow, will do for the framework. Just gather thin, pliable material and strip off the foliage. If it's a little stiff, soak in a pan of warm water for a few minutes.

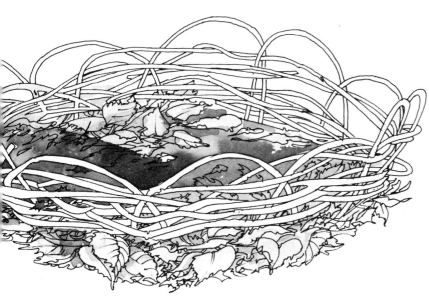

## MATERIALS

**(For a 9-inch bun basket)**
**Pruning shears**
**6 18- to 20-inch lengths of pliable woody stems about ⅛ inch in diameter**
**Longer pieces of pliable woody stems about ⅛ inch in diameter**
**Large.bunch of long-stemmed herbs, such as artemisia, bedstraw, chamomile, hyssop, marjoram, mint, rosemary, rue, summer savory, tarragon, thyme, or wormwood, with the leaves attached**

1. To start the basket, put three of the 18-inch woody stems next to each other parallel on a flat surface. Put the other three on top at a right angle to and in the center of the first group.
2. Take one of the longer woody stems and begin weaving over and under the groups of three pieces. Go around the "square" twice. Next, begin going over and under the pieces individually. Spread the spokes out so that they are evenly spaced, except for two, which should be combined to create an uneven number of spokes.
3. Go around about eight times. When you finish with one piece of woody stem, overlap with a new piece. A circle will not be taking shape.
4. Now, start weaving with herb stems, continuing around the circle and overlapping the ends when you add another piece. When you've made about 2 inches of herb weaving, begin shaping the sides of the basket, bringing the "spokes" upward.
5. After a total of 3 or 4 inches of

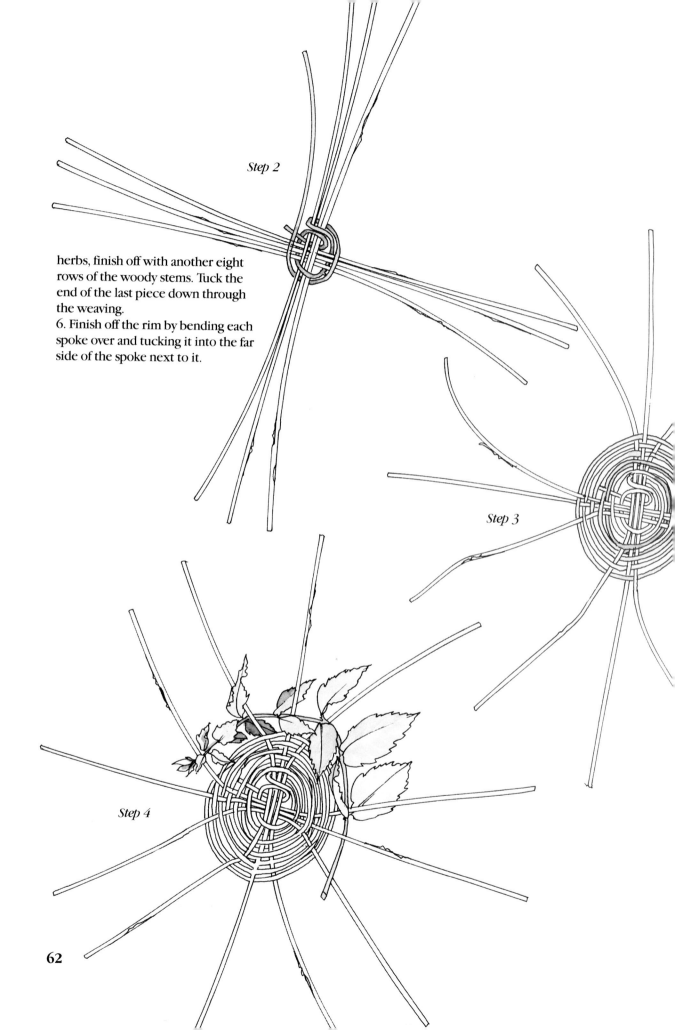

*Step 2*

herbs, finish off with another eight rows of the woody stems. Tuck the end of the last piece down through the weaving.

6. Finish off the rim by bending each spoke over and tucking it into the far side of the spoke next to it.

*Step 3*

*Step 4*

# Miniature Dried Flower Nosegays

Tiny nosegays, or tussie-mussies as the Victorians called them, are a captivating little conceit with a multitude of uses. Let them be ornaments on a sophisticated turn-of-the-century Christmas tree, package trims for gifts, place-card holders at a luncheon or dinner party, or favors at an open house. Hang them at a window, wear them on a lapel, attach to a comb or barrette for a hair ornament or to a silken cord for a necklace, and keep several on hand for giving at a moment's notice.

Scraps of lace and bits of dried flowers left over from other projects are the basis for these nosegays. I keep a shoebox handy with these materials so that it's easy to put several together without a great deal of effort.

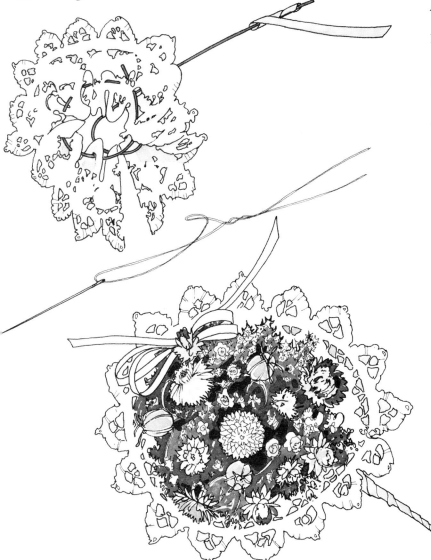

## MATERIALS

Wire cutters
#24-gauge floral wire
Scissors
Ruler
8 to 10 inches of 1- to 1½-inch-
  wide lace
Needle-nose pliers
Needle
Thread
Floral tape
Assortment of dried flowers in
  various sizes
Hot glue gun with clear glue
  sticks, or white craft or house-
  hold glue
⅛-inch-wide satin ribbon
  (optional)

1. Take a length of the floral wire and weave it through one 6-inch side of the lace. Bend the wire into a small circle, gathering the lace tightly. Bring the wire together and twist several times with the pliers. Cut this "stem" to 1½ inches.
2. Spread the lace evenly into a circle. With needle and thread, sew the ends together.
3. With the floral tape, wrap the wire stem, twirling the stem and stretching the tape. Trim the end.
4. Make an arrangement of flowers on top of the lace, gluing each piece in place. Put airy flowers like German statice or baby's breath on first, then the larger flowers like globe amaranth or rosebuds.
5. Tie a bow with the ribbon, if desired, and attach with glue under the bouquet but on top of the lace.

**63**

## MATERIALS

Container
Knife
Floral foam
Rubber cement, hot glue gun
   with clear glue sticks, white
   craft glue, or sticky floral tape,
   depending on the container
   (See Step 1, below)
Dried Spanish moss or dried
   sheet moss
Wire cutters
#22-gauge floral wire
Assorted dried grasses
Clear plastic craft spray sealer

1. Prepare the container by cutting a block of dry floral foam to fit snugly in the container with an inch extending above the rim. Firmly attach the foam to the container, using one of the following methods: rubber cement with glass and china; clear hot glue or white craft glue with baskets and wooden or metal containers. Alternatively, the foam may be anchored with strips of the sticky tape going from rim to rim of the container in at least two directions.
2. Lightly cover the foam with the dried Spanish moss. Attach with small "hairpins" cut and bent from the floral wire.
3. Create your arrangement, inserting the stems securely into the foam.
4. Step back and evaluate the arrangement. Add or remove as you see fit, or push and pull as necessary. When satisfied, spray the arrangement with sealer to keep the grass heads from shattering.

# Dried Grass Arrangements

The popularity of ornamental grasses for landscaping was foreshadowed by their widespread availability for years as dried material in florist and craft shops. There's no reason to depend on these retail sources for the lovely soft-textured grasses, however, as both the perennial and annual ornamental grasses are easily grown throughout the United States.

The perennial grasses are usually purchased as one-year-old field-grown plants. They offer the most in terms of landscaping potential, providing striking silhouettes in the garden from spring through winter. The annuals, which are readily started from seed, may be grown in a cutting garden or used in beds and borders like other annual flowers.

There are several native grasses with decorative flowers that you can find in fields and roadsides during the summer. These include foxtail, brome grass, switch grass, and common reed.

The key to successfully drying your own grasses is in picking the flower head just as it is emerging from the leaves of the plant. This may seem premature, but it ensures that the head will not shatter as it dries. A few grasses can be successfully picked later, but generally aim for early picking.

To dry grasses, simply hang bunches of them upside down in a cool, dry, dark, well-ventilated room. If you want stems that have more curve, place the cut grasses upright in a container with no water. Drying usually takes one to two weeks.

For added texture in dried arrangements, two grass varieties have leaves that are particularly attractive when dried. These are maiden grass, *Miscanthus sinensis* 'Gracillimus', and plume grass, *Erianthus ravennae*.

When dry, most grasses are beige, brown, or sometimes pale green. If desired, they can be dyed by dipping in fabric dye. However, grasses are so striking and blend so well with other natural materials, such as yarrow, money plant, cattails, teasel, and everlastings, that it seems a shame to alter them in any way.

Keep a supply of dried grasses on hand for general use with your dried flower projects. They'll add wonderful texture and form, whether you're making wreaths, swags, formal table arrangements, dried nosegays, or casual bouquets.

# ORNAMENTAL GRASSES

## Perennial Ornamental Grasses with Decorative Flower Heads

| Botanical Name | Common Name |
|---|---|
| *Ampelodesmos mauritanicus* | Mauritania vine reed |
| *Andropogon scoparius* | Little bluestem |
| *Arundo donax* | Giant reed grass |
| *Bouteloua gracilis* | Side oats grama |
| *Briza media* | Quaking grass |
| *Calamagrostis epigeous* | Reed grass |
| *Cortaderia selloana* | Pampas grass |
| *Deschampsia* spp. | Hair grass |
| *Elymus interruptus* | Nodding lyme grass |
| *Eragrostis* spp. | Love grass |
| *Erianthus ravennae* | Plume grass |
| *Luzula* spp. | White woodrush |
| *Millium* spp. | Millet grass |
| *Miscanthus* spp. | Eulalia grass |
| *Panicum virgatum* | Switch grass |
| *Phleum pratensis* | Timothy |
| *Sitanion hystrix* | Squirrel's-tail grass |
| *Sorghastrum nutans* | Indian grass |
| *Spartina pectinata* 'Aureo-Marginata' | Prairie cord grass |
| *Stipa pennata* | Feather grass |
| *Uniola* spp. | Sea oats |

## Annual Ornamental Grasses with Decorative Flower Heads

| Botanical Name | Common Name |
|---|---|
| *Agrostis nebulosa* | Cloud grass |
| *Aira capillaris* 'Pulchella' | Hair grass |
| *Apera* spp. | Silky bent grass |
| *Avena* spp. | Oats |
| *Briza maxima* | Large quaking grass |
| *Briza minor* | Small quaking grass |
| *Bromus* spp. | Brome grass |
| *Desmazeria sicula* | Spike grass |
| *Hordeum vulgare* | Barley |
| *Lagurus ovatus* | Hare's-tail grass |
| *Phalaris* spp. | Canary grass |
| *Polypogon monspeliensis* | Rabbit's-tail grass |
| *Setaria italica* | Foxtail millet |
| *Triticum* spp. | Wheat |
| *Zizania aquatica* | Wild rice |

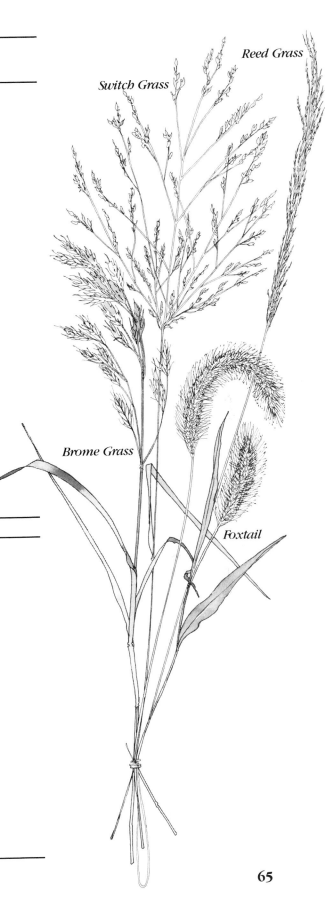

Reed Grass

Switch Grass

Brome Grass

Foxtail

# *Eulalia Grass Wreath*

## MATERIALS

Wire cutters
#22-gauge floral wire
Needle-nose pliers
12-inch straw wreath form
50 or more heads of dried eulalia
   grass
Scissors
Floral pins
Dried flowers and herbs
   (optional)
Hot glue gun with clear glue
   sticks, or white craft or house-
   hold glue
Clear plastic craft spray sealer
Ribbon bow (see Tying the
   Perfect Bow, page 165); optional

1. Make a hanger for the wreath by bending a length of the #22-gauge floral wire in half, knotting the two ends together, then pulling the knot tight with the pliers. Loop the wire around the wreath, putting one end of the wire through the other. Pull it tight on the back side of the wreath.
2. Cut the stems of the grass 2 to 3 inches long.
3. Put three together and attach to the wreath form with a floral pin.
4. Continue adding the grass around the form, overlapping so the stems don't show. It will take two or three clumps across to cover the front of the wreath; stagger them slightly.
5. When you have gone completely around, raise your first clump up to cover the last one.
6. Trim with dried flowers or herbs, if desired, using glue.
7. Spray with craft sealer.
8. Add a ribbon bow, if desired.

One of the most popular of the ornamental grasses, the form of eulalia grass with the scientific name of *Miscanthus sinensis,* is an outstanding garden plant. The gracefully arching or curving leaves add delicate texture to either perennial borders or naturalized areas. The plants are able to grow well in a variety of soil types, but need full sun. And for anyone who has dealt with the rampantly spreading roots of its cousin, *M. sacchariflorus,* the sedately spreading clumps of this eulalia are most enjoyable. At most, they will reach 4 feet across and 7 to 10 feet tall.

There are three interesting variants of this species of eulalia grass that are worth searching out and growing. 'Gracillimus', or maiden grass, is a smaller-growing, finer-textured, more graceful plant with curly leaves and heads. 'Variegatus', or striped eulalia grass, has yellow-, white-, and green-striped foliage. While the species and maiden grass are hardy through Zone 4, striped eulalia grass is only hardy through Zone 7. 'Zebrinus', or zebra grass, is one of the most unusual of the ornamental grasses in that the leaves are striped horizontally. It is hardy through Zone 5.

Even though the leaves of all these grasses turn brown in winter, the large, fluffy, plumelike flowers remain attractive outdoors until early spring and, if cut, are excellent for drying and dyeing for craft projects. Pick them just as they are expanding from the leaves of the plant. Hang them upside down in a cool, dry, dark, well-ventilated place for one to two weeks.

Besides being a wonderful grass for dried arrangements, the plumes of eulalia grass make a stunning wreath that can be used as is, or accented with ribbon or other trim.

66

# Chapter 2
# Crafts from Pressed Flowers

## Flowers and Grasses for Pressing

Aster
Baby's breath
Bleeding heart
Browallia
Buttercup
Cardinal flower
Celandine poppy
Clematis
Cloud grass
Columbine
Coral bells
Coreopsis
Cosmos
Crocus
Daisy
Delphinium
Dogwood
Dutchman's breeches
Feverfew
Forget-me-not
Freesia
Geranium florets
Goldenrod
Honeysuckle
Hydrangea florets
Larkspur
Lobelia
Love-in-a-mist
Mimosa
Miniature rose
Mock orange
Monkshood
Oxalis
Pansy
Phlox florets
Queen Anne's lace
Salvia

## Materials and Methods for Pressing Flowers and Herbs

Preserving flowers and herbs by pressing them allows you to make a wide range of appealing objects and keepsakes. With the removal of their dimension and scent as well the frequent alteration of their color, the botanical subjects verge on becoming abstract elements. As such, they are not restricted to any particular style, and can be developed into designs that are traditional or contemporary, simple or elaborate, sophisticated or frilly.

As a pastime, flowers and herbs can be pressed and used with only a minimum of paraphernalia. If you get deeply involved, you may find additional items useful, but they're certainly not necessary to begin.

## The Plant Press

The most obvious necessity is a means of pressing the plant materials and absorbing their moisture as they dry. A thick telephone directory is the best choice for beginners because it works well and the price is right. Just don't use this year's!

Stacks of unprinted newspaper stock are another good pressing material. You can also use printed newspapers, but you'll have to put the plant material between pieces of typing paper to avoid ink staining the flowers and leaves. If you're using newspaper, cut the pages into 7½-by-11-inch quarters. Blotter paper also works well; cut sheets into 9½-by-12-inch quarters.

Don't use paper towels, as the wafflelike texture is undesirable. Facial tissues should also be avoided; the fragile flowers will often cling to them and break as they're removed. Similarly, don't use presses with corrugated cardboard that will give pressed plant material a wavy appearance.

To maintain pressure on the paper and plant materials, you can use bricks, concrete blocks, books, or other heavy objects. A press can be made with two pieces of ½-inch plywood, held together with four C-clamps or by drilling holes in each corner of the wood and inserting four long screws with matching wing nuts.

## Plant Materials

Usually the best plant materials for drying are those that are already flat and thin-centered, but there are exceptions. Use the list on this page as a guide, but be adventurous and try different things.

## The Process

Pick flowers on a dry, sunny day, either in the morning just after the dew has dried or in the late afternoon. Press the flowers and leaves as soon as possible. Placing face down, arrange the material in pleasing shapes, pressing flowers at different stages of development, with some flat and others in profile. Make sure they do not touch one another or overlap. Thin out leaves so they do not overlap or lie on the stem. Curve some of the stems. To make sure you get the shape you want, apply small pieces of masking tape at several points along the stem to create a particular curve.

If you're using a phone directory or newsprint, have at least ½ inch of paper between each page of plant material. Or use several sheets of blotter paper between layers.

Use masking tape to make tabs extending from the side of each sheet for labels with plant name and date. If you're the organized type, you'll have only one color on each layer and use that color ink for the label.

When the stack is ready for drying, put it in a warm, dry place with good air circulation. Avoid damp floors or areas with high humidity. Add weights, clamps, or screws.

Check the plants in several weeks. The time necessary for drying will depend on the plant material, the weather, and the location. When the flowers and leaves are thoroughly dry, they can be left in the press or transferred to thin, flat boxes or drawers for storage.

Speedwell
Squirrel corn
Statice
Verbena
White clover
Wild grasses

### Leaves for Pressing

Autumn foliage
Betony
Chrysanthemum
Clematis
Clover
Columbine
Dusty miller
Garlic chives
Geranium
Honeysuckle
Ivy
Jacob's ladder
Lady's bedstraw
Lamb's-ear
Oxalis
Raspberry
Rose
Rue
Sage
Variegated goutweed
Vetch

### Ferns for Pressing

Bracken
Christmas
Lady
Maidenhair
Narrow breech
Polypody
Royal

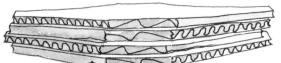

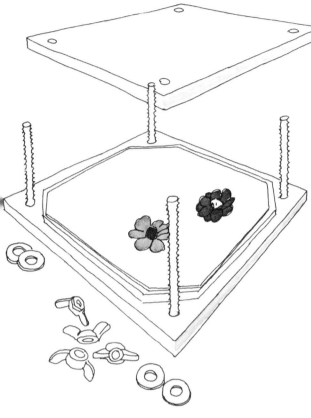

# Pressed Flower Pictures

If you're ever in Phildelphia in March, be sure to visit the fantasy world of the Philadelphia Flower Show. It is remarkable not only for the complete landscapes assembled indoors, but also for the display of pressed flower pictures entered into competition. You'll be tremendously inspired – it is an opportunity to see the ultimate possibilities of using pressed flowers.

Actually, one of the nicest aspects of making pressed flower pictures is that sometimes the simplest ones seem the best. One of my favorites is a single curved stem with two leaves and one yellow miniature rosebud pressed in profile and placed on black velvet in a brass frame.

Another delightful option is placing one or two perfect flowers against a line drawing. Or make a composition entirely of colorful autumn foliage. Why not gather flowers on your vacation and make a "souvenir" picture when you return home? A thoughtful thank-you for a hostess would be a picture using flowers gathered from her garden.

Wedding invitations or special photographs embellished with pressed flowers are a lovely keepsake. Try making a "basket" out of cornshucks or pressed wheat stems. Fern fronds placed vertically can create a miniature forest. Pressed wreaths are another option. Some people even create scenes with animals, fairies, and people, either by using the natural shape of the pressed material or by trimming it with scissors.

## Selecting the Background

Begin assembling a pressed flower picture by coordinating your plant materials with a suitable background. Traditional materials include matte board and fabrics such as velvet, wool, burlap, felt, grasscloth, matte-finish silks, and moiré. The background should enhance, not compete with, the flowers and foliage. Generally, choose a background color that will suit the flowers but in a shade that contrasts. For example, if most of the flowers are light, a dark background will set them off, and vice versa.

## Choosing the Frame

Next, choose a frame that coordinates with your plant materials as well as with the design you have in mind. There is a wide range of inexpensive, ready-made frames available. You can also have a frame professionally made. Or you may want to make a twig frame or one from old barn siding. Flea markets and antique shops are both excellent sources of picture frames.

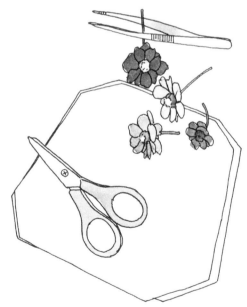

*To use a flower press, arrange flowers on sheets of cardboard or paper. Cover with another sheet. When you've run out of flowers or the press is full, screw on the wooden top.*

## Preparing the Background

Once the background and the frame have been selected, cut the background to size, using the the glass from the frame as a guide. If using fabric, mount it on a sheet of stiff cardboard the same size. Put a very narrow bead of white craft glue right on the edge of the cardboard, then attach the fabric. An alternative method is to use artist's spray adhesive, which is available from art and craft stores.

## Designing the Picture

With the prepared background in front of you, consider your design. Use a camel's hair paintbrush or small makeup brush and eyebrow tweezers to move the plant materials around.

Start with the outer ("framing") flowers and leaves. These are usually the lightest in color and texture. Using fern fronds and grasses lends an element of airiness to a picture. Work in the larger, darker flowers toward the center and base. Keep the size of the flowers and leaves in scale.

Overlap some of the leaves and flowers to create the effect of depth and dimension, but remember that the finished project must be flat unless you intend to add matting to the picture. If necessary, cut away stems and plant parts that are hidden. Don't crowd your arrangement; it's better to err on the side of too little rather than too much.

Now, you must either make a sketch of the arrangement and disassemble it or turn it upside down. To do the latter, place a sheet of stiff cardboard on top, hold tightly, and turn it over. Carefully remove the background sheet and turn it right side up.

## Assembling the Picture

Use water-soluble white craft glue that dries clear. Squeeze some out into a saucer, and use a toothpick to dab tiny amounts on key places on the backs of the flowers and foliage. Put them in place on the background you've chosen, following the design you've planned. Let the picture dry thoroughly, at least overnight, before framing.

Clean the glass well and insert into the frame. Then gently insert the pressed flower picture. Carefully put in small picture nails or glazing points to hold the cardboard in place. Attach masking tape to seal the point where the cardboard and frame meet. Next, cut a piece of aluminum foil to fit inside the frame and tape it into place; this helps to seal out moisture. Finally, cut a piece of plain brown paper to cover the back and glue it on. Attach two screws designed for picture frame backs about one-third of the way from the top; thread picture wire between the screws or attach a self-leveling hanger at the top.

*Design a pressed flower picture before you assemble it.*

# *Pressed Flower Stationery and Bookmark*

## MATERIALS

**Scissors**
**Ruler**
**Pencil**
**Plain note cards, paper, or heavy stock**
**Pressed flowers, leaves, and so forth**
**White craft or household glue**
**Clear plastic self-sticking paper (available from craft stores)**
**Hole punch and yarn (optional for bookmark)**

1. Decide what you want to make, the paper to use, and the design. Piece by piece, transfer the dried material to the surface you're decorating, putting a tiny drop of glue on the back of the pressed flower or leaf before setting it in place. Make sure it is thoroughly dry before proceeding to the next step.
2. Cut a piece of the clear self-sticking paper a half-inch or so larger than the paper with the pressed arrangement. Remove the backing from the self-sticking paper, center it over the other paper, and put in place. Trim the edges.
3. The bookmark can be made as above or with both the top and bottom made of the clear self-sticking paper. If desired, punch a hole at one end and make a yarn tassel.

With only the smallest amount of pressed flowers, sometimes just the scraps from other projects, you can design delicate, one-of-a-kind note cards and papers, bookmarks, and place cards. Adding a few pressed leaves, bits of moss, and butterfly wings will further enhance your creations. A calligraphic message or quote makes them even more special.

The note paper and cards can be made in any size and with a variety of materials. Rice paper, available from craft stores, provides additional textural interest. Small print shops and stationery stores are sources of rich-looking papers in delicate pastels. The traditional size for place cards is 3 by 2 inches, folded to 1½ by 2 inches. An average size for a bookmark is 1½ by 5 inches.

A particularly nice touch, especially if giving pressed flower stationery as a gift, is to make a flower-covered box or writing portfolio to match the contents.

# Pressed Flower Placemats

You can remember those flower-filled summer days all year long with placemats decorated with pressed flowers. Or, during autumn, set the table with placemats showcasing colorful leaves. Customize placemats to match a friend's china or dining room. For a special dinner party, the flowers in the placemats could match the fresh flowers in the centerpiece.

## MATERIALS

**Newspapers**
**Yardstick or long metal ruler**
**Single-edge razor or X-acto knife**
**Matte board (a 32-by-40-inch sheet will make two 14-by-18-inch placemats)**
**Pressed flowers and leaves**
**Scissors**
**Camel's hair brush or small makeup brush**
**Tweezers**
**White craft or household glue**
**Saucer**
**Toothpick**
**Clear self-sticking paper (you'll need a piece slightly larger than 14 by 18 inches for each placemat)**

1. On a large, flat surface, well-protected with newspapers, use the yardstick and the razor or knife to cut the matte board into 14-by-18-inch pieces for each placemat. (Or have a frame shop cut the board for you.)
2. Lay out a design, following the principles suggested in Pressed Flower Pictures (page 70).
3. Put some glue in a saucer and, using a toothpick, put a small amount of glue on the back of the pressed plant materials and transfer the design to the matte board.
4. When all the flowers and leaves are glued down, let the the glue dry completely, preferably overnight.
5. Cut a sheet of the clear self-sticking paper several inches larger than the placemat. Remove the backing and carefully place on top of the decorated placemat. If the self-sticking plastic adheres to the work surface, gently lift it up.
6. Turn the placemat over and, working again on a flat, well-protected surface, use the razor or knife to trim the edges or fold the plastic to the back, mitering the corners.

73

## MATERIALS

**Glass microscope slides**
**Pressed flowers, leaves, and so
    forth**
**Tweezers**
**Scissors**
**White craft or household glue**
**Toothpick**
**⅛-inch-wide ribbon**

1. Placing a slide vertically, develop a design with pressed flowers and leaves. Put another slide on top and, holding tightly together, turn over.
2. The design is now upside down and can be transferred to the first slide, attaching each piece with tiny amounts of glue applied with a toothpick.
3. Cut a 5-inch length of ribbon and make a loop. Glue the ribbon to the top end of the flower-decorated slide.
4. Put a drop of glue in each corner and put the second slide on top.
5. Put a thin layer of glue around the raw edges of the glass and cover with ribbon. Put a small bow at the base of the hanger, if desired.

# *Pressed Flower Glass Hanging*

Sometimes we make or do things just because they're fun, pretty, enjoyable, or impractical. I firmly believe that every day needs a little caprice. Pressed flower glass ornaments definitely fall into that category.

Sunlight is the bane of pressed flowers, bleaching out the colors. Yet while the colors are still vibrant, these ornaments bring a great deal of satisfaction. So what if it's fleeting? By the time the colors fade, we'll be anxious to try a new design.

If you already have the skills to do copper foil or leaded glass, or have a shop nearby that teaches these crafts, then sandwich a pressed flower arrangement between two sheets of glass and finish them with one of the two techniques. For the rest of us, a metal sectional frame can substitute.

A simple, but wonderfully inspired, idea is to make small ornaments from microscope slides. This design is from the booklet, *Deck the Halls with Artemisia: Christmas Decorating with Herbs,* by Barbara Radcliffe Rogers (available for $3.00 from Herbitage Farm, Route 2, Richmond, NH 03470).

## MATERIALS

**Pressed flowers and leaves**
**Scissors (optional)**
**5-by-7-inch metal sectional**
   **frame with two sheets of**
   **glass cut for it and metal clips**
**Tweezers (optional)**
**White craft or household glue**
**Toothpick**
**Epoxy glue**
**Two ½-inch metal washers**
**Nylon filament thread or fishing**
   **line or metal chain**

1. Develop design with pressed flowers and leaves. Transfer it to one sheet of glass (with tweezers, if desired), attaching with tiny amounts of glue applied with a toothpick. When the arrangement is complete, let it dry thoroughly, preferably overnight.
2. Put a second piece of glass on top and insert into the frame. Put metal clips along the edges between the glass and frame to hold the glass in the frame.
3. Use the epoxy glue to attach a washer to each upper corner of the frame. Thread a length of fishing line between the washers for a hanger, or use chain.

## MATERIALS

**Candles at least 2 inches in diameter**
**Pressed flowers and leaves**
**Scissors**
**White craft or household glue**
**Small bowl**
**Water**
**Tweezers**
**½-inch-wide brush**

1. Create your pressed flower and leaf design for the candle.
2. Pour some glue into a bowl. If necessary, thin it with water to the consistency of light cream.
3. Holding the pressed material with tweezers, use a brush to lightly coat the underside of the pressed material with glue. Attach to the candle. Continue until you have the design you want. Let it dry thoroughly, preferably overnight.
4. Make up a new batch of thinned glue. Use it to paint over the pressed flowers and leaves, extending the glue slightly beyond the pressed materials. This should seal the flowers to the candle, yet dry clear.

# Candles Trimmed with Pressed Flowers

Put your pressed flowers in a new light and let them shine. Decorating the surface of large pastel candles that hold their shape as they burn is a lovely way to use pressed flowers and leaves. A cluster of five or seven candles makes a stunning centerpiece. Candles trimmed this way will also be much-appreciated gifts.

# Pressed Flower Serving Tray

A serving tray decorated with your best pressed flowers combines the aspects of beauty and function in an almost ideal manner. Whether left sitting on a flat surface or leaning against a wall, the tray is literally "as pretty as a picture." Use it to serve refreshments for a party or a meal just for you, as it makes any occasion special.

A project such as this allows a great deal of leeway as to the appearance of the finished product. By varying the color and design of the frame and handles as well as the color of the matting and the flowers, you can create a tray that will fit just about any home or personality. The size, too, can be varied, although the 14-by-18-inch dimensions of the tray shown are very useful. I specially selected the frame for this tray at a picture framing shop, but you might find something you like already made.

## MATERIALS

Background matting to fit frame
Assorted pressed flowers, leaves, and butterflies
Double picture matting to fit frame, with opening cut to size and shape you desire
White craft or household glue
Toothpick
2 cabinet handles
Wooden picture frame (with area for matting and glass at least ⅝ inch thick)
Drill
Glass cut to fit frame
¼-inch-thick plywood or ⅛-inch-thick fiberboard cut to fit frame
Glazing points (optional)
Hammer (optional)
Felt to fit the back of the frame, or four round self-adhesive rubber frame-back tips (available from frame shops)

1. On the background matting, create a design with pressed flowers, leaves, and butterflies that will fit inside the opening of the double picture matting.
2. Use white glue to attach the pressed material, putting small drops on the main veins, flower centers, and so forth. Spread the glue with a toothpick, if necessary. Let it dry completely, preferably overnight.
3. Attach cabinet handles to the center of each end of the frame, using a drill to predrill the holes.
4. Insert the glass in the frame, then the double matting. Next, put in the pressed flower arrangement. Finally, put in the plywood or fiberboard. Attach glazing points with a hammer to hold these layers in the frame. (If preferred, take the frame and layers to a picture-framing shop for this step.)
5. To protect furniture, cover the back of the frame with felt, attaching it at the edges with white glue, or attach rubber tips at the corners.

77

# Pressed Flower and Leaf Christmas Decorations

## MATERIALS

Pressed flowers and leaves
⅛- or ¼-inch-wide ribbon, or
   gilt or satin cord
Hot glue gun with clear glue
   sticks, or white craft or household glue
Dried flowers or red peppers
   (optional)

1. Design the ornament, wreath, or garland.
2. Attach the pieces together or to ribbon or cord with glue. Make a loop for hanging an ornament with a 7-inch length of ribbon or cord.
3. Trim with dried flowers or red peppers, if desired.

Snowflakes of Queen Anne's lace, garlands and wreaths of crimson leaves, and translucent coins of money plant pods are delicate decorations that will make your Christmas holidays blossom.

Look at pressed flowers and leaves with a fresh eye. Five separate pointed leaves glued together in an overlapping pattern make a star; put a flower in the middle and a loop of ribbon or cord at the top. String a pair of mitten-shaped sassafras leaves together with ribbon and make "fur" cuffs with dried flowers.

When pressed and dried, Queen Anne's lace so closely resembles a snowflake that I make a concerted effort each summer to press a great many for the Christmas holidays. Glue several money plant seedpods on the back of one of these flowers and attach a cream-colored ribbon loop. Or make a garland by spacing them at intervals along the same colored ribbon. Make other ornaments by combining Queen Anne's lace with dried white poplar leaves or the leaves of dusty miller.

Make tiny wreaths of grapevine or honeysuckle and glue pressed leaves or flowers on top. Make another garland, this time with pressed leaves evenly spaced at intervals on the ribbon. Try unusual combinations of pressed flowers and leaves on top of one another or trimmed with dried flowers. Dried red peppers call up the holiday mood, too.

For traditional Christmas colors, dry green leaves during the summer *and* red ones in autumn. Or try the naturally red leaves of barberry, Joseph's-coat, Japanese maple, and coleus. Be sure to dry lots of white or pale leaves and flowers, too.

# Wooden Objects Trimmed with Pressed Flowers

Part of the fun of getting involved in craft projects is brainstorming and considering the possibilities. For instance, think about combining an assortment of dried flowers and leaves with flat wooden surfaces and a clear sealer, such as lacquer, vinyl resin, or decoupage coating.

My list of objects that would be attractive trimmed with dried flowers includes bookends, hairbrush and and mirror sets, light switch covers, wastebaskets, clocks, jewelry boxes, pendants and pins, plaques, napkin holders, bed trays, coffee or end tables, cabinet knobs, and coasters. I expect you can come up with more.

## MATERIALS

**Fine-grit sandpaper**
**1-inch-wide paintbrush**
**Lacquer, decoupage coating, or vinyl resin kit**
**Wooden object**
**Pressed flowers, leaves, and so forth**
**Scissors**
**Tweezers (optional)**
**Old can or cup for cleaning brush**

1. Sand, then coat or lacquer the surface of the wooden object.
2. If using decoupage coating or a vinyl resin kit, follow the directions on the packaging, adding the pressed flowers at the step suggested by the manufacturer.
3. To use lacquer as the sealer, apply one coat to the wood and let it dry.
4. Create the pressed-flower design.
5. Sand the wood lightly. Apply a second coat of lacquer. While it is still wet, gently place the flowers on top, using tweezers, if desired. Let dry.
6. Apply a third coat of lacquer. Let it dry. If some of the pressed flowers or leaves protrude, apply a fourth coat.

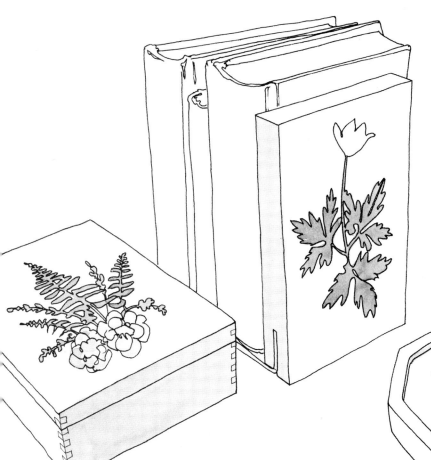

79

## MATERIALS

**Clean eggs**
**Corsage or hat pin**
**Bowl**
**Hot glue gun with clear glue
   sticks, or white craft or house-
   hold glue**
**¼-inch-wide ribbon or
   decorative braid**
**Pressed flowers and leaves**
**Saucer**
**Toothpick**
**Scissors**
**Tweezers (optional)**
**Dried flowers and herbs
   (optional)**
**Thin gold cording (available at
   craft or fabric stores)**
**Clear plastic craft spray sealer**

1. Fresh eggs are more difficult to blow than eggs that have set a few weeks. Have them at room temperature. With the pin, make a hole ¹/₁₆ inch wide at one end. Make a hole three times as large at the other end. Pierce the yolk and agitate. Place your mouth over the smaller hole, and blow the white and yolk into a bowl. Rinse the egg by filling the empty shell with water, shaking, and blowing out the water. Set the shell upright in an egg carton to dry.
2. Glue the ribbon or braid lengthwise around the egg to cover the holes.
3. Create your pressed flower design. Pour some glue into a saucer. With a brush or toothpick, lightly coat the underside of the dried materials and attach them to the front and back of the egg, using tweezers to handle the flowers and leaves, if desired. Let it dry thoroughly, preferably overnight.
4. Glue a 6-inch length of the gold cord to the top of the egg as a hanger. Trim the top with dried flowers and herbs, if desired, attaching with white glue or a hot glue gun with clear glue sticks.
5. Spray the surface with plastic sealer.

# Pressed Flower Egg Ornament

Blown eggs have been decorated for centuries. They take readily to being trimmed with pressed flowers and leaves. Decorate a tree with them at Christmas, and use them as open-house gifts. Of course, they're equally appropriate for an Easter-egg tree in the spring.

If eggshells seem too fragile, consider using egg gourds instead.

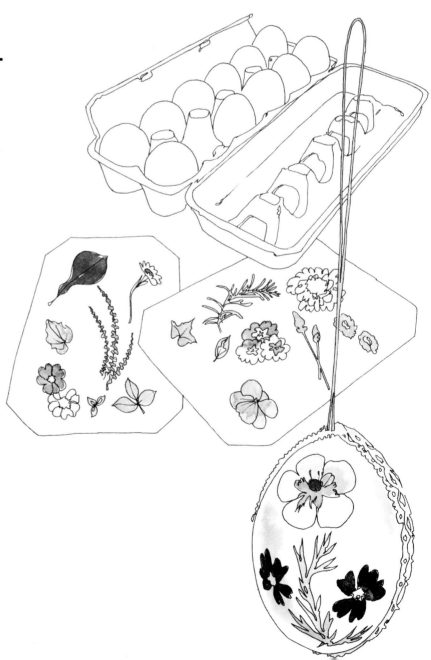

# Chapter 3

# Potpourri and Related Crafts

## Potpourri Materials and Methods

Fragrances have the same ability to conjure up memories that pictures or songs do. Catching a whiff of the sweet smell of roses, mint, lavender, and other herbs and flowers on a snowy winter's day can transport us back to a shade-dappled summer's afternoon in the garden. The woodsy scent of pine is synonymous with Christmas festivities.

Our love affair with flowers and herbs through the centuries is due in great part to their fragrances. The perfumes of plants have been used to woo, entice, and appease the opposite sex, as well as to make our homes and surroundings pleasant since time immemorial. Scents affect our emotions, even evoking strong reactions.

Creating and using fragrance has become big business in the twentieth century. The fragrances we use today need not be harsh and artificial, however. Fragrant plants and flowers are easily grown and readily used in mixtures that can scent our rooms, closets, linens, lingerie, or even be hung around our necks. Such is the magic of potpourri.

The term *potpourri* is derived from the French *pourrir,* which means "to rot," and literally translates as "rotten pot." The actual meaning is fairly accurate, in that early potpourris were damp mixtures of rose petals pickled or preserved with salt and spices.

Such moist mixtures, as well as both fresh and dried herbs and flowers, were widely used in less hygienic times to mask the odors brought on by the filthy living conditions of rich and poor alike. Although today's homes and bodies are kept incredibly clean by comparison, we still want the fragrances of plants surrounding us.

Dry potpourri is the easiest to make and is also the prettiest. It is basically a mixture of dried herbs and flowers mixed with spices and essential oils. Potpourri is usually displayed in attractive, closed containers that can be opened occasionally to release the scent.

Making traditional moist potpourri is more involved, but it has a richer, fuller scent that lasts longer. There are lots of different "recipes," but essentially rose petals are partially dried, then layered with salt alone or salt and other ingredients; if layered with salt only, the other ingredients are added later.

Both dry and moist potpourris have three main ingredients: the blossoms, leaves, and seeds of plants for bulk, color, and scent; at least one essential oil providing extra, intense fragrance; and a fixative that holds the perfume of the plant materials and oil.

## Scent

Intensely fragrant essential oils enhance the natural fragrance of potpourris. Usually, you will want to choose an oil that is the same as the plant material used in the greatest quantity. Craft shops and perfume shops may carry essential oils; they are also available by mail order. (See Sources, page 169.) If you can't find your first choice, then choose one that is complementary. Never use more than two or three different essential oils in one batch of potpourri.

Fragrant oils have become much more commercially available in the last 20 years. Many of these are synthetic and of varying quality. Sniff and compare before buying whenever possible.

## Fixatives

Since the reason for using potpourri is the fragrance released as the oils evaporate, we want these oils to last as long as possible. Certain materials have the ability to retard, or slow down, the evaporation of the fragrant oils. The best ones for potpourri are derived from plants. The first two listed below can be grown in the garden. All three can also be purchased from craft shops or potpourri suppliers.

Orris root (*Iris* ×*germanica* var. *florentina*) has a delicate, violetlike scent. It is the most popular fixative, blending particularly well with woodsy and oriental-type mixtures.

Calamus root, or sweet flag (*Acorus calamus*), grows in boggy ground. Its goes well with spicy, earthy, and vanilla-scented potpourris.

Oak moss (*Evernia pranastri*) is actually a lichen. It blends well with lavender, gives freshness to citrus and floral blends, and depth to potpourris containing patchouli, vetivert, vanilla, and tonka bean.

For dry potpourris, use the fixatives in chopped form. The powdered form is better for moist potpourris and pomanders. To make your own, scrub the roots of orris or calamus thoroughly, dice into ¼-inch pieces, and allow to dry thoroughly in a warm, dark, well-ventilated place.

There are many other materials that are often listed as fixatives, but there is some debate as to whether they actually give permanence to the main scent or merely enhance it. The above three are the most reliable.

In her book *Potpourri...Easy as One, Two, Three!* (for information on ordering, write Berry Hill Press, 7336 Berry Hill, Palos Verdes, CA 90274), Dody Lyness suggests that the gum resins, such as gum arabic, gum benzoin, frankincense, myrrh, and gum styrax, act as fusing agents, uniting all the fragrances in the mixture. Her recommendation is to add 2 tablespoons of one of them to each gallon of potpourri.

## Plant Materials for Potpourri

Both whole flowers and individual petals can be dried and used in potpourri. The classic components of potpourri are lavender flowers and rose petals, as these hold their scent best when dried. Some other fragrant flowers to consider include:

| | |
|---|---|
| Carnation | Lily-of-the-valley |
| (Clove pinks) | Linden |
| Chamomile | Mignonette |
| Citrus | Mock orange |
| Heliotrope | Stock |
| Honeysuckle | Sweet pea |
| Hyssop | Tuberose |
| Jasmine | Wallflower |
| Lilac | |

The leaves of many of the herbs grown in our gardens also add special fragrances to potpourri.

The ones used most often include:

| | |
|---|---|
| Angelica | Myrtle |
| Basil | Rosemary |
| Bay | Sage |
| Costmary | Scented geranium |
| Hyssop | Summer savory |
| Lovage | Sweet woodruff |
| Marjoram | Tarragon |
| Mint | Thyme |

Potpourri with a fruity or citrusy aroma has a particularly clean, fresh appeal to it. This effect can be achieved in several ways. Most obviously, we can remove the outer rind from lemons and oranges (with none of the white inner peel) and dry it in thin strips. Another way is by using the various herbs with a lemon scent, including:

| | |
|---|---|
| Lemon balm | Lemon grass |
| Lemon basil | Lemon thyme |
| Lemon geranium | Lemon verbena |

Spices add an exotic undertone to potpourri. Most spices come from seeds, but there are a few exceptions. For example, cinnamon is from the bark of a tree, while ginger and sassa-

# Gathering Plant Materials

Cut flowers and herbs after the dew has dried on a morning following a few days of clear, dry weather. Pick flowers just as they begin to open and herbs just before they start to flower.

Of the "old" roses, the best all-around landscape plant, as well as the most fragrant, is the rugosa rose (*Rosa rugosa*). Of the modern hybrid roses, there are many fragrant varieties, including 'Mister Lincoln', 'Chrysler Imperial', 'Mirandy', 'Tiffany', 'Intrigue', 'Amber Queen', 'Sweet Surrender', 'Paradise', and 'Sheer Bliss'. Roses are mainly used as individual petals in potpourri, so the petals are pulled from the flowers and spread to dry. A rose potpourri is more attractive if you also dry a few tiny rosebuds, such as those from 'Bonica' or 'Cecile Brunner'. (See Sources, page 169.)

## Drying Plant Materials

After the flowers are picked, trim off the stems or cut the individual florets, such as on delphinium, from the stalks. Spread them in a single layer on cheesecloth, a non-metal screen or tray, or a cookie sheet with a non-stick coating. Put in a dark, dry, well-ventilated place to dry. If on a solid tray or sheet, stir occasionally.

Herbs are usually hung upside down in small bunches held together with rubber bands and placed in a dark, dry, well-ventilated place. When the leaves are completely dry, strip them from the stems.

An alternative is to strip the leaves when just picked and spread them in a single layer as with the flowers. The disadvantage of this method is that if it is not done very gently, many of the essential oils will be released from the bruised leaves.

Drying is complete when the flowers or leaves are crackly crisp. You can speed up the drying time with an oven set on the lowest possible temperature. Often, the pilot light in a gas oven will give off enough heat to work perfectly.

## Storing Plant Materials

What seems like a great quantity of fresh material will dry to a much smaller amount. You may have to dry several batches before you have enough of the varieties you want to make a certain potpourri.

Once the flowers or leaves are dry, they can be stored in glass containers with airtight, screw-top lids. Label the jars and store in a dark place. Check the jars a few days after first putting in the dried material to be sure that the material is indeed dry; if not, remove and let it dry further before returning it to the jar.

fras are roots. Don't use ground spices, as they will settle to the bottom and quickly lose their scent. Instead, purchase whole spices and lightly crush them with a mortar and pestle. Many of these spices can be purchased at grocery stores; the more esoteric, as well as many of the other potpourri ingredients, are available from mail-order companies specializing in potpourri supplies. Spices to consider include:

| | |
|---|---|
| Allspice | Ginger |
| Anise | Juniper |
| Caraway | Nutmeg |
| Cardamom | Sassafras |
| Cinnamon | Star anise |
| Cloves | Vanilla bean |
| Coriander | |

Other plant materials that can contribute scent to potpourri include:

Cedar shavings and chips
Evergreen needles
Sandalwood shavings and chips
Tonka bean
Vetiver root

In combining mixtures of flowers, leaves, seeds, and other plant materials, think about how the various scents complement and go with each other. Just as in perfumes, there are combinations with the overall effect of floral, woodsy, citrusy, or spicy scents. Usually, it is best to try to achieve a particular effect, although sometimes it's fun to go for an unusual undertone. The rule of thumb for potpourri is to use no more than four to six different flowers and leaves and three or four spices and other ingredients.

Besides the plant materials that contribute scent to the potpourri, colorful or unusually shaped flowers are often included for appearance alone. Tiny hemlock cones are frequently added to a pine-based potpourri. The flowers that retain their color best when dried or have an interesting shape include:

| | |
|---|---|
| Aconite | Geranium |
| Annual statice | Larkspur |
| Bee balm | Nasturtium |
| Blue sage | Pansy |
| Borage | Pineapple sage |
| Calendula | Primrose |
| Coreopsis | Scarlet sage |
| Cornflower | Strawflower |
| Delphinium | Yarrow |
| Feverfew | Violets |

## DRY POTPOURRI MATERIALS

**10 to 20 drops essential oil**
**2 to 4 tablespoons fixative (if using orris or calamus root; for oak moss, use 1 cup)**
**4 cups (about ¼ to ⅓ pound) dried flowers and herbs**
**1 to 3 tablespoons crushed spices**
**1½ teaspoons powdered gum resin**
**½ cup dried, crushed citrus peel (optional)**
**½ cup cedar or sandalwood chips (optional)**

1. Prepare for potpourri-making at least two days in advance by sprinkling essential oil over the fixative in a small glass jar and capping tightly.
2. In a large bowl, combine dried flowers and herbs, crushed spices, gum resin, citrus peel, and wood chips.
3. Sprinkle on the oil-and-fixative mixture and stir in thoroughly.
4. Pour the mixture into the aging jar and cap tightly, selecting a jar that leaves plenty of room for the potpourri to be shaken.
5. Put the jar in a warm, dark place. About twice a week, turn the jar end for end and shake gently to redistribute the ingredients. The potpourri should be well blended and no longer "raw smelling" in about four weeks.

## Equipment

To make potpourri, you will need a 6-quart glass, enameled, ceramic, or stainless steel bowl; measuring cups and spoons; and a long-handled wooden spoon. A mortar and pestle is useful for crushing spices, but a rolling pin and a paper bag can also be used. Sometimes a food processor, coffee grinder, or blender comes in handy for this task.

You will also need an aging jar, which is any wide-mouthed glass jar with an airtight, screw-top lid. Restaurants often throw away gallon-size jars that are very good for this purpose. A smaller, 6- to 8-ounce jar is needed for preparing the oil-and-fixative mixture.

# Basic Dry Potpourri Recipe

There are more ways to make potpourri than there are people making it, so don't feel that there is a right or wrong way. Perception of fragrances differs widely, so combine scents that please you. There are, however, proportions that have become rather standard as guidelines for making potpourri. These are featured in the recipe at left.

## Using and Displaying Dry Potpourri

Potpourri can continue to be stored in the aging jar, or transferred to smaller containers for use around the house and for gifts. It can also be made into various other projects.

Choose containers with covers so that the scent can be released or not, as you please. Search through your cupboard as well as department and import stores, flea markets, and antique shops.

Some attractive possibilities include ginger jars, ceramic mustard crocks with cork lids, porcelain rice bowls with lids, sugar bowls, soup tureens, glass-lined silver serving dishes, gourds, and apothecary jars.

## Rejuvenating Dry Potpourri

Sprinkling a few drops of brandy on potpourri is often recommended as a means of refreshing the scent. What actually works most efficiently, according to Dody Lyness, is 90 to 96 percent pure rectified alcohol. Add 10 to 12 drops per cup of potpourri, then put in the aging jar, and toss and turn as before for four weeks. In my opinion, you might as well make a fresh batch!

# *Moist Potpourri*

Some moist potpourri recipes call for first making a "cake" by alternating layers of partially dried rose petals and salt, then adding other ingredients later, while others suggest adding everything at once. The following recipe follows this second method.

## MOIST POTPOURRI MATERIALS

**1 quart rose petals**
**2 cups partially dried, fragrant flowers of your choice**
**1 cup partially dried, fragrant leaves, such as those of rose geranium, lemon verbena, rosemary, or lemon thyme**
**1 tablespoon powdered orris root**
**¾ cup non-iodized salt**
**¼ cup ground allspice**
**¼ cup crushed cloves**
**¼ cup brown sugar**
**2 crushed bay leaves**
**2 tablespoons brandy**

1. Dry rose petals for three days, as described above.
2. Add partially dried, fragrant flowers and leaves.
3. Toss these ingredients with powdered orris root.
4. In a separate bowl, combine salt, spices, sugar, and bay leaves.
5. In a crock or wide-mouthed jar, alternate layers of the petals and herbs with the salt and spices. Sprinkle brandy over the top, and cap the crock or jar tightly, using a lid or plastic wrap. Stir daily with a wooden spoon.

The potpourri will be ready in about a month, and it will last for years.

# Potpourri-Covered Forms

## MATERIALS

**Potpourri**
**Food processor, coffee grinder, blender, or plastic bag and rolling pin**
**White craft or household glue**
**Small bowl**
**Water**
**½-inch-wide paintbrush**
**Polystyrene balls, wreaths, or other shapes or papier-mâché forms**
**Dried flowers and herbs**
**Ribbon or satin cord**

---

1. Process, grind, or roll potpourri to a coarse texture. It can still be used, even if you overdo it.
2. Pour some glue into a bowl. If it is of fairly thin consistency, use it directly. If not, thin it with a little water to the thickness of light cream.
3. "Paint" the glue onto the form.
4. Sprinkle the potpourri on, covering as thickly as possible.
5. Decorate with dried flowers and herbs, ribbon, and so forth. If using as an ornament or wreath, glue on a cord or ribbon for hanging.

Making potpourri is a little like cooking a stir-fry. I start with what seems like only the barest minimum of ingredients, and all at once I have enough for an army. Eating all the stir-fry never seems to be a problem, but as my house is small, there are just so many places for me to use all the potpourri.

Rather than making less, it's more fun to share potpourri with others and to think up different ways of using it. Some of my potpourri bounty is donated every year to the local herb society's booth at a craft fair. You might try putting some in zip-top plastic bags and selling it at a church bazaar.

Another way to use potpourri is to crush or grind it to a coarse texture and glue it to forms such as polystyrene wreaths and balls or papier-mâché ducks, teddy bears, and so forth. You can even cover a ready-made basket or make a basket out of a peat pot by gluing a bent-twig handle inside the pot. With a few dried flowers and herbs and a little ribbon, you'll soon have all manner of decorations and gifts.

# *Potpourri-Filled Embroidery Hoop Hanging*

One of the strongest memories of my grade school days is of constantly gazing out the classroom window. This is no reflection on the quality of my education, but rather on my lifelong preoccupation with windows and light. Both are a dominant feature in my home and office today.

Besides the obvious joys and benefits of the beautiful vistas that these windows provide, they also scent my rooms. I have embroidery hoops covered with lace or eyelet and filled with potpourri hanging at the windows. Their fragrance is naturally released as the sun warms the oils of the dried plants.

The many sizes of embroidery hoops available now in craft stores and departments indicates that their use has left embroidery far behind. The little 1½- or 2-inch hoops are perfect for making into potpourri-filled Christmas ornaments, package trims, or even necklaces! Use 3-, 4-, or 5-inch hoops for hanging at windows or on walls and doors. Vary the type of fabric used as well as the color to create different looks. The dried flowers and herbs you choose as trim can also make your hanging fit into many different situations and please a variety of people.

## MATERIALS

**Embroidery hoop**
**Lace or eyelet fabric**
**Pencil**
**Scissors**
**Potpourri**
**Hot glue gun with clear glue sticks, or white craft or household glue**
**Lace or eyelet ruffling, pregathered and bias-bound, ½ to 1 inch wide, depending on the size of the hoop**
**Dried flowers and herbs (optional)**
**Ribbon bow (see Tying the Perfect Bow, page 165); optional**

1. Open the embroidery hoop and lay the inner hoop on the fabric. With the pencil, draw a circle ½ inch beyond the outside of the hoop. Cut this out.
2. Draw and cut another circle of fabric the same size as the outer hoop.
3. Placing the fabric so the right side will face out, center the larger fabric circle over the inner hoop, then lay the outer hoop over the top and tighten the screw.
4. Lay the hoop on a flat surface, fabric down, and fill it with potpourri.
5. Attach the second circle of fabric to the hoop with glue.
6. Cut a piece of pregathered, bias-bound ruffling to fit the circumference of the circle. Glue to the back of the hanging, with the lace facing out.
7. Trim with dried flowers and herbs, plus a ribbon bow, as desired.

**87**

# Sachets, Pillows, and Other Potpourri-Filled Objects

Surround yourself with homegrown fragrance by using your potpourri in all shapes and sizes of "sweet bags" around the house and even in the car! These also make wonderful little presents.

The basic concept of sweet bags is to crush or grind potpourri, contain it in fabric, then place the encased herbs among sheets, towels, sweaters, and nightgowns, in cupboards, on bookshelves, in boxes of writing paper, on hangers, on the backs of chairs, on bedposts, under pillows, in pockets, or even over the vents in the car.

A simple way to crush potpourri is to put it in a plastic bag and go over it several times with a heavy rolling pin. A blender, coffee grinder, or food processor can also be used, but with these it's difficult to keep the potpourri from becoming a powder.

What were known as herbal amulets in days gone by pass as jewelry today; a scrap of satin, calico, or old quilt sewn in a heart or other shape, filled with potpourri, and trimmed with a long thin satin ribbon or cord becomes a necklace.

The distinction between sachets and pillows (or cushions) is basically one of size and function. Sachets are generally no larger than 3 by 4 inches and are for tucking into places. Lavender, violets, rosemary, and roses are old-fashioned favorites for sachets, mainly because that was what was readily available.

Pillows are usually in the 6-by-8-inch size range, and are most often associated with inducing sleep, relieving headaches, or affecting dreams. Hops are the classic soporific, while an assortment of mints combined with bee balm (bergamot) soothes an aching head. Try lemon balm for keeping bad dreams at bay. As some people are allergic to orris root, you may want to leave it out of the potpourri intended for this purpose.

The simplest way to make any of the sweet bags is to cut two rectangles of fabric (the size depends on your preference, but 3 by 6 inches is an average size), put the right sides together, sew up

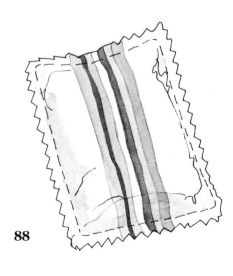

three sides, leaving an end open, turn right side out, fill halfway with potpourri, and tie with a ribbon. To make a car freshener, just sew the two long sides and tie each end tightly with ribbon, then place over a vent in the car.

From there on, the possibilities are endless. Consider using different fabrics, such as satin, lace, moiré, silk, voile, gingham, muslin, batiste, calico, organdy, crocheted doilies or other holders, or pretty handkerchiefs. Embellish the cases with embroidery, needlepoint, applique, ribbon, or lace. Potpourri can also be put into placemats, pincushions, and stuffed toys.

Another way to enclose crushed potpourri is to recycle greeting cards by filling with the herb mixture and gluing or sewing them shut. They're then ready for tucking into gifts, Christmas stockings, or lingerie drawers.

Don't neglect the men in your life and on your gift list. Sachets for their dresser drawers and clothes closets are appreciated, too. Try potpourris made of pine and lavender; lavender, lemon verbena, and sandalwood; or lavender, lemon balm, and lemon thyme. Coarsely crushed nutmeg, cinnamon sticks, and allspice berries can be added to any of the mixtures.

# Padded Hanger

## MATERIALS

**Ruler**
**Wooden hanger (the kind without a pants bar)**
**Scissors**
**Package of 2-inch-wide satin blanket binding (available at fabric stores)**
**Straight pins**
**Needle**
**Thread**
**Sewing machine (optional)**
**Polyester fiberfill**
**Potpourri**
**12 inches of ½-inch-wide ribbon**

1. Measure the hanger from the base of the hook to the end. Add 2 inches to this number. Cut two pieces of blanket binding to this length.
2. Turn the binding inside out and pin, if desired. Sew a ¼-inch seam along the edge and one end. Trim corners and turn right side out. Repeat with second piece.
3. Poke a small amount of the fiberfill into the end of each piece, then pull each piece of binding over the ends of the hanger.
4. Fill each piece of binding with slightly crumbled potpourri, evenly covering the hanger on all sides.
5. Turn under the raw edges of the binding in the middle of the hanger and whip stitch the two edges together with needle and thread.
6. Wrap the ribbon around the middle seam and hook base several times, then tie in a bow.

I'm a firm believer in treating not only myself but also my possessions with care and respect. Clothing for me is an expression of self, and so I take a great deal of interest in color, design, and fabric. One of the ways of keeping clothes in good condition for many years is by using padded hangers.

With only minimal sewing skills and an abundance of potpourri, you can readily create wonderfully scented hangers that gently shape the shoulders of your garments while at the same time imbuing them with a delicate fragrance. Fill some hangers with dried moth-repellent herbs, such as rue, tansy, wormwood, santolina, and southernwood, to protect your woolens. (See Moth Bags, page 96.)

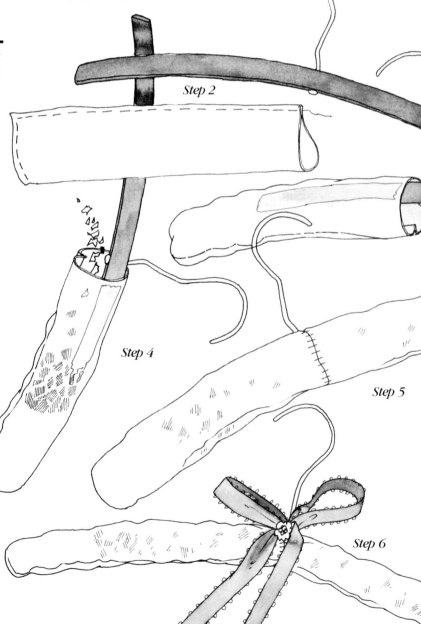

*Step 2*

*Step 4*

*Step 5*

*Step 6*

90

# Catnip Mice

Although there are several hundred species of catnip, or catmint, the favorite of cats the world over is *Nepeta cataria*. Native to Europe and Asia, this member of the mint family is a perennial through USDA Hardiness Zone 4, but it sometimes acts as a biennial. It self-sows so readily, however, that once you have it established, you can usually keep it for some time.

Start the seeds early indoors, sow directly outdoors, or buy transplants. Whichever method you choose, be sure to protect young seedlings from cats until the plants are well established with plenty of growth. Plant in a location that gets full sun, and space plants 18 inches apart.

Harvest your catnip when the flower buds start to open. Hang the stems in clusters upside down for about a week in a dark, dry, well-ventilated area. When completely dry, rub the leaves gently off the stalk.

Now you are ready to start your catnip toy. Whether you make a basic gray-colored mouse or dress it up to be a chef, raconteur, or hausfrau, your pet will show his gratitude with a display of playfulness – a real game of cat-and-mouse.

## MATERIALS

**Ruler**
**Scissors**
**Sturdy fabric scraps**
**Yarn cut into three 5-inch lengths**
**Straight pins**
**Sewing machine (optional)**
**Needle**
**Thread**
**Polyester fiberfill**
**Dried catnip leaves**
**Felt**
**Permanent black felt-tip marking
   pen**
**Black embroidery floss**

1. Cut out two matching, 6-inch-long, egg-shaped pieces of fabric.
2. Using the three pieces of yarn, plait a tail, just as you would braid a pigtail.
3. Put the two pieces of fabric together, wrong side out. Insert the tail between the two pieces at the broad end of the egg; pin in place. Be sure that it is caught only in the one point of the seam line.
4. Using a ¼-inch seam allowance, sew around the mouse, leaving a 1½-inch opening. Clip the curves and turn right side out.
5. Stuff the mouse with fiberfill and a generous amount of catnip. Then sew it closed.
6. Cut out two ½-inch-round felt ears.
7. Sew ears on toward the pointed end of the "egg."
8. With the marking pen, put a dot on for the two eyes just in front of the ears.
9. Cut six strands of embroidery floss, each 2½ inches long. Sew them on at the tip of the nose.
10. Fluff up the mouse from time to time to release the oils in the catnip.

## MATERIALS

**Water**
**Double boiler**
**Knife**
**Beeswax**
**Old saucepan or large tin can**
**Newspaper**
**Flexible plastic candy molds**
**Potpourri**
**Blender, coffee grinder, food processor, or mortar and pestle**
**Metal spoon**

*Optional:*
**Ice pick**
**Gold cording**
**White glue**
**Camel's hair artist's paintbrushes**
**Gold leafing paint**
**Acrylic paint**

1. Put water in the bottom of a double boiler and bring to a boil; reduce heat to simmer. With a knife, grate beeswax into an old saucepan or tin can and place in the top of the double boiler.

2. Spread out newspaper and set flexible candy molds on top.

3. Grind the potpourri to a fine powder. Add enough to the melted wax to scent. The proportion depends on the strength of the herbs as well as your own preference.

4. Remove the melted, scented wax from the stove. With a metal spoon, fill each mold to the top.

5. When the wax has hardened, gently flex the mold to remove the ornaments. If you're not satisfied, remelt and try again.

6. Heat an ice pick in a flame and make a hole through the ornament about ¼ inch from the top.

7. Cut a 6-inch length of gold cording and run through the hole. Tie the ends in a knot.

8. If desired, glue additional cording to the edge of the ornament. Burnish the ornament with gilt paint, following the instructions on the bottle, or paint with acrylic paints.

# Scented Wax Ornaments

One type of early pomander was made by combining beeswax with herbs and spices, then rolling it into balls. German craftsmen in the late nineteenth and early twentieth centuries carefully carved and painted beeswax into Christmas ornaments. These two crafts from other eras can be combined into one by scenting melted beeswax with potpourri and pouring the mixture into candy molds. The ornaments can be left unadorned or trimmed and painted.

# Scented Candles

Nothing puts any of us or our homes in as nice a light as candles. Their soft glow makes the humblest of meals or dwellings seem special. Although there are plenty of scented candles available in the stores, to me the fragrance often seems too strong and rather artificial. Homemade candles scented with herbs from my garden are much more special and the fragrance more pleasing.

Candlemaking requires very little special equipment and can be done rather inexpensively. Even beeswax candles are not an unattainable luxury, if you can find a beekeeper with a surplus of wax that he's willing to sell at a reasonable price.

Homemade candles can be scented in various ways, which can be done either separately or in combination. Dry potpourri can be ground to a fine powder and added to the melted wax, or you can add fresh herbs or essential oils.

## MATERIALS

**Water**
**Double boiler**
**Knife**
**Paraffin (available in 1-pound boxes at the supermarket) and/or beeswax**
**Old saucepan or large tin can**
**Crayons or commercial candle coloring (optional)**
**Candle wicking**
**Pencil, small stick, or dowel**
**Molds (waxed milk cartons, tin cans, salad molds, plastic soft drink bottles, or traditional candle molds)**

*For scent:*
**Potpourri**
**Blender, coffee grinder, food processor, or mortar and pestle**
or
**Fresh herbs, such as rosemary, lavender, hyssop, bergamot, any of the mints or thymes, lemon balm or verbena, and pineapple sage**
**Scissors**
or
**Essential oils, such as jasmine, rose, lavender, and gardenia**

1. Put water in the bottom of a double boiler and bring to a boil; reduce heat to simmer. With a knife, grate paraffin or beeswax into an old saucepan or tin can set inside the top of the double boiler. You can use all paraffin, all beeswax, or equal parts of each. Color the wax, if desired, using candle colors available from craft shops or old crayons.
2. While the paraffin or wax is melting, prepare wicks in the molds. Cut the wicking so it is about 2 inches longer than the mold is tall. Tie one end of the wicking to the pencil, stick, or dowel and set it on top of the mold, so the wicking hangs in the center of the mold and

reaches the bottom with an inch extra.

3. To scent the wax with potpourri, grind the potpourri until it is a fine powder and add some to the melted wax. If using fresh herbs, snip into small pieces with scissors before adding to the wax. The essential oil can be added directly to the wax.

4. Slowly pour the melted, scented wax into a mold or molds prepared with wicking.

5. As the wax cools, a depression will form around the wicking. Fill in with more melted wax until level.

6. Allow candles to dry thoroughly. Tear or cut away disposable molds. Remove candles from reusable molds by holding the mold in hot water briefly or running hot water over it.

7. To give your candles a shine, wipe them with a cotton ball dipped in vegetable oil. Trim with pressed flowers, if desired. (See Candles Trimmed with Pressed Flowers, page 76.)

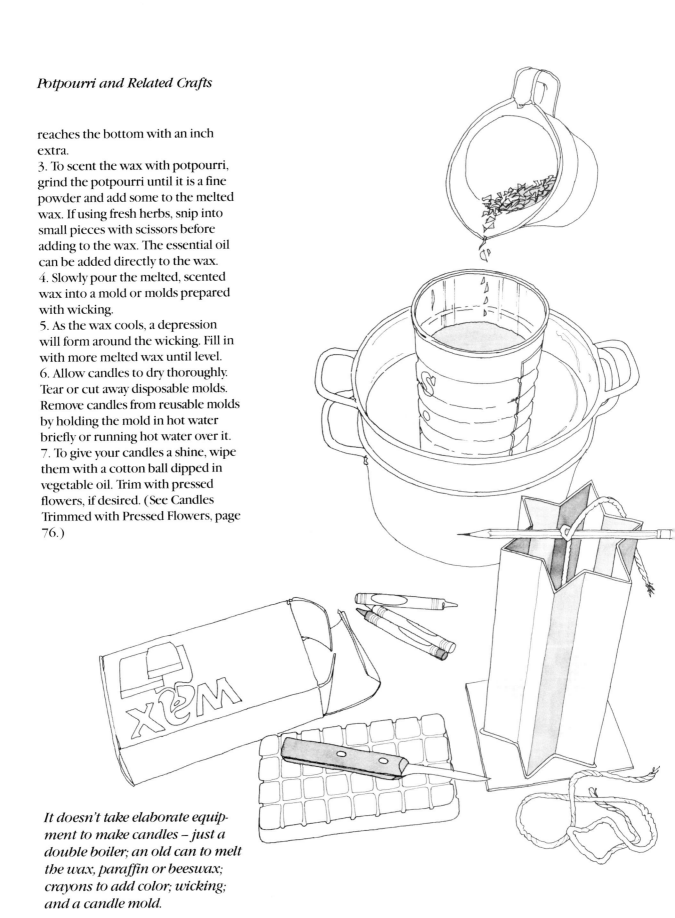

*It doesn't take elaborate equipment to make candles – just a double boiler; an old can to melt the wax, paraffin or beeswax; crayons to add color; wicking; and a candle mold.*

# *Incense*

People who grew up in the sixties may think they invented incense, but it has actually been used for thousands of years. Its importance in ancient times is evident from the inclusion of frankincense and myrrh with gold as the gifts brought by the wise men to the Christ Child.

Long before antiseptic properties were scientifically understood, it was accepted that burning herbs purified the air. In the Middle Ages, the common cleansing herbs included angelica seeds, lavender flowers, and the leaves of bay, juniper, lemon balm, lovage, rosemary, rue, sage, santolina, southernwood, sweet marjoram, tansy, and thyme. These herbs were dried, powdered, and burned over charcoal or in special containers. Recipe books from this time also mention making dried herbs into a paste and forming them into pastilles, which were burned.

If today's chemical air fresheners are not to your liking, you can try any of the herbs mentioned above. Simply dry and make into a powder by grinding in a mortar and pestle, blender, food processor, or coffee grinder. Store the powder in glass jars; put a teaspoonful in an incense burner or other metal dish and light with a match. A simple way to have a natural incense is to strip the flowers off dry lavender stems, then insert several of the stems in a flowerpot filled with sand and light the tips.

Following is a recipe for old-fashioned flower-and-herb incense pastilles.

## MATERIALS

¼ **cup loosely packed fragrant red rose petals**
**Mortar and pestle, blender, food processor, or coffee grinder**
2 **tablespoons dried, powdered lavender flowers**
1 **tablespoon dried, powdered orris root**
1 **tablespoon dried, powdered gum benzoin**
**Rosewater**
**Wax paper**
**Small iron skillet**

1. Thoroughly mash rose petals in a mortar and pestle, blender, food processor, or coffee grinder, then work in lavender, orris root, and gum benzoin.
2. Add rosewater until the mixture forms a thick paste.
3. Shape into marble-size balls and flatten. Put on wax paper in a sunny window and let dry, turning occasionally.
4. Heat in a small iron skillet to scent the air.

# *Moth Bags*

When I first started taking an interest in herbs about 15 years ago, I purchased several moth-repellent sachets at the Philadelphia Flower Show. I really didn't expect them to work, but the scent was rather nice. Amazingly enough, they actually kept the moths out of my stored clothing.

My knowledge of herbs at the time was rather limited, so some of the names on the ingredient list, such as southernwood, mugwort, and wormwood, were unfamiliar. Since then I've learned that these are all members of the artemisia family (named for Artemis, goddess of the moon) and that they have beautiful, feathery gray foliage. Each is now an integral part of my garden, and I tolerate their rampant growth because I like the texture they add to the landscape. You may choose to isolate them in a sunny part of the yard, as their spreading roots may be a nuisance.

Some of the other readily grown herbs that can be dried and used to make sweet-smelling, moth-repellent potpourri mixtures include tansy, santolina, the various thymes and mints, sweet woodruff, rosemary, sage, sweet marjoram, lavender, rue, pennyroyal, lemon verbena, and costmary. Purchased items that are often added to moth bags include orris root chips as well as any of the following items, partially crushed: cinnamon sticks, cloves, peppercorns, coriander seeds, and dried lemon and orange peel. Cedarwood shavings can also be used. Experiment with combinations that please you. Just be sure to include some southernwood, wormwood, or tansy, as these three have the greatest moth-repellent properties.

There are four ways that I like to use moth-repellent potpourri: padded hangers (see Padded Hanger, page 90), triangle-shaped sachets to put on hangers, small square bags to tuck among folded items, and larger bags sized to serve as a complete drawer liner. (See Sachets, Pillows, and Other Potpourri-Filled Objects, page 88.)

# Chapter 4
# *Beauty Basics*

## Beauty from Plants

With our scientific knowledge today, we are aware that the foundation of an attractive appearance is good health, and that this desired level of health is based on sufficient fresh air, exercise, sleep, relaxation, and wholesome food. Bath oils, soaps, powders, lotions, and other cosmetic preparations are useful in enhancing the natural beauty of a healthy, happy person. As such, they should be a pleasure to use and contribute to a safe, natural look and lifestyle.

Herbs and flowers have been used since time immemorial for their beautifying and cleansing properties. The leaves of henna, an ornamental tropical shrub, have been used as both a reddish-brown hair dye and rouge since the time of ancient Egypt. Ovid wrote a book on perfumes, and included information on facials for Roman women. The water in Roman baths was often scented with flowers and herbs, and bathers were rubbed down with fragrant oils. Records of other civilizations also indicate the use of cosmetics based on plants.

All parts of the body, including the face, hair, eyes, nails, feet, hands, and skin, can benefit from herb and flower preparations. There is such a wide variety of cultivated herbs and flowers with useful properties that you can choose ingredients to suit your needs and preferences. A homemade beauty concoction will have a light, delicate scent that is not abrasive and tends to have a relaxing yet stimulating effect. Without preservative chemicals, these preparations do not last as long as commercial products, but neither do they contain harsh ingredients.

No matter which of the preparations you use or how often, growing and using flowers and herbs for beauty concoctions is a delightful addition to craft projects from the garden. Finding beautiful bottles and jars for storing the cosmetics is an adventure in itself. Put a few into a handmade basket, perhaps with a homegrown luffa sponge, and you have a very special gift, too.

The following herbs and flowers are the plants most widely used in beauty concoctions, and they are the ones that are relatively easy to find and grow in most parts of the country. The directions for the various preparations follow. Many of these plants are not only attractive ornamentals but have other uses as well, including cooking, fresh flower arrangements, and dried flower projects.

## A Garden for Beauty

**Bergamot** *(Monarda didyma)*. Leaves used for their lemony scent and in hair and suntan preparations.
**Borage** *(Borago officinalis)*. Leaves used for softening and cleansing effect on the skin.
**Calendula** *(Calendula officinalis)*. Flowers and leaves used for soothing the skin and lightening the hair.
**Chamomile** *(Chamaemelum nobile)*. Flowers used for cleansing and softening skin, as a lightening hair rinse, and as an antiseptic. Mildly astringent.

**Chervil** *(Anthriscus cerefolium)*. Leaves used as a skin cleanser.

**Clove pink** *(Dianthus caryophyllus)*. Flowers used for scent.

**Comfrey** *(Symphytum officinale)*. Leaves used for soothing skin.

**Costmary** *(Chrysanthemum balsamita)*. Leaves used for bathing and hair care.

**Dandelion** *(Taraxacum officinale)*. Leaves used in hair care, to revitalize tired skin, and to improve circulation.

**Elder** *(Sambucus canadensis)*. Flowers used for softening, soothing, cleansing, and whitening the skin.

**Fennel** *(Foeniculum vulgare)*. Leaves used to soften and smooth the skin.

**Feverfew** *(Chrysanthemum parthenium)*. Leaves used in creams for the skin.

**Garlic** *(Allium sativum)*. Bulbs used for dandruff control.

**Geranium, scented** *(Pelargonium* spp.*)*. Leaves used in bathing.

**Horsetail** *(Equisetum arvense)*. Leaves used as an astringent and toner for the skin and for strengthening hair and nails.

**Hyssop** *(Hyssopus officinalis)*. Leaves used as a cleanser and for healing.

**Lady's mantle** *(Alchemilla vulgaris)* Leaves used to refine and whiten skin.

**Lavender** *(Lavandula* spp.*)*. Flowers and leaves used for scent and as an astringent and antiseptic for the skin.

**Lemon balm** *(Melissa officinalis)*. Leaves used for scenting soap and as an astringent for the skin.

**Lemon verbena** *(Aloysia triphylla)*. Leaves used as a skin freshener in soaps and bath water.

**Linden** *(Tilia cordata)*. Flowers whiten skin, improve circulation, and smooth wrinkles.

*Lavender is easy to grow, harvest, and dry. Its fragrance is delightful in beauty products from soap to powder. Lavender leaves and stems are also fragrant and can be dried and used with the flowers.*

**Marjoram** *(Origanum majorana)*. Leaves used for scent and antiseptic properties.

**Marsh mallow** *(Althaea officinalis)*. Leaves and roots used in face packs and hair care as an emollient and for healing.

**Mint** *(Mentha* spp.*)*. Leaves used for scent and as an astringent for their stimulating, antiseptic properties.

**Mullein** *(Verbascum thapsus)*. Flowers used for lightening hair.

**Nettle** *(Urtica dioica)*. Leaves used in skin toners and in hair preparations for dandruff.

**Parsley** *(Petroselinum crispum)*. Leaves whiten skin and improve circulation.

**Pennyroyal** *(Mentha pulegium* var. *decumbens)*. Leaves used in bathing.

**Rose** *(Rosa* spp.*)*. Flowers used for scent.

**Rosemary** *(Rosmarinus officinalis)*. Leaves used for scent and astringent properties and for darkening hair.

**Sage** *(Salvia officinalis)*. Leaves used for astringent properties in bathing and for darkening hair.

**Salad burnet** *(Poterium sanguisorba)*. Leaves used to soften and refine skin.

**Southernwood** *(Artemisia abrotanum)*. Leaves used as an antiseptic and to encourage hair growth.

**Sweet basil** *(Ocimum basilicum)*. Leaves used for their scent and in hair rinses.

**Thyme** *(Thymus vulgaris)*. Leaves used for deodorant and antiseptic properties in bathing.

**Violet** *(Viola odorata)*. Leaves used as an antiseptic; flowers used for their scent.

**Yarrow** *(Achillea millefolium)*. Leaves used for their astringent effect on oily skin and to improve circulation.

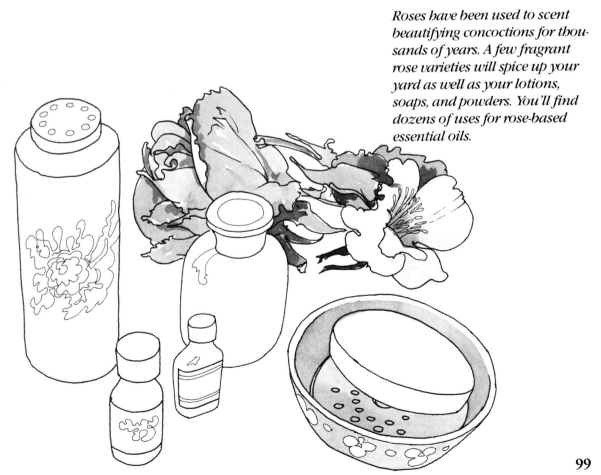

*Roses have been used to scent beautifying concoctions for thousands of years. A few fragrant rose varieties will spice up your yard as well as your lotions, soaps, and powders. You'll find dozens of uses for rose-based essential oils.*

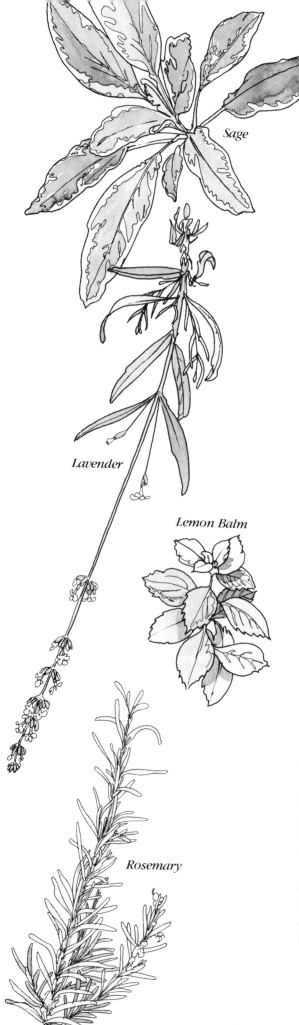

Sage

Lavender

Lemon Balm

Rosemary

# Infusions and Decoctions

It's easy to refresh your face and body with a splash of aromatic water. Stored in old or unusual glass bottles in the bath or bedroom, they can get your day off to a rousing start or provide a soothing relief at the end. Use them to cleanse and tone the skin and improve circulation.

An infusion is a solution made by pouring boiling water over fresh or dried leaves and flowers. After letting this stand for 15 minutes to several hours, depending on the strength desired, the water-soluble substances will have been extracted. The solution is then strained and bottled.

To make a solution from the harder plant parts, such as stems and roots, the material must be soaked and then boiled in water before straining and storing. This is called a decoction.

To make an infusion or decoction, use at least 3 or 4 tablespoons of fresh herbs or 2 tablespoons of dried herbs to 2 cups water. For an infusion, let the mixture stand for at least 15 minutes, but 2 to 3 hours will extract the greatest amount of fragrance. For a decoction, soak the plant material in the water for 10 minutes, then heat to the boiling point, simmer for 15 minutes, and let stand for another 10 minutes. Use a glass, stainless steel, or enameled container.

With flowers, you'll need to use a greater quantity of material – at least 1 or 2 cups fresh flowers per cup of water. For roses and calendulas, remove the petals from the stem; for elder flowers, snip away as much of the stem as possible.

Infusions and decoctions are fairly short-lived. They should be used within several days if not refrigerated, or in a week or so if stored in the refrigerator. Although waters made from any of the herbs listed are not harmful to humans, it is always best to label the bottle as not for internal use.

Some of the plants most often used in making infusions and decoctions for cosmetic use include the leaves of rosemary, mint, lemon balm, lady's mantle, salad burnet, fennel, yarrow, parsley, sage, hyssop, thyme, lavender, marjoram, and lemon verbena, and the flowers of elder, linden, rose, lavender, and calendula.

# *Extractions*

The various toiletries such as colognes, toilet waters, and afterbath and aftershave lotions are actually a form of alcohol extraction, or tincture. Commercially, these are produced by distillation, but at home they are made by steeping flowers or leaves in pure grain spirits or 100-proof vodka. After straining, the extract may be diluted with plain or scented water. Glycerine is sometimes added as a softening agent, or emollient. A few drops of musk oil or tincture of benzoin act as a preservative.

Extractions have a drying effect on the skin, as they tighten pores and remove excess oils. The herbs and flowers that are especially astringent include sage, rosemary, salad burnet, yarrow, rose petals, ladys' mantle, and southernwood. Some of the other herbs that are often used in extractions are scented geranium, basil, bergamot, bay, hyssop, southernwood, and lemon thyme; other flowers that are used include violets, lavender, jasmine, wallflower, and chamomile.

Although extractions can be made of individual flowers and herbs, I find it more interesting to use various combinations of plants from the garden as well as citrus and spices. Homemade aftershave lotions are a unique, personal present for that special man, while other mixtures are ideal for the women on your gift list. Scout craft fairs and flea markets for unusual bottles.

## MATERIALS

**Fresh herbs and flowers**
**Pint or quart jar with lid**
**Pure grain spirits or 100-proof**
 **vodka**
**Blotter paper**
**Glycerine**
**Musk oil or tincture of benzoin**

1. Coarsely chop enough of the herbs and flowers to fill a pint or quart jar half full.
2. Add enough grain spirits or vodka to cover. Screw the lid on tightly.
3. Shake daily.
4. After several weeks, check the scent by dipping a small strip of blotter paper in the extract and letting it dry. If, after several months, the fragrance is not as strong as you would like, strain the alcohol and repeat the process with fresh herbs.
5. When the desired fragrance is attained, strain the alcohol, then add 2 teaspoons glycerine to each cup of alcohol and several drops of musk oil or tincture of benzoin.
6. Bottle and label by name, adding that it is not for internal consumption.

*Bay*

*Scented geranium*

## Classic Toilet Water

¼ cup fresh rosemary, crushed

3 tablespoons fresh lemon balm, crushed

3 tablespoons fresh rose petals, crushed

1 tablespoon each grated lemon and orange peel

1 cup pure grain spirits or 100-proof vodka

1 cup rose petal infusion (See Infusions and Decoctions, page 100.)

4 teaspoons glycerine (available at drugstores)

Steep all ingredients except rose infusion and glycerine together in a glass jar for several weeks. Strain and add rose infusion and glycerine. Bottle and store for another few weeks to mature. Label.

## Spicy Aftershave Lotion

¼ cup fresh rosemary, crushed

¼ cup fresh mint, crushed

1 teaspoon each grated lemon and orange peel

1 cracked nutmeg

1 broken cinnamon stick

1 cup pure grain spirits or 100-proof vodka

1 cup elder flower infusion

4 teaspoons glycerine

Several drops of musk oil

Steep all ingredients together in a glass jar except elder flower infusion, glycerine, and musk oil. Let stand for several weeks. Strain, add remaining ingredients, and store in bottles. Label.

## English Cologne

¼ cup each fresh rosemary, lavender flowers, and myrtle, crushed

1 cup pure grain spirits or 100-proof vodka

1 cup rose petal infusion

4 teaspoons glycerine

Several drops of tincture of benzoin

Steep ingredients except rose petal infusion, glycerine, and benzoin in a glass jar. Let stand for several weeks. Strain, add remaining ingredients, and store in bottles. Label.

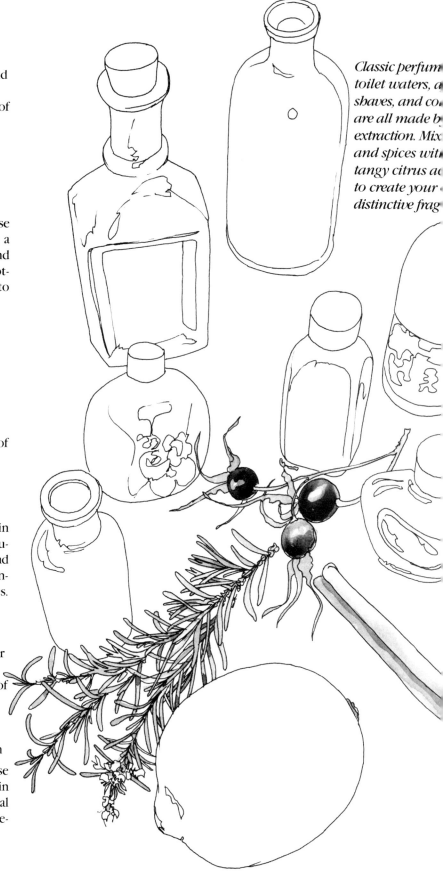

*Classic perfum... toilet waters, a... shaves, and co... are all made b... extraction. Mix... and spices with... tangy citrus a... to create your... distinctive frag...*

102

# Vinegars

Herb- and flower-scented vinegars aren't just for your tossed salad. They also can be used as beauty preparations, because vinegar refines the skin's pores and restores the natural acid balance of the skin after washing.

The scent of beauty vinegars is similar to that of an infusion, but vinegars have the advantage of a longer shelf life. Vinegars have been used for many centuries, not only for their scent but also for their disinfectant property. In fact, ladies at one time wore a vial of scented vinegar in case they felt faint, got a headache, or needed to refresh sweaty palms.

The herbs that are often used in beauty vinegars include basil, dill, sage, horsetail, rosemary, marjoram, lemon verbena, mint, southernwood, thyme, and parsley. The flowers to use in vinegars are roses, lavender, violets, pinks, chamomile, elder, and calendula.

Dilute beauty vinegars before using on the skin, either by adding several tablespoons to the wash basin when you rinse your face or by combining equal parts of vinegar and an infusion or plain water. Other ways to use beauty vinegars is by adding them to bath water or the rinse water for hand laundry. They also make excellent hair rinses.

**MATERIALS**

**1 cup fresh petals or leaves**
**Glass jar with lid**
**2 cups apple cider vinegar or white wine vinegar**

1. Put the petals or leaves in a glass jar and cover with vinegar.
2. Set on a sunny windowsill and shake daily for several weeks.
3. Strain and bottle. Label.

# Rubbing Lotions

Whether for the jogger with aching muscles or the invalid confined to bed, ordinary rubbing alcohol becomes a special stimulating treat when aromatic herbs and flowers are steeped in it. That clinical smell becomes a pleasant, refreshing fragrance, often with an attractive, pale green tint.

To scent rubbing lotions, use the leaves of basil, lavender, lemon verbena, mint, rosemary, thyme, marjoram, lemon balm, bergamot, and hyssop. For floral fragrance, try the flowers of rose, elder, calendula, violet, and chamomile.

**MATERIALS**

**Glass jar with lid**
**Fresh petals and/or leaves, crushed**
**Unscented rubbing alcohol**

1. Fill a jar a quarter to half full with petals and/or leaves.
2. Fill the jar with the rubbing alcohol. Put on the lid.
3. Let it stand for two weeks, shaking daily.
4. Strain and store in bottles. Label with the name or names of the plant or plants used, and add that the lotion is not to be taken internally.

**103**

**Fresh petals or leaves, crushed**
**Glass jar with lid**
**Mild oil, such as corn, olive,**
    **almond, safflower, or sesame**

1. Pack petals or leaves loosely in a jar to fill.
2. Fill the jar with oil and cover. Set in a warm place.
3. After 24 hours, strain and repeat the process with new petals or leaves.
4. Repeat daily for a week or two, or until the desired fragrance is attained.
5. After the final straining, store in tightly stoppered glass bottles, and label.

   If you want a more lightly scented oil to use for massaging, do not change the herbs daily, but rather keep the same ones in the jar for two weeks, shaking daily. Strain, bottle, label, and store.

# Essential Oils

   The little vials of intensely scented oils that are available at herb and craft shops are commercially extracted by distillation or are synthetically produced. It is possible to make your own essential oils at home, although much patience and huge quantities of herbs and flowers are required.

   However, if a certain flower or herb is a particular favorite of yours and you can't find that oil in a shop, there's no reason not to forge ahead. The results are definitely worth the effort. As you get involved in making herb and flower cosmetics, you'll find yourself wanting essential oils to use as perfume or bath oils and for scenting creams, potpourri, candles, soaps, and so forth.

   Homemade oils are not as long-lived as commercial oils, but even so they'll last for several months if covered tightly and refrigerated. Adding several drops of oil of musk will act as a preservative, too.

   Although you can make essential oils out of just about any flower or herb, some of the most popular leaves are rosemary, sage, bay, mint, marjoram, basil, and thyme; favorite flowers are calendula, lavender, honeysuckle, lilac, roses, and violets.

*Basil*

*Rose*

*Violet*

# Hand Care

Any gardener knows the effect that working in the soil, pulling weeds, and the like can have on hands. Combine gardening with cold weather and harsh detergents, and even the hands of a young person will look old if they're not cared for properly.

As much as possible, we should try to wear rubber gloves for household tasks, cotton gloves when gardening, and dress gloves outdoors in winter. Using herb- and flower-based creams and rinses regularly will help to soothe even the most chapped and roughened hands and protect hands from chapping.

A comprehensive hand-care program would include soaking the hands in rinsing solution each morning, especially during cold weather, and using a hand lotion, jelly, or cream before and after going outside in the winter, as well as after doing dishes, working in the soil, and so forth.

The best skin-care plants for hands are the flowers of elder, chamomile, and calendula, and the leaves of comfrey, lady's mantle, fennel, and marsh mallow.

## Hand Rinse

Make an infusion of any of the skin-care herbs or flowers. In the morning, after washing your hands, soak your hands for several minutes in the solution. Dry on a soft towel. If stored in the refrigerator, the infusion can be reused for about a week.

## Hand Lotion

¼ cup herb or flower infusion
¼ cup glycerine
2 tablespoons witch hazel
1 tablespoon mild oil, such as almond, olive, or safflower
½ teaspoon borax

Mix all ingredients together. Store in a tightly closed jar, label, and shake well before using.

## Hand Jelly

2 tablespoons glycerine
2 teaspoons arrowroot powder (usually found in the spice department of the grocery)
½ cup herb or flower infusion

Warm the glycerine in a small bowl set in a saucepan of simmering water. Stir in arrowroot powder, making a smooth, thick cream. Warm the infusion in a separate pan and gradually stir it into the arrowroot mixture. Continue heating gently until the mixture clears. Remove from heat, cool, store in a tightly closed jar, and label.

## Hand Cream

2 tablespoons lemon juice
2 tablespoons beeswax or cocoa butter
¼ cup mild oil, such as almond, olive, or safflower
1 cup herb or flower infusion
½ teaspoon borax

Heat lemon juice, beeswax or cocoa butter, and oil in a saucepan. In a separate saucepan, combine the infusion and the borax, and heat until the borax is dissolved. Slowly stir the infusion mixture into the oil mixture, stirring until the cream is smooth. Cool, store in a tightly covered jar, and label.

## Body Powder
## with Herbs and Spices

1 tablespoon dried flowers, herbs,
   citrus peel, and/or spices
1 tablespoon powdered orris root
   (your own or from an herb or craft
   supplier)
2 tablespoons cornstarch, arrowroot,
   or unscented talcum
Several drops essential oil (optional)

Using a blender, coffee grinder,
or food processor, grind all the ingredients together until they form a well-
blended fine powder. Store and label.

## Body Powder
## with Potpourri

2 tablespoons potpourri
2 tablespoons cornstarch, arrowroot,
   or unscented talcum

Using a blender, coffee grinder,
or food processor, combine the ingredients and grind until they form a
well-blended fine powder. Store and
label.

## Body Powder
## with Fresh Flowers

Very fragrant fresh flowers, such as
   lilac, gardenia, hyacinth, or
   magnolia
Cornstarch, arrowroot, or unscented
   talcum
Glass jar with lid

Fill the jar with the flowers and
add as much arrowroot, cornstarch,
or talcum as possible. Cover and shake
several times a day. Replace the flowers every other day until the powder
attains the scent you want. Remove
the flowers for the last time, store,
and label.

# Body Powders

Body powders fragrant with herbs and flowers are especially lovely to use in the summertime, as they absorb moisture while soothing and scenting the skin. Body powders are a particularly indulgent ending to an herbal bath. Luckily, not only are most of the ingredients easily procured from the garden and kitchen, but powders are among the simplest of garden crafts.

Arrowroot, cornstarch, or unscented talcum are the tradi-tional bases for body powders. Ground orris root can be added as a fixative. Be careful, however, as some people are allergic to orris root; eliminate it from the recipes if that is a problem.

The most difficult part of making body powders is deciding what to use for scenting them. Sometimes I want the simplicity of an individual flower or herb, while in other moods I'll choose one of my favorite potpourris. If I'm giving a body powder as a gift to a man, I'll scent it with ground spices and citrus peel. It used to be hard to find a container for handmade powders that weren't already commercially labeled, but recently I've found gift shops carrying beautiful glass jars with perforated silver tops made expressly for body powders; similar items can also be found in antique stores and flea markets.

*Magnolia*

*Lilac*

# Soaps

Anyone who has actually had to make lye-based soaps – or even just been around when they were being made – knows that soap-making is anything but a romantic experience. Happily, I can report that memories are selective enough that today I cannot only use but actually make soaps with the sweet fragrances of flowers and herbs from my garden without any adverse reaction.

One reason for this is that it is quite easy to make your own scented soaps using bars of glycerine or other pure, mild, unscented soaps. Another is that, even if you're making a traditional soap from scratch, materials are readily available, eliminating much of the drudgery of soap-making.

Some of the first soaps were made from the roots and leaves of plants containing saponins, which create a soapy lather in warm water. Soapwort is the best known of these plants; others include lamb's-quarters, California soap plant, soap tree yucca, Spanish bayonet, papaya, guaiac, soap pod, and wild gourd.

Other early soaps were made from lye, which is a strong alkaline solution. This lye usually had to be laboriously made at home from wood ashes saved from the fireplace or stove. The other major ingredient was animal fat, most notably rendered lard from hog butchering. Fine soaps manufactured in Spain used an olive oil base rather than lard. Because of its Spanish origins, "castile" soap has become a generic term for a delicate soap. Besides olive oil, "vegetarian" soaps can be made from almond, safflower, avocado, or other mild oils, as well as coconut oil or pure solid vegetable shortening.

There are several ways to scent soaps made at home; the methods may be used singly or in combination. These include using essential oils, strong infusions or decoctions, and adding ground or finely chopped fresh or dried herbs, flowers, spices, and citrus peel. Use any of the flowers and herbs listed on page 97, or others that you would like to try. The most popular choices for soaps are comfrey root, mint leaves, and chamomile and lavender flowers.

Shaping the soap can be as simple as rolling it into balls (1½ inches in diameter is an average size) or as complex as buying and using special soap molds. You can also use individual salad molds, egg poaching cups, or other containers. Line the molds with wax paper, plastic wrap, or dampened cheesecloth. Or put soap in a milk carton, then remove and slice the soap into bars when hardened. Another alternative is to pour the soap into a shaving mug.

## MATERIALS

¼ cup herb or flower infusion
Several drops essential oil
2 tablespoons fresh herbs and/or flowers, finely chopped, or 1 tablespoon dried herbs, flowers, potpourri, spices, and/or citrus peel, finely ground
1 tablespoon coarsely ground oatmeal or bran (optional)
Double boiler
Water
2 cups grated glycerine soap or other pure, mild, unscented soap (available at drugstores)
Spoon or whisk
Molds and liner (optional)

1. Combine infusion, oil, herbs, flowers, and oatmeal, or whatever is desired, in the top of a double boiler. Heat the mixture until simmering.
2. Add soap and stir until mixed well.
3. Pour into prepared molds. When cool, remove and age for several weeks.
4. Alternatively, let the hot mixture set for 15 minutes, stir, and shape it into balls. Set on wax paper or plastic wrap and let dry.

For more complete information about soap-making, consult *Soap – Making It, Enjoying It* by Ann Bramson (Workman Publishing Company, 1975).

### Moisturizing Lotion

¼ cup herb or flower infusion or
    decoction
2 teaspoons witch hazel
1 teaspoon glycerine

Mix all ingredients together in a bowl. Pour into a glass bottle or jar to store.

### Simple Cream

½ ounce beeswax or paraffin
3 ounces mild oil, such as almond,
    olive, or safflower
3 tablespoons herb or flower
    infusion or decoction, heated
¼ teaspoon borax

In an old pan or tin can set in the top of a double boiler, melt beeswax or paraffin and oil together. Slowly stir the hot infusion or decoction thoroughly into the wax-oil mixture. Pour into a small widemouthed jar and cool. Cover tightly and let set 24 hours before using.

### Quick Cream

1 tablespoon herb or flower infusion
    or decoction
4 ounces unscented cold cream

Set the jar of cold cream in a pan of simmering water and warm gently. Remove from heat and whip in the infusion or decoction. Cover tightly.

An alternative to cold cream is to whip together 1 part olive oil with 4 parts pure solid vegetable shortening and a few drops of tincture of benzoin (available from drugstores or herb suppliers).

### Herb or Flower Egg Cream

1 egg yolk
1 teaspoon honey
1 teaspoon mild oil, such as almond,
    olive, safflower, or lanolin; or
    glycerine
1 tablespoon herb or flower infusion
    or decoction

Beat the egg yolk with honey, oil, and the infusion or decoction. Pour into a small jar, cover tightly, and store in the refrigerator.

# Facial Moisturizers and Creams

Face creams and moisturizers serve several functions as beauty preparations. An important facet of skin care is to clean the skin well. A proper cleansing removes dirt and makeup as well as dead cells.

The cleansing process is started by smoothing a cream or moisturizing lotion over the skin; after a few moments, it is wiped off with a tissue. This is followed by washing the face with a mild soap and warm water. The final step depends on your skin type. If you have oily skin, use a freshening lotion or astringent first, followed by a light moisturizer. If your skin is dry, use a moisturizer or cream.

This second use of moisturizers and creams serves to hold in skin moisture by protecting the skin from harsh weather and the low humidity that goes with central heating and air conditioning.

Herb and flower moisturizers and creams are easy to make. Most ingredients can be found at the grocery and drugstore and in your garden. The basic principle involves combining an infusion or decoction with a mild oil and one or more emollients. Homemade moisturizers and creams should be used within a month, even when you use borax as an emulsifier and preservative.

The herb leaves used most often in the infusion or decoction include rosemary, salad burnet, fennel, lady's mantle, marsh mallow, and comfrey. The flowers to consider are calendula, roses, elder, violets, linden, and chamomile.

# *Hair Care*

There are many factors that contribute to healthy hair, including eating a balanced diet, increasing the flow of blood to the hair roots by massaging the scalp, thorough brushing daily to remove dust and distribute natural oils, and using herbs and flowers to strengthen hair and stimulate its growth.

Every possible – and impossible – ingredient has at one time or another in history been used in hair preparations. If you read the labels on modern hair products, that is obviously still the case. Natural or mild soaps, conditioners, rinses, and colorants made from plants are gentle to the delicate structure of hair and, over a period of time, will enrich it as well as impart a wholesome fragrance.

The specific properties of herbs and flowers are very important in hair care. These include:

**Burdock** – Root helps to prevent dandruff.
**Calendula** – Flowers lighten hair color.
**Catnip** – Leaves encourage hair growth and sooth scalp.
**Chamomile** – Flowers soften and lighten hair.
**Comfrey** – Leaves condition dry hair.
**Elder** – Berries darken hair and flowers condition dry hair.
**Garlic and onions** – Bulbs encourage hair growth and help prevent dandruff.
**Henna** – Leaves condition hair and impart a red color.
**Horsetail** – Non-fertile stems strengthen hair and prevent dandruff.
**Linden** – Flowers soften and cleanse hair.
**Marjoram** – Leaves encourage hair growth.
**Mullein** – Flowers lighten hair.
**Nasturtium** – Leaves encourage hair growth.
**Nettle** – Leaves help prevent dandruff and condition dry hair.
**Parsley** – Leaves make hair glossy and prevent dandruff.
**Rosemary** – Leaves make hair glossy, add body, prevent dandruff, and encourage hair growth; the most important hair-care plant.
**Rhubarb** – Root colors hair blonde.
**Sage** – Leaves condition dry hair and darken hair.
**Soapwort** – Leaves and roots cleanse hair.
**Southernwood** – Leaves encourage hair growth, help prevent dandruff, and brighten hair.
**Walnut** – Shells darken hair.
**Witch hazel** – Leaves and bark cleanse and condition oily hair and help prevent dandruff.

## Oil Conditioners

A warm oil conditioner used once a week is especially good for dry, brittle, or unmanageable hair, but anyone can benefit. Make a strong essential oil as described on page 104, using one or several of the hair-care herbs and flowers.

To use, warm 2 tablespoons of the oil and rub it thoroughly into the scalp and then through the hair. Cover the hair with a plastic shower cap and then with a towel dampened with very hot water and wrung out well. Remove the towel and cap after 30 minutes. Shampoo and apply a final herb or flower rinse.

## Shampoo

Homemade shampoos will not cover your head with an abundance of suds; they will, however, completely clean the hair.

1 tablespoon grated or powdered
    soapwort root or mild, white soap
    flakes
A handful of finely minced fresh herbs
    or flowers, or 1 tablespoon crushed
    dried herbs or flowers
1 tablespoon borax
1 cup boiling water

Combine soapwort or soap, herbs or flowers, and borax. Pour on boiling water. Stir until well blended. Infuse until cool and use.

## Rinses

Not only do herb and flower rinses impart their beneficial properties to the hair, including intensifying and highlighting hair color, but they also leave it delicately scented.

For a final rinse, make an infusion from any of the flowers or herbs listed, either singly or in combination, by pouring 1 cup boiling water over ¼ cup of the plant material. Let steep for 20 minutes. Strain and pour over hair that has been washed and rinsed with plain water. Work the final rinse in well.

Alternative rinses are the beauty vinegars described on page 103. These help restore the natural acid balance of the scalp, stop the scalp from itching, help prevent and control dandruff, and very effectively remove all traces of soap.

The three aspects of herb and flower hair care are oil conditioners, shampoos, and rinses. The oils can be made ahead of time, but the shampoos and rinses are made as needed. To give hair-care projects as gifts, package the dried herbs and flowers in attractive containers, combine with the oil, and present in a pretty basket, perhaps also including a hat, bow, barrette, or other hair ornament decorated with dried flowers and herbs.

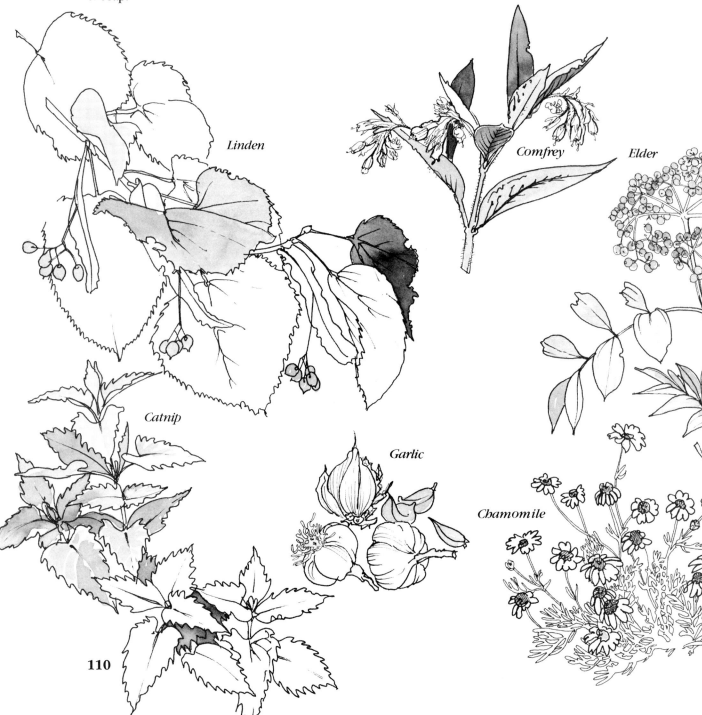

Linden

Comfrey

Elder

Catnip

Garlic

Chamomile

# Bath Bags and Salts

You don't have to spend thousands of dollars at a chic spa to get the royal beauty treatment. You can have the luxurious spa experience right in your own bath with a few simple items from your garden and kitchen. Depending on the herbs and flowers you choose, a soak in the tub can be either leisurely and relaxing or refreshing and energizing.

The basics for a beauty-spa bath include first taking a quick soap-and-water shower, then filling the tub with water at 90° to 98° F. It can be slightly warmer if muscles are particularly sore. Add bath bags, bath salts, or other items as the tub fills. Allow yourself at least 15 or 20 minutes to soak in order to get the full effect of the warm water and bath ingredients; any longer than that will dry the skin.

There are two ways that either fresh or dried herbs and flowers are used in the bath. One is to make a strong infusion with 1 cup of herbs and flowers in a quart of water; simmer for 20 minutes and steep for 30 minutes. Strain the herbs and flowers and add the water to the bath.

Another way is to put ½ to 1 cup of herbs and flowers in a muslin bag with a drawstring, and hang this under the tap as the water runs into the tub. This, of course, implies that you have the time to make muslin bags. I've found that discount stores often sell washcloths inexpensively in bundles of 12; I fill these with herbs and flowers and tie them with ribbon or rubber bands.

Usually several different herbs and flowers are combined in bath bags, each with a certain property that contributes to the overall effect. One of the most famous mixtures was allegedly used daily by a great French beauty of the seventeenth century. It included lavender and rose flowers, leaves of rosemary, mint, and thyme, and comfrey root. Any number of herbs and flowers can be used in the bath, including the leaves of lemon balm, lemon verbena, bay, comfrey, borage, catnip, parsley, thyme, basil, sweet woodruff, valerian, horsetail, lovage, fennel, sage, yarrow, dandelion, nettle, blackberry, black currant, and bergamot, as well as the needles of pine, fir, larch, and juniper. Some flowers to consider are calendula, roses, chamomile, elder, cowslip, daisies, meadowsweet, linden, and lavender.

Other additions to the bath bag are oatmeal or bran, which act as gentle abrasives. You can also add a tablespoon of sea salt, or a cup of powdered milk or honey to the bath water. Herb and flower vinegars can be added, too, for softening skin, soothing muscles, and relieving skin irritations. Use bath salts instead of the bath bag for a change.

## MATERIALS

**2 cups borax or Epsom salts**
**1 cup baking soda**
**1 cup dried flowers and/or herbs or potpourri, finely ground**
**1 dram essential oil (optional)**
**Glass jar with lid**

1. Combine all ingredients.
2. Store in the glass jar, tightly covered and labeled.
3. Use 2 to 4 tablespoons in the bath.

# Chapter 5
# *Crafts from the Landscape*

Trees, shrubs, and woody vines provide the framework of our gardens. Their height, depth, texture, color, and form give yards dimension and year-round interest. The goal when landscaping is to use a wide range of both evergreen and deciduous flowering and nonflowering trees, shrubs, and vines.

An average-size lot can contain a great many more plants than most people realize. Even if you don't have the money to invest in having the entire yard landscaped at once, you can develop a long-term plan, then add several plants or work on a specific area each year.

How to develop a plan? Whether you buy graph paper and draw the plan yourself or have a nursery, garden center, or landscape architect design one for you, you must first make some decisions about your garden.

Study magazines and books and gather together pictures of the garden style that suits you and your home. Decide how much time you want to spend working in the garden. Who will be tending the garden? How much money can you reasonably spend on maintenance? Do you want a lot of different plants? How much privacy or screening is desirable? Is a play area needed for children? Do you need, and can you afford, major construction for decks, walls, and terraces? Do you want fruits and vegetables as well as ornamental plants? Will you be entertaining outdoors much?

Once you formulate answers to these questions, you'll be ready to analyze your site. Are there existing plants? Do you want to keep them? What is your soil type? How much sun does the yard get now? Where do you want shade? Is the site sloping? What are the needs for parking and walks?

Think of landscaping as an extension of the home. As such, your goal is to create a unified whole, with the house and garden in the same scale and style. Most important, though, is a yard that is not only functional but also attractive all year long. As with so much else in gardening – and life – there are many different approaches, but most of all you want to be proud of your yard and delighted to spend time there.

Many of the following projects use pine boughs and cones. White pine grows best in the area where I live. Other varieties may be better for your area. But no matter where you are, the needled evergreens offer a lot to the landscape and to crafts. They provide excellent windbreaks, soothing sounds as the wind whispers through them, beautiful visual contrast to deciduous plants, a haven for birds and other wildlife, and a wonderful supply of aromatic greenery for the Christmas holidays.

The projects with leaves use both deciduous and broadleaved evergreen trees and shrubs. Many different varieties can work for these projects. Experiment with what you have and can find.

The basket and wreath projects feature vines such as wisteria, honeysuckle, bittersweet, clematis, trumpetvine, carolina jessamine, and silverlace vine. These vary in hardiness and vigor. Some can become pests; know your space and maintenance requirements, then choose wisely. Vines add vertical form and color to the landscape. Including them in your garden will be one of the best decisions you make.

# A Christmas Tree for the Birds

Birds are one thing that I cannot imagine my life without. Their colors, music, grace, beauty, and antics are an integral part of my existence. Providing food and water for them in my garden has become an enjoyable year-round project.

Since they are so much a part of my life, it seemed only logical to include a special Christmas tree for them as part of the holiday tradition. To make your own, simply trim an evergreen or deciduous tree that is already growing in your yard with an assortment of foods that birds enjoy. An alternative is to use a cut tree – either pre- or post-Christmas. If you use a cut tree, stabilize it with a concrete block or two criss-crossing boards nailed to the bottom.

Following are suggestions for some taste-tempting trims:

**Garlands** – String popcorn, cranberries, raisins, and dates. Loop garlands through the branches.

**Bird cakes** – Combine one part peanut butter with two parts mixed birdseed, five parts cornmeal, and one part melted beef suet. (To melt beef suet, cut in small pieces and cook over low flame in a heavy skillet.) Spoon into paper-lined muffin tins. When partially hardened, insert 6-inch loops of cord in the middle by first poking a hole in the cake with an ice pick. Remove cakes and hang when thoroughly hardened, or store in the freezer until you're ready for them.

**Pinecone ornaments** – Make a mixture of peanut butter, birdseed, cornmeal, and melted beef suet, as above. When cooled to working consistency, spoon it between the scales of the pinecones.

**Bacon balls** – Add four parts cornmeal and two parts birdseed to one part room-temperature bacon grease until you have a dough-like consistency. Add sand or fine gravel for grit, if desired. Shape around 6-inch loops of cord into balls about 2 inches in diameter.

**Fruit and nut cups** – Save orange or grapefruit rinds cut in half from breakfast. Using a heavy needle and thread, run the thread through the rind at three evenly spaced points around the edge and make a hanger. Fill the cups with stale doughnut pieces, peanuts, birdseed, apple wedges, raisins, dates, and suet chunks.

**Suet bags** – Fill plastic net onion bags with chunks of beef suet and attach to tree branches.

**Wheat dollies** – Tie small bunches of wheat together with red outdoor ribbon and attach to tree.

*A treat cup made from half an orange rind adds a decorative touch to the yard and creates a smorgasbord for the birds.*

**113**

*Your birds will appreciate suet bags, peanut butter pinecone ornaments, bird cupcakes and wheat dollies at Christmas and throughout the winter.*

**114**

# Holiday Greens

Treat your senses of sight, touch, and smell this Christmas by festooning your house, inside and out, with evergreen wreaths, swags, balls, and garlands that you've made yourself. They'll be welcome gifts, too.

Each one is simply assembled with only a few inexpensive materials. If at all possible, carefully prune the greens from your own shrubs and trees. Otherwise, they can be purchased.

Of the cone-bearing, or needled, evergreens, the most suitable are balsam fir, Douglas fir, Austrian pine, white pine, Scotch pine, red pine, yew, red cedar, juniper, and false cypress. Avoid hemlock and spruce for indoor use, as they quickly drop their needles.

Broadleaved evergreens are also used in holiday decorations, especially where they are hardy in the landscape. Some of the best choices are holly, boxwood, barberry, Oregon grape holly, English ivy, magnolia, and rhododendron. If harvesting these from your own garden, be careful not to damage the ornamental value of the plant.

Most of the evergreen decorations usually last long enough, but freshness can be prolonged with the use of sprays, called anti-dessicants, that minimize moisture loss. These sprays are available from nurseries and garden centers. A flame-retardant spray can be made by dissolving ¼ cup boric acid with 9 tablespoons borax in 2 quarts water; another mixture with the same effect combines 5 tablespoons borax and ¼ cup Epsom salts in 2 quarts water. Apply either of these mixtures with a mister bottle or garden sprayer.

Why did we begin decorating our homes with evergreens? Historians trace the custom back to Egyptians bringing palm branches into their homes in late December as a symbol of growing things. The Roman harvest festival held in December, called Saturnalia, was a time for exchanging gifts and trimming trees with trinkets; Romans also exchanged green tree branches for good luck on January 1.

The Germans are usually credited, however, with incorporating evergreens into the Christian winter celebration, Christmas. Legend has it that about 1,200 years ago, when the missionary Saint Boniface, traveling in northern Germany, chopped down a sacrificial oak, a fir tree appeared as the tree of life, representing Christ. It was not until about 400 years ago, though, that the use of a decorated tree became a tradition in Germany. By the 1800s, the custom had spread throughout Europe and Britain, and to the United States.

## MATERIALS

**For the Wreath:**
**Pruning shears**
**4- to 6-inch-long cuttings of evergreen branch tips**
**15-inch three-wire wreath form (available from craft stores)**
**Wire cutters**
**#24-gauge floral wire, cut into 6-inch lengths**
**Ribbon (optional)**
**Cones, berried branches, or other decorative accents (optional)**

1. Gather three or four evergreen sprigs with the stem ends together. Lay these on the wire wreath frame, then use the short lengths of floral wire to bind the stems to the frame with at least three turns of the wire.
2. Continue this procedure around the frame on each of the three wires of the frame, overlapping the groups like shingles on a roof. To finish attaching the greens, gently pull back the first sprigs and bind in the last bundle.
3. Add ribbon, cones, berries, ornaments, or bells, if desired. Attach each decoration separately with its own wire.

## MATERIALS

**For the Evergreen Ball:**
**Stout cord**
**Large, round potato about 4 inches in diameter**
**Pruning shears**
**Sharp knife**
**4-inch-long cuttings of needled or broadleaved evergreens**
**Ribbon, mistletoe, holly, berried branches, or other decorative accent materials (optional)**

*(continued)*

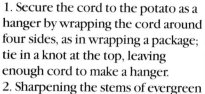

1. Secure the cord to the potato as a hanger by wrapping the cord around four sides, as in wrapping a package; tie in a knot at the top, leaving enough cord to make a hanger.

2. Sharpening the stems of evergreen cuttings with a knife, if necessary, insert the sprigs into the potato until completely covered. As many as 75 sprigs will be needed.

3. Trim with ribbon, mistletoe, holly, berried branches, or other decorative accent materials, as desired.

## MATERIALS

**For the Garlands or Roping:**
**Heavy, flexible clothesline cord, as long as desired**
**3- to 4-inch-long cuttings of evergreen branch tips**
**Pruning shears**
**Wire cutters**
**#24-gauge floral wire, cut into 6-inch lengths**

1. Knot or bind the end of the cord so it does not unravel. Fasten the cord to a hook or doorknob so that it can be stretched taut.

2. Gather three or four sprigs of greens with the stem ends together. Starting at one end, lay these on the cord with the stem ends facing you.

3. Then use short lengths of floral wire to bind the stems to the cord with at least three turns of the wire.

4. Continue fastening bundles to both sides of the cord, overlapping the bundles like shingles on a roof.

# Yule Log

Derived from the word for December and January, *yule* is an old Anglo-Saxon name for the Christmas season. The tradition of the yule log probably started with early Norsemen honoring Thor, their god of war, by burning a huge oak log once a year. After becoming Christians, the Norse continued the log-burning as part of the Christmas celebration. Later, the English incorporated the custom into their festivities, and it is now considered to be good luck to save a piece to start next year's fire.

Most of the fireplaces in our homes today would not accommodate the real yule logs of long ago. A way to maintain this ancient tradition, however, is with a small replica aglow with candles and surrounded with greens. Although oak would be most authentic, the bark of other trees is more interesting, such as that of birch, hackberry, and sassafras.

## MATERIALS

Chain, circular or bow saw
Section of log or branch, 3 inches or more in diameter and 12 inches long
Brown felt, approximately 2 by 12 inches
Drill with ⅞-inch paddle bit
Hot glue gun with clear glue sticks, or white craft or household glue
Bow, optional (See Tying the Perfect Bow, page 165)
Holly, pinecones, dried flowers, or greens (optional)
2 candles

1. Use a saw to cut off about a quarter inch along the length of one side of a log so that it will sit flat.
2. Attach felt to the bottom with glue to protect furniture.
3. Measure in 3 inches from each end, and drill a hole 1 inch deep at each point.
4. Glue a bow in the middle, if desired, or decorate with dried flowers, cones, or whatever you prefer if desired. You may also surround the log with greens. Insert candles in the holes.

Step 1

Step 2

Step 3

117

## MATERIALS

**Pruning shears**
**Hemlock cones**
**Wire cutters**
**#24-gauge floral wire**
**Green floral tape**
**Sprigs of multiflora rose hips or holly berries**
**Assortment of foliage, such as holly or ivy leaves, or sprigs of spruce, fir, or cedar**
**½-inch-wide ribbon**
**Corsage or hat pin**

Part of the joy of the Christmas holiday season lies in remembering others with thoughtful gifts. A corsage styled with tiny hemlock cones, multiflora rose hips, holly berries and leaves, plain or variegated ivy leaves, and evergreen foliage can be worn on a coat or purse all through the month of December.

*Step 1*

*Step 2*

1. To wire the hemlock cones, wrap an inch or so of wire around the base of the cone, then bring the wire down and twist it around itself directly under the cone. Wrap with the floral tape, starting just under the cone, then twirling it down the wire stem, stretching and keeping it taut as you work.

2. Wire the hips or berries and the foliage by using the "hairpin" technique. First, bend a length of wire in half. For broad leaves, like holly or ivy, pierce the leaf with one end of the "pin" on each side of the main vein about a half inch from the base. Wrap with floral tape, as above, starting at the stem. For the berries or hips and the sprigs of evergreen, place the "hairpin" parallel to the backside of the bottom inch or so of stem, then wrap the stem.

3. Purchase a bow from a craft or florist shop, or make your own by forming loops from the ribbon and securing in the middle with an 8-to 10-inch piece of ribbon; fluff out the loops.

4. Assemble the corsage by interspersing the cones with the sprigs of hips or berries and the foliage. Twist the wires together as you work.

5. Cut the stems at the base of the corsage to about 1½ inches long. Wrap with additional floral tape.

6. Tie the ribbon bow on. Insert the pin through the stem.

# Pinecone Christmas Ornaments

Pine trees are the most important group of lumber trees in the world, and they are equally significant as ornamentals in the landscape. They adapt to a wide range of soils and climates, while providing shades of green, soft textures, and wonderful scent year-round.

For crafts, the best thing about pine trees is their cones. Depending on the variety, cones may be long and skinny or short and plump, ranging in length from an inch or so to over 12 inches.

Pinecones have always been one of the souvenirs of my travels around the country. Whether from the long leaf, loblolly, or slash pine in the South or the western white or ponderosa pine in the West, using the cones in Christmas decorations brings pleasant memories of summertime pursuits. Of course, I also combine these with the cones of the white, Scotch, and jack pines that are readily accessible where I live in the Midwest.

Pinecones serve a multitude of purposes around the house during the Christmas holidays, made into wreaths, plaques, fire starters, or simply tucked in among pine branches or casually strewn along ribbon streamers as a table centerpiece. They're also quite appropriate as ornaments on the tree or hung at windows and doors.

## MATERIALS

**Scissors**
**Gilt or satin cord**
**Hot glue gun with clear glue sticks, or white craft glue**
**Pinecones (one for each ornament)**
**Ribbon (use a width in scale with the cone)**
**Dried flowers, herbs, and berries**

1. Cut a 7-inch length of cord and glue both ends to the top of a pinecone to make a hanger.
2. Use glue to attach several loops of ribbon among the dried flowers, herbs, and berries.
3. As a variation, instead of attaching the loop of cord, hang the pinecones from the ribbon streamers of a bow hung on a door, as curtain tiebacks, or as mantel trim.

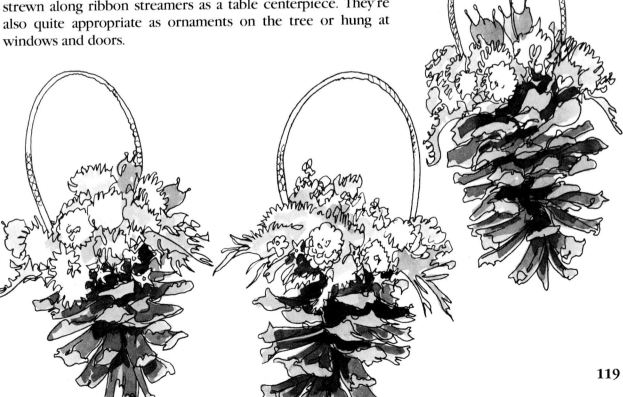

119

## MATERIALS

**Pinecones (75 to 100)**
**Tub, sink, or large pan of warm**
**water**
**12-inch or larger three-wire**
**wreath form**

1. Soak pinecones in the warm water for 30 minutes. This will cause them to close up.
2. Push about an inch of the base of each cone into the frame between the wires. Space close enough together so they stay in the frame readily. Vary the size of cone used and the angle of placement.
3. Set aside to dry. The cones will expand as they dry, wedging them in tightly and filling in the spaces.
4. Decorate as desired.

# Pinecone Wreath

Trimmed simply with a plaid bow or embellished with dried flowers, paint, and ornaments, a bristling pinecone wreath is the basis for all manner of Christmas holiday decorations. Besides hanging it on a door or wall, try it as a base for a punch bowl or as a table centerpiece surrounding a large candle and hurricane shade.

Although any kind of pinecone will work, cones from white pines *(Pinus sylvestris)* are among the most readily available, and they have a natural "snow" trim – the white resin that clings to them.

# Fire Starters

For those with a practical bent, fire starters made from pinecones are among the most worthwhile of crafts. One of these placed under the kindling in your fireplace or stove will be sure to have the fire glowing brightly in no time.

At Christmas, trim a beautiful basket with holly and ribbon, fill with fire starters, and set beside the hearth to enhance the holiday atmosphere. This also makes one of the best and most appreciated gifts, and is an especially good present for that person who seems to have everything.

## MATERIALS

**Medium-size pinecones**
**Water**
**Double boiler**
**Knife**
**Paraffin**
**Old saucepan or large tin can**
**Newspaper**
**Red or green crayon (optional)**
**Old muffin pan**
**Scissors**
**Candle wicking or heavy cord**

1. Select cones that will fit in muffin cups. If cones are still partially closed, they can be made to open completely by baking them on an old cookie sheet in a 200° F oven for 30 minutes.

2. Put water in the bottom of a double boiler and bring to a boil; reduce heat to a simmer. With a knife, grate paraffin into an old saucepan or tin can set inside the top of the double boiler.

3. When the paraffin has melted, dip each pinecone to coat completely. Remove and cool on newspaper.

4. Melt more paraffin, as needed. When all the cones have been dipped, add red or green crayon to the melted wax to tint, if desired.

5. Pour melted paraffin ½ inch deep into each of the muffin cups.

6. Cut wicking or cord into 2-inch lengths. Place one wick in each muffin cup, placing it to one side with at least an inch extending above the paraffin.

7. Allow paraffin to partially harden, then press a pinecone into each cup. Let harden completely.

8. Run hot water into the sink and dip the bottom of the muffin pan into it to loosen the fire starters. Lift each one out.

## MATERIALS

**White glue**
**Bowl**
**Water**
**½-inch paintbrush**
**Pinecones**
**Fire-color crystals (available from fireplace specialty shops)**
**Newspaper**

1. Pour white glue into a bowl and thin with water, if necessary, to the consistency of paint.
2. With the paintbrush, put a coat of glue all over a pinecone.
3. Sprinkle the glue-covered pinecone with fire-color crystals.
4. Set on newspaper to dry.

## MATERIALS

**Ruler**
**4-inch-diameter polystyrene ball**
**Large knife**
**2 candle holder cups (available at craft stores)**
**Brown spray paint (optional)**
**Assortment of nuts, cones, and seedpods**
**Hot glue gun with clear glue sticks, white craft glue, or linoleum cement**
**Clear polyurethane spray**

1. Measure the midway point on a polystyrene ball and cut it in half with a knife.
2. In the top center of the rounded side, carve a space large enough for a candle holder cup and insert the holder. Repeat for the other half.
3. Paint the balls, if desired.
4. Attach larger nuts, cones, and pods to the polystyrene, using glue or cement. Fill in with smaller ones until you have covered it to your satisfaction.
5. Spray with clear polyurethane varnish.

# Colored-Fire Pinecones

Children often like to be involved with craftwork at the same time as adults, and this project is an excellent companion to Fire Starters, page 121. It is also a project that can easily stand on its own as a quick and simple treat for yourself or friends.

Some of my older craft books suggest buying individual chemicals, but I feel it is safer to use the fire-color crystals sold at fireplace equipment stores.

Fill a basket with these color cones, and toss one on the fire whenever you want a rainbow of color to brighten up a wintry evening.

# Cone-and-Nut Candle Holder

As a person who is fascinated by texture and form, I am always struck by the beauty of the various nuts, cones, and seedpods that characterize autumn's bounty. And if you've ever thought brown a boring color, look again at the tremendous range of shades in these woody "fruits."

Let candlelight play on these textures, forms, and colors, and you have created something quite extraordinary. The candle holders described here are easy to make, and there are endless variations. Try covering different shapes and sizes of forms.

Be adventurous in collecting materials for your candle holders. Look for a variety of acorns, beechnut hulls, walnuts, heartnuts, hibiscus and rose-of-Sharon pods, buckeyes, sweet gum balls, and all manner of conifer cones. Don't forget that the grocery offers a backup with bags of mixed nuts!

# Leaf Imprints

Use the great variety of different leaf shapes to create an impression – with the pun obviously intended. The imprint left by leaves, especially if they are deeply veined or unusually shaped, is a limitless design tool, whether for making wall plaques, ornaments, jewelry, or paving stones. You can make imprints using plaster of paris, flour-and-salt clay, potter's clay, or cement.

Another benefit of making leaf impressions is that it appeals to people of different ages and skill levels. Anyone from a preschooler to an artist can take advantage of the opportunities presented by this technique.

Step 2

Step 3

Step 6

## MATERIALS

**Leaves**
**Watercolor, tempera, or acrylic paints, in colors as desired**
**Small, fine camel's hair artist's brushes**
**Clear plastic craft spray sealer**
**Yarn, satin cording, ribbon, leather thong, or earring and pin backs, as desired**

### For Flour-and-Salt Clay Projects:

1 cup salt
2 cups all-purpose white flour
½ cup water
2 tablespoons vegetable oil
Bowl
Spoon
Rolling pin
Knife
Cookie cutters
Metal egg turner
Nonstick cookie sheet
Sharp object
Screw eye (optional)
Oven, preheated to 250° F

1. Stir salt, flour, water, and oil together in a bowl until well mixed; work with your hands to blend, if necessary. The consistency should be like rolled cookie dough.
2. Roll out clay to ⅜ inch thick, then shape as desired, using knife, cookie cutters, and so forth. Clay can be stored in a tightly closed plastic bag in the refrigerator.
3. Press a leaf or leaves, vein side down, onto the clay. Carefully remove the leaf and place the piece on the cookie sheet with the egg turner. Use a sharp object to make a hole or holes in the top for attaching a cord or other hanger; another idea is to insert a screw eye in the top.
4. Bake for three hours in a 250° F oven.
5. Paint, if desired, or spray with clear craft sealer.
6. Attach cord or other hanger, if desired.

## MATERIALS

**Large sheet of plastic**
**Newspaper**
**Tempera paint, or oil or acrylic block printing ink, or fabric ink or paint**
**Large glazed dinner plate or 12-by-12-inch piece of ground-edge plate glass**
**3- or 4-inch soft rubber roller, called an ink brayer**
**Assortment of leaves**
**Paper or fabric, as desired**
**Paper towels**

1. Spread a sheet of plastic over a large flat work surface, and cover this with newspapers.

2. Put a small amount of paint or ink on a plate or piece of glass. Spread it out with the roller, picking the roller up between strokes to help distribute the ink evenly.

3. Place a leaf vein side up on the plate or glass and roll the inked brayer over the entire surface until uniformly coated. You can ink the stem or not, as desired.

4. Gently pick up the leaf by the stem and carefully place vein side down on your paper or fabric. Put a paper towel on top and gently rub. Be careful not to let the leaf slide.

5. Finally, carefully remove first the paper and then the leaf. Repeat the process, as desired, being cautious about smearing with inky leaves, paper towels, and fingers. Clean up as you work. Sometimes you can get two or more prints with one inking, with each gradually fainter. The time it takes for the ink to dry will depend on the ink and the atmospheric humidity.

As an alternative, you can simply take a ¼- or ½-inch-wide paintbrush and paint the back side of the leaf. Place it on the fabric or paper, then rub with your fingers to transfer the ink or paint.

124

# *Leaf Printing*

Leaves benefit us as well as the plants they nourish by their beauty. It is interesting just to observe and compare the amazing variety of leaf shapes, colors, and forms. Look even closer and notice the network of veins in leaves. The craft of leaf printing allows us to use the astonishing diversity of leaves in limitless possibilities of expression.

Use leaf print designs with permanent oil or acrylic paint or ink to decorate clothing, wall hangings, tablecloths, placemats, curtains, pillows, or ceiling stencils. Make borders, random cascades, or overlapping imprints. Embroider or quilt around leaf shapes. Kids have fun decorating their own T-shirts and pants, and even the walls of their rooms!

Water-soluble paints are most often used to make gift wrapping and tags, although permanent paint or ink can also be used on these.

Different paints and inks will vary the look of your projects. Try them all to see which ones you like best. Besides those suggested, look for iron-on transfer paints at art and craft stores. Dull-finish paper and cotton or cotton-polyester blend fabrics are best. Consider a beautifully colored burlap for a wall hanging or a homespun-look cotton for a table runner.

Some leaves to begin with might include sycamore, tulip tree, maple, ginkgo, basswood, elm, locust, ash, oak, willow, walnut, buckeye, and sassafras.

*Leaf printing is easy and fun.
All you need are leaves, paper or
cloth, coloring ( like ink or
acrylics ), a roller, and a surface
to work on.*

## MATERIALS

**Individual leaves or branches of leaves to 2 feet long**
**Pruning shears**
**Glycerine**
**Hot water**
**1½-quart glass loaf pan and plastic wrap or lid (for individual leaves)**
**Coffee can or quart jar (for branches)**
**Hammer (optional)**

1. Pick leaves or prune off branches of leaves that are as perfect and as free from dust as possible. Picking them after a dry spell is important, as this improves absorption. If leaves look dusty, wipe them with a damp cloth.

2. Make a solution of 1 part glycerine and 2 parts hot water. For example, if you are using a 4-ounce bottle of glycerine, pour it into your container, then add two bottles (8 ounces) of hot water. If preserving individual leaves, pour the solution into a glass loaf pan to a 3-inch depth. If preserving branches, use a coffee can or quart jar filled with 3 to 5 inches of solution.

3. To preserve individual leaves, stack them in the pan, making sure that the solution surrounds the surfaces of all the leaves. Cover and set aside. Tilt the container every couple of days to make sure the solution is still touching all the leaves. When the coloring of the individual leaves is uniform, they are done. Remove each leaf separately, and drain solution back into a jar for storage. Separate the leaves and place them in a single layer on newspaper. Let dry for a week or so. Store in a box with tissue between the leaves.

# *Glycerinized Leaves*

One of the things often missing from dried flower arrangements and other projects is attractive foliage. Leaves add texture, form, and color, as well as providing background and filling in spaces. Rather than losing these important elements or using artificial foliage, why not preserve a variety of leaves in glycerine? It's very easy, and the leaves last for years.

Leaves from an assortment of trees and shrubs in the garden, when glycerinized, remain pliable and leatherlike, with a slightly oily surface. The color will vary depending on the time of year when picked, the time the material is in the glycerine, and the type of plant. Usually, the leaves will take on a lovely, glossy bronze, burgundy, or brown color. Southern magnolia *(Magnolia grandiflora)* leaves become almost black, and are quite striking surrounding a wreath or table arrangement of fruit.

Although it's worth experimenting, the best results are usually obtained with leaves that have heavy textures. Those with the most consistent track record include magnolia, viburnum, pittosporum, red maple, sumac, beech, oak, camellia, galax, elaeagnus (olive), ivy, barberry, crabapple, plum, forsythia, and Christmas fern.

Glycerinized leaves keep indefinitely. If they begin to look a little bedraggled, leave them for several hours in a steamy bathroom to brighten and restore freshness, or just wipe large leaves with a damp cloth.

The 4-ounce bottles of glycerine available at most drugstores have gotten rather expensive, but luckily the treatment solution can be reused. A drop or two of bleach in it will help to prevent mold. I did some calling around in my area, and finally found both a drugstore and a craft shop that sold larger quantities more cheaply, so a little investigative effort is worth the trouble if you're going to be doing a lot of preserving by this method.

126

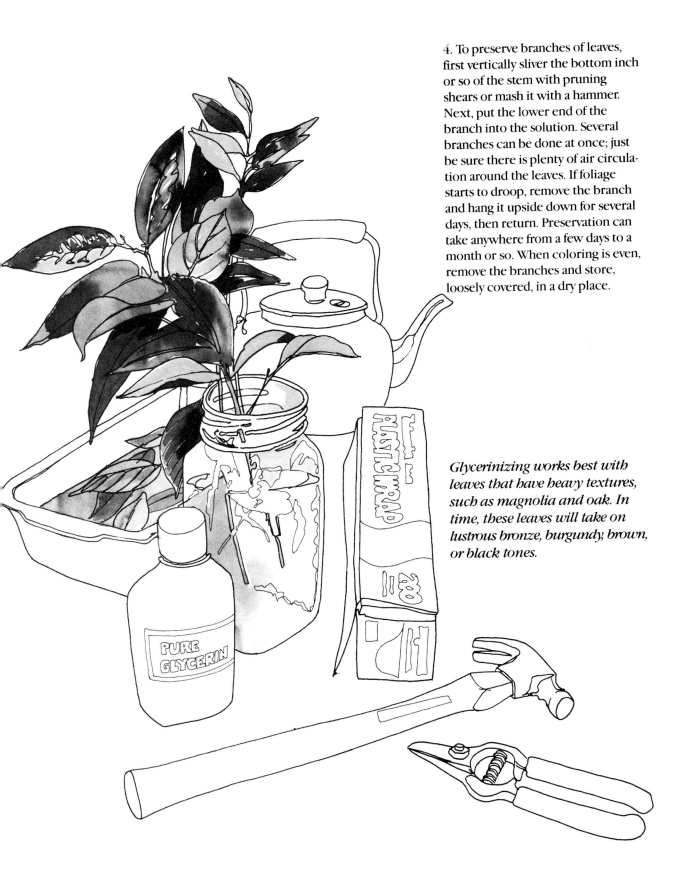

4. To preserve branches of leaves, first vertically sliver the bottom inch or so of the stem with pruning shears or mash it with a hammer. Next, put the lower end of the branch into the solution. Several branches can be done at once; just be sure there is plenty of air circulation around the leaves. If foliage starts to droop, remove the branch and hang it upside down for several days, then return. Preservation can take anywhere from a few days to a month or so. When coloring is even, remove the branches and store, loosely covered, in a dry place.

*Glycerinizing works best with leaves that have heavy textures, such as magnolia and oak. In time, these leaves will take on lustrous bronze, burgundy, brown, or black tones.*

## MATERIALS

**Washing soda**
**Fresh mature leaves**
**Stainless steel or enameled pot**
**Dull knife**
**Household bleach**
**#24-gauge floral wire**
**White floral tape**
**Hot glue gun with clear glue
    sticks, or white craft or house-
    hold glue**
**Glycerine (optional)**

1. Adding a teaspoon of washing soda to each quart of water used, put water, soda, and leaves into a pot.
2. Bring to a boil and continue slowly boiling for 30 minutes. Let stand until cool.
3. Spread leaves out on newspaper. With a dull knife, carefully scrape both sides of the leaves, which will remove the fleshy part between the leaf veins.
4. Rinse the pot and prepare a solution with 2 tablespoons of bleach to each quart of water.
5. Add the leaves and let soak for about an hour, or until white.
6. Remove leaves, rinse with water, and gently wipe with a soft cloth.
7. Spread the leaves between pieces of paper towel and place between the pages of a book for 24 hours.
8. Remove and use the leaves or store them in a cool, dry place in a covered box with paper towel between the layers.
9. To use in arrangements, bend a length of floral wire in half and place the bend along the leaf stem. Holding the leaf and wire in your left hand, use your right hand to wrap the stem and wire with floral tape, twirling the wire and stretching the tape as you work. Put a drop of glue on the wire at the back of the leaf.
10. Leaves may be dipped in glycerine, if desired, to keep them pliable.

**NOTE:** An alternate method is to stack glycerine-treated leaves (see Glycerinized Leaves, page 126) and wrap in wax paper. Store in a box for about six months. After this time, remove the leaves and use a small, soft brush to carefully flick away the fleshy part of the leaves instead of scraping. Bleach and wire.

# Skeletonized Leaves

Victorians used them to make wintertime "phantom bouquets," but, belying their pale, ethereal, ghostlike form, skeletonized leaves are really rather sturdy and hold their shape well. Specially preserved, these leaves, also called angel's wings, have had the outer "skin," or leaf surface, removed, leaving only the skeletonlike framework of the plant's vascular system.

Skeletonizing leaves is not an easy project, as it is tedious and requires patience. The rather stunning result does make the challenge worthwhile, however.

The best leaves for skeletonizing are ones that are thick and have prominent veins, such as magnolia, rhododendron, holly, ivy, maple, beech, oak, avocado, croton, and crabapple.

# Round Market Basket

As with any item with a history of long use, there are wonderful bits of folklore attached to baskets. For instance, in Germany at one time (probably long, long ago as all good folk tales go), it was supposedly the custom for a girl who was being courted to lower a basket from her window to receive gifts from her suitor.

If the girl wasn't particularly pleased with her beau, she would let down a loose-bottomed basket, so the bottom would fall out along with the gift. It even got to the point where girls would use baskets with no bottom at all! The phrase *to give a basket* came to mean giving a refusal, and the term *fell through* refers to a plan that failed.

The integration of baskets into our lives and language is evidenced just by looking around the home. The list could include bushel, laundry, waste, shopping, sewing, and fruit and berry baskets, to say nothing of the decorative ones sitting about.

A sturdy, homey market basket can take many sizes and shapes, but the round is the "granddaddy" of them all and the easiest to make. The main difference between this and the Fireside Basket (page 131) is the shape.

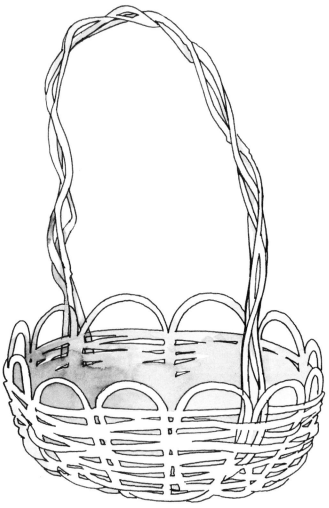

## MATERIALS

(For a 9-inch basket)
Pruning shears
Nine 22-inch lengths of thin, pliable woody stems about ⅛ inch thick, such as honeysuckle, wisteria, or willow
Longer pieces of the same thin, pliable stems, about 4 to 6 feet long
Large sink or tub of warm water

1. Soak the stems in the warm water for about 10 minutes, if necessary, before beginning to weave.
2. To start the basket, put three 22-inch woody stems close together and parallel on a flat surface. Put three more on top at a right angle to the first group, forming a large plus sign.
3. Use one of the longer woody stems to begin weaving over and under the groups of three pieces. Go around this "square" twice.
4. Begin going over and under the pieces individually. Spread the spokes out evenly, except for two spokes, which should be combined to create an uneven number of spokes. Continue over and under, around and around. When you finish with one long woody piece and start with another, either tuck the ends in securely next to a spoke or overlap the ends.
5. When the diameter of the weaving is about 8 inches, begin bringing the spokes up as you work to create the sides of the basket. Continue over and under, around and around.
6. When there are only about 4 inches of spoke left, tuck the end of the last piece down through the weaving alongside one of the spokes.
7. Finish off the rim by bending each spoke over and tucking it securely beside the spoke next to it.
8. Lightly twist the remaining three 22-inch pieces together. Securely insert one end of these stems down beside one spoke, then arch them over to the other side and insert beside the spoke opposite the first one.

**129**

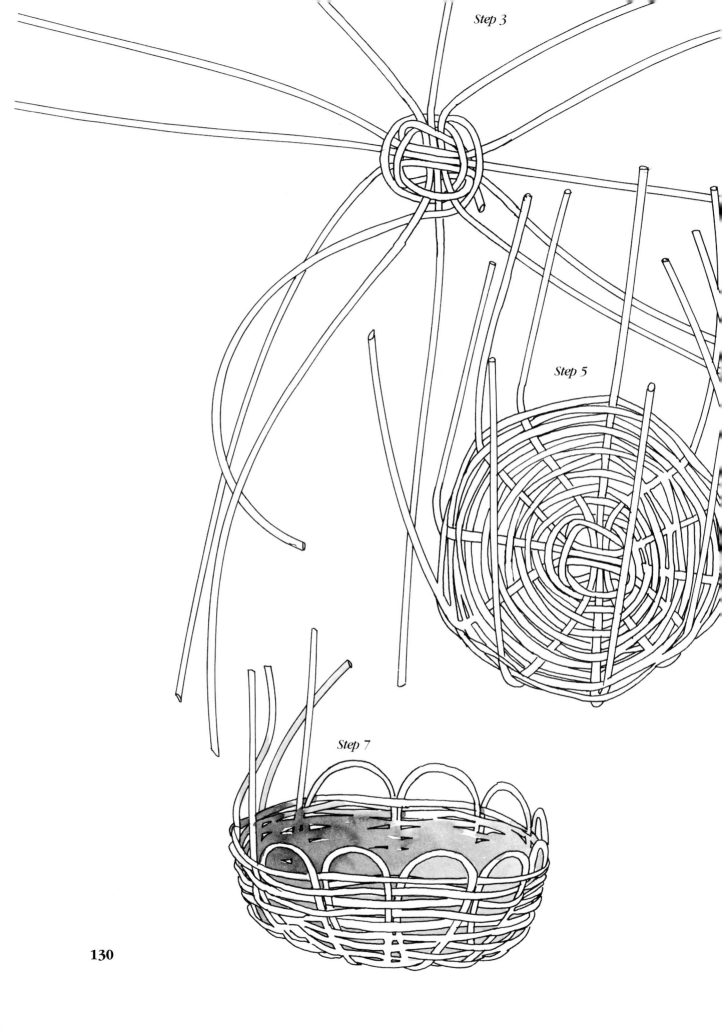

Step 3

Step 5

Step 7

130

# *Fireside Basket*

Basketweaving is one of our oldest and most venerable crafts. Cultures and civilizations throughout the ages have made and used baskets from the native plant materials that were readily available. Pine needles, hickory, willow, palmetto, honeysuckle, sweet grass, cornshucks, raffia, rushes, rattan, and straw are some of the materials that come to mind.

Objects and vessels woven from plant materials have been used for everything from the most obvious task of holding food to lining storage pits, and serving as water containers, fishnets, boats, cradles, horse carts, even "people containers" for hot-air balloons.

Baskets are still a vital part of our lives today, playing both useful and decorative roles. People continue to enjoy making baskets because it is simple to do, inexpensive, and relatively quick, yet it can also be challenging. Each person tends to bring something personal to the process, making every basket special and unique.

A fireside basket is a simple project for learning both basketry techniques and the possibilities of plant materials from the garden, roadside, and woodland. Basically, it is a round mat with two of the sides brought up and a handle attached. Depending on the material used, it could be no more than an inch across, or reach a width of several feet.

There are any number of ways to make even such a basic basket as this. I have used a method that is one of the simplest ways to construct a basket so that success will come readily. If you become fascinated with the process, delve further into the subject. There are many books and classes on basketmaking available; take advantage of them.

## MATERIALS

(For a 14- to 16-inch basket)
Pruning shears
Nine 24-inch lengths of thin, pliable woody stems about ⅛ inch thick, such as honeysuckle, wisteria, or willow
Longer pieces of the same thin, pliable stems (4 to 6 feet long)
Large sink or tub of warm water

1. Soak the stems for about 10 minutes before beginning to weave.
2. To start the basket, put three of the 24-inch woody stems close together and parallel on a flat surface. Put three more on top at a right angle to the first group, making a large plus sign.
3. Use one of the longer woody stems to begin weaving over and under the groups of three pieces. Go around the "square" twice.
4. Begin going over and under the pieces individually. Spread the spokes out evenly, except for two spokes, which should be combined to create an uneven number of spokes. Continue over and under, around and around. When you finish with one piece of long woody stem and start with another, either tuck the ends in securely next to a spoke or overlap them.
5. When there are only about 4 inches of spoke showing, tuck the end of the last piece down through the weaving by one of the spokes.
6. Finish off the rim by bending each spoke over and tucking it securely beside the spoke next to it.
7. Lightly twist the remaining three 24-inch pieces together. Gently bend up two sides of the circle and securely insert the three stems down beside the spokes on opposite sides.

**131**

# Cookie-Cutter Vine Wreaths

The ubiquitous vine wreath takes on a whole new dimension when shaped into gingerbread men, rabbits, chickens, stars, or the shape of your favorite cookie cutter. Once the technique is mastered, you can use those honeysuckle vines that are such a nuisance to you and your neighbor. Use these miniature wreaths as ornaments for hanging in windows, decorating a package, or as gifts themselves, to fit any season or occasion.

## MATERIALS

**Large cookie cutter**
**Scrap of board larger than the cookie cutter**
**Pencil**
**Hammer**
**#4 finishing nails**
**Pruning shears**
**Fresh honeysuckle vines**
**Large sink or tub of warm water**
**Tiny ribbon and dried flowers (optional)**

1. Make a guide for the wreath, called a jig, by placing a cookie cutter on a board and tracing around it with a pencil.
2. Remove the cookie cutter and drive nails into the wood along the outline, spacing them ½ inch apart. The nails should be secure, but still have at least 1½ inches showing above the board.
3. Strip the leaves from honeysuckle vines. Soak the vines in the warm water for a few minutes, then pull the outer bark off. Weave the vines in and out around the guide nails in several layers until you have the wreath the thickness you want.
4. Slide the vines up about ½ inch above the board. Take another vine and wrap it around the vines on the jig to hold the wreath together. Tuck in the ends to secure.
5. Let the vines dry completely. To speed up the drying process, place the vine-covered jig on a cookie sheet and put it in a 150°F oven for several hours.
6. Slip the dried wreath off the nails. If this is difficult, just pull out the nails with the claw of a hammer or a pair of pliers. Trim the wreath with narrow ribbon tied into a bow and with dried flowers, if desired.

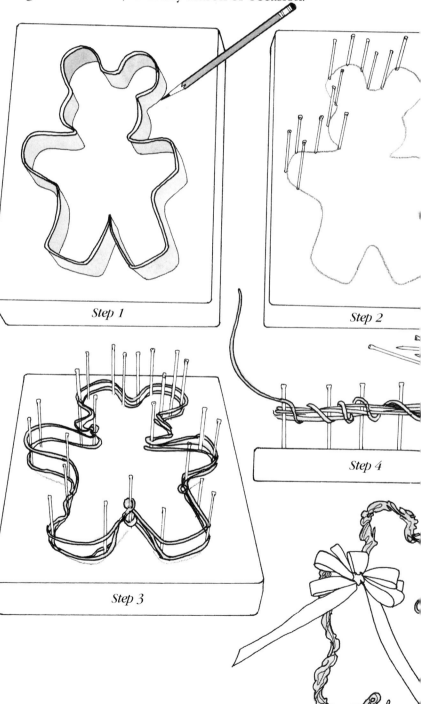

*Step 1*

*Step 2*

*Step 3*

*Step 4*

# Wall Basket Towel Holder

The most exciting aspects of baskets are their amazing diversity and versatility. There are at least as many, if not more, ways to make and use baskets as there are people. The great range of styles, shapes, and materials possible provides us with a unique opportunity for creativity.

If you're new to basketmaking, yet want something a little different, this simple, primitive basket that doubles as a towel holder and a wall pocket is a good project. Use it in the kitchen or bath, at a vacation house, or next to an outdoor shower or where you clean up from gardening.

## MATERIALS

**Pruning shears**
**3- to 6-foot lengths of thin, supple branches or vines, such as willow, honeysuckle, bittersweet, or grape**
**Large sink or tub of warm water**
**Tape measure**
**Scissors**
**Raffia (available at craft stores)**
**Towel**

1. Cut branches or vines and soak in sink or tub of warm water for 30 minutes.
2. Select a branch or vine 36 inches long and about ¼ inch in diameter. Form an oval about 12 inches long and 9 inches across, overlapping the ends by several inches. Tie the ends together with a piece of raffia. Place this point where they are joined in the middle of a long side.
3. Select another branch or vine about 30 inches long and slightly less than ¼ inch in diameter. Tie one end of this new piece to the first piece directly opposite the tied joint. Twist this new piece around the first piece, going halfway around the oval; this forms the handle. Making a smaller oval within the larger one, bring the end around to the point where you started, overlap, and tie with raffia.
4. Select a branch or vine about 5 feet long and slightly less than ¼ inch in diameter. Place one end at a right angle to an overlap joint and lash them together with raffia. Take this branch straight across to the opposite side and tie again. Wrapping around the outside of the large oval, go back to the other side, letting the branch dip about 1¼ inches below the first one. Tie and

**133**

go around and back to the other side, again going about 1¼ inches below the previous one. Repeat this twice again. You will have three cross pieces on each side of your ovals. This forms the side of the wall pocket.

5. Select thinner branches or stems, about ⅛ inch in diameter. Starting in the center, weave toward the side, tucking in the ends behind the spokes. When one half is completed, start in the middle again and work toward the other side. This helps to keep the basket even.

6. Fill the basket wall pocket with dried flowers or homemade soaps and creams. Hang a pretty hand towel on the lower loop.

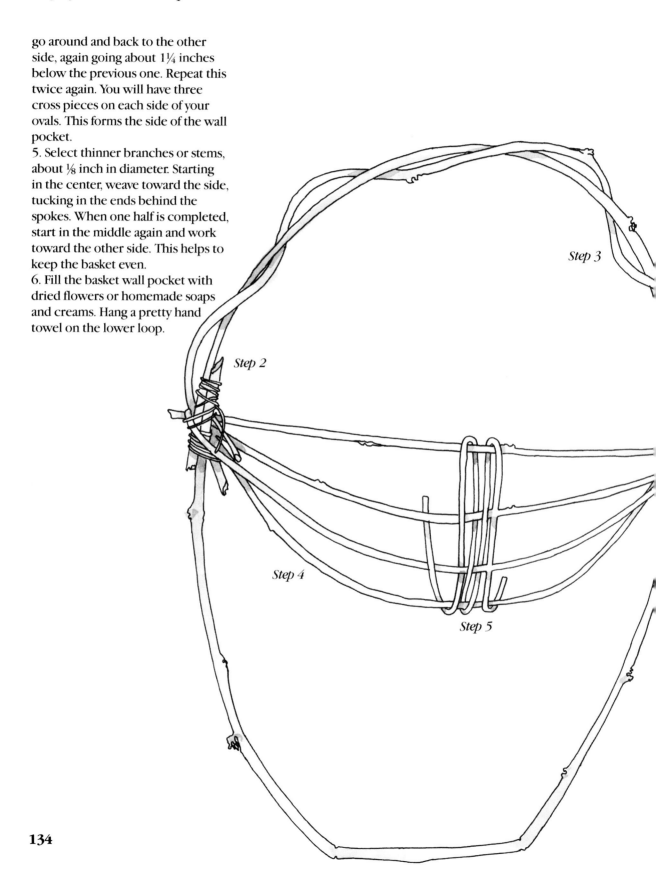

Step 3

Step 2

Step 4

Step 5

# Chapter 6
# Crafts from Corn and Wheat

## Cornshuck Materials and Methods

Along with wheat, rice, and potatoes, corn is one of our most important foods. Economically, it is the most valuable crop grown in the United States. Corn is native to North America. Fossilized corn pollen grains more than 60,000 years old have been found in Mexico. When Christopher Columbus arrived in 1492, corn was an integral part of the lives of all the native cultures in both North and South America. Prior to Columbus's discovery, however, Europeans had never seen corn.

Corn was important to the native Americans not only for the food it provided but also for the objects made from the shucks, or outer covering of the ears of corn. These included bedding, hats, bags, mats, shoes, toys, and ceremonial masks. The Indians developed elaborate ceremonies around the planting and harvesting of corn. Designs using corn as a motif decorated pottery, sculpture, and other items.

Passing seeds as well as their knowledge about planting, growing, and using corn and its shucks on to the early European settlers, the Indians gave our ancestors an incredible heritage. Corn played a vital role not only in keeping many a settler alive, but also in providing him with materials to barter.

It's easy to appreciate how important corn is to us today: Try to imagine life without corn-on-the-cob, cornflake cereal, grits, popcorn, tortillas, or bourbon whiskey. In this time of high technology, it is somehow comforting to know that not only does some of our food hearken back 60,000 years, but that there are people still making crafts from something as plain and old-fashioned as cornshucks.

The best cornshucks for craft projects are from field corn, because they are the largest. The shucks from sweet, or garden, corn can also be used if the ears are left to ripen on the stalks. Harvest when the corn is hard and the shucks are dry.

Most shucks are a creamy golden color, but certain varieties are a lovely maroon (see Sources, page 169). For other colors, shucks can be dyed with commercial fabric dyes or food coloring. Let the shucks set in the dye for at least five hours, then drain and let them dry in the sun. Natural dyes can also be used. In this case, boil shucks and the dye material together until you have the color desired; drain and dry. Use crushed green walnuts for brown, red oak bark for rust to brown, maple leaves for pale blue-gray, pokeberries for red-blue to fuchsia, charcoal for black, powdered copper for green, and indigo for blue.

Craft shops and mailorder craft suppliers also offer packages of cornshucks ready to use in projects.

## MATERIALS

**Cornshucks**
**Pan of warm water**
**Scissors**
**Polystyrene ball, 1 inch in**
   **diameter**
**Spool of #26-gauge covered wire**
**#16-gauge floral wire**
**Heavy thread**
**Dried flowers (optional)**
**Triangle of calico, 3½ by 3½ by**
   **4½ inches (optional)**
**Cornsilk or polyester fiberfill**
**Hot glue gun with clear glue**
   **sticks**

1. Soak the shucks in the warm water for a few minutes to soften.

2. Cut two shucks 1½ inches wide and as long as possible. Criss-cross them and put a polystyrene ball in the center. Bring the shucks tightly up around the ball, making sure the surface is smooth. Secure with a piece of covered wire. This forms the head; set it aside.

3. To make the arms, cut a piece of shuck 1½ by 7 inches long and a piece of #16-gauge floral wire 6 inches long. Center the wire at one end of the shuck by placing it ½ inch from each edge; roll the husk tightly around the wire. With two 2-inch pieces of covered wire, wrap a piece around each end roll, ½ inch from the end; trim off excess.

4. To make sleeves, cut four pieces of shuck, each 4 by 4 inches. For the first sleeve, put two of the pieces on top of one another. Insert 1 inch of the armpiece between these pieces, 2 inches from the side.

5. Gather the sleeves evenly around the arm, and secure with a piece of covered wire; trim off excess wire.

6. Now pull the two pieces toward the center of the armpiece, over-lapping so they will be closed and

**136**

# *Cornshuck Doll*

Among my earliest recollections of crafts is making cornshuck dolls and, quite simply, I can't remember ever not having one in my possession. My mother's passion for history and crafts, combined with her teaching abilities, made learning fun. While forming toys from cornshucks, she would weave stories of Indians and early settlers. Mother intertwined information about their daily life with historical dates and facts.

Cornshuck dolls were and still are a fascinating part of our heritage and culture. They seem to know no social, monetary, or age boundaries. Perhaps the fascination is with the ingenuity of the Indians and pioneers in creating something so magical from material so mundane. Whatever the reason for their appeal, there is no excuse for not making one of these dolls to share with a special young friend, or just for yourself. With practice, you can create dolls doing various tasks, or angels and a nativity for the Christmas season.

There are many different versions and methods for making cornshuck dolls. A doll can be very simple and made in minutes, or incredibly elaborate, taking many hours to produce. This one is relatively simple to make, yet it can be trimmed quite elaborately.

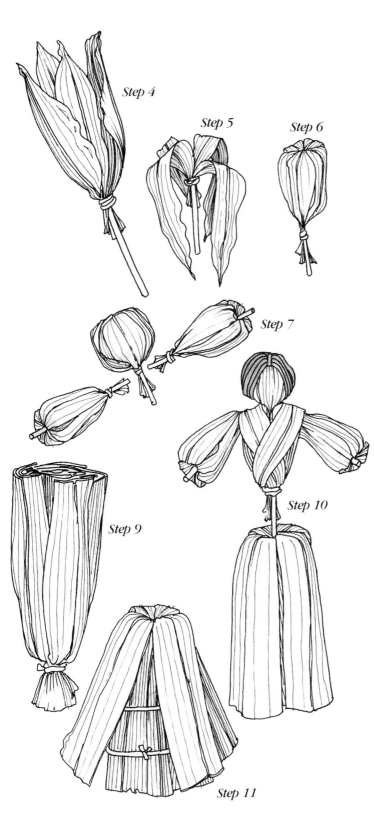

Step 4

Step 5

Step 6

Step 7

Step 9

Step 10

Step 11

puffed, and secure with covered wire. Repeat at the other end.

7. Attach the head by tucking the armpiece in among the shucks below the covered ball.

8. To make the top of the dress, cut two pieces of shuck, each 2 by 6 inches. Place one piece over each shoulder. Wrap at waist with covered wire.

9. Cut four pieces of shuck 4 by 6 inches for the skirt. Place them evenly around the body, up over the doll's head and with the edges overlapping the waist by ½ inch or so. Secure with covered wire.

10. Gently fold the skirt down.

11. Tie lightly with thread until the skirt dries, then remove. Trim bottom of skirt so doll stands evenly.

12. Bend arms around and, if desired, glue a dried flower bouquet in one hand.

13. Wrap calico around the head and glue the three points together in the back. Tuck in and glue a bit of cornsilk or fiberfill in front for hair.

# *Looped Cornshuck Wreath*

## MATERIALS

About 100 cornshucks, cut into
   6-by-2-inch pieces, for a 12-inch
   wreath
Pan of warm water
Straw wreath form
Floral pins
Ribbon and/or lace for bow and
   streamers, as desired
Hot glue gun, with clear glue
   sticks, white craft glue, or wired
   wooden floral picks
Dried baby's breath, or other
   dried flowers, seeds, and
   so forth

The appeal of some craft projects is the intricacy or skill demanded, while with others it is having something nice to give or use quickly and easily. This is exactly what makes a looped cornshuck wreath so delightful. Although it can be elaborately trimmed, the procedure for making the basic wreath is quite simple and repetitive, taking less than an hour to complete.

Use shucks in their natural color or dye them; and leave the wreath plain or add bows, ribbon, lace, and all manner of dried flowers, cones, and seedpods. This is really a chance to let your imagination shine.

1. Soak the cornshucks in the warm water to make them pliable.
2. Bring the ends of one of the cornshuck pieces together, forming a loop. Gather slightly in your fingers. Place it on a wreath form and insert a floral pin through the cornshuck and into the straw form at a 45-degree angle. If making a heart-shaped wreath, begin at the bottom point and work upward, doing first one side and then the other.
3. Continue adding loops of cornshuck across the top and sides of the form, staggering the placement somewhat and placing them approximately three across.
4. When the front of the wreath form is covered, trim with loops made from 6-inch lengths of ribbon or lace inserted among the cornshucks and attached with glue or picks. You can also add sprigs of baby's breath or other dried material; attach with glue or pins. Trim with a larger bow, if desired, that combines ribbon and lace and has long streamers.

# Shredded Cornshuck Wreath

Versatile and economical, cornshuck crafts and decorations needn't be limited to use in the fall. This double-heart wreath offers an unusual accent for Valentine's Day or makes a thoughtful present for someone who collects heart-shaped objects. Why not use it as a wedding, anniversary, or shower present? The same technique can also be used to make a traditional single-circle wreath.

As cornshucks color readily with commercial fabric dyes, you can have them match an occasion or decor. Follow manufacturer's directions.

## MATERIALS

**Cornshucks**
**Pan of warm water**
**Coat hanger**
**18-inch piece of #14-gauge wire**
**Needle-nose pliers**
**Scissors**
**Dried flowers**
**Ribbon**

1. Soak the cornshucks in the water for 5 to 10 minutes to soften.
2. Form a coat hanger into a heart shape, putting the hook at the top as shown.
3. Shape an 8-inch piece of wire into a heart shape, twisting the ends with pliers.
4. Put the small heart on top of the larger one, overlapping at the top. Using pliers, twist the coat hanger hook around the small heart to secure.
5. To cover the wreath form, cut cornshucks into strips 6 inches long and 1 to 1½ inches wide. Take a strip and bring the two ends together. The center will form a loop.
6. Place this folded strip under the wire form, with the ends toward the center and the loop an inch beyond the wire.
7. Bring both ends up and over the wire.
8. Pull through the loop, gently tightening. This is variously called a ring hitch, lark's head, cow hitch, or bale-sling hitch.
9. Repeat this many times, bunching up the cornshucks so that as they dry the frame is completely covered.
10. Decorate with dried flowers and ribbon, as desired.

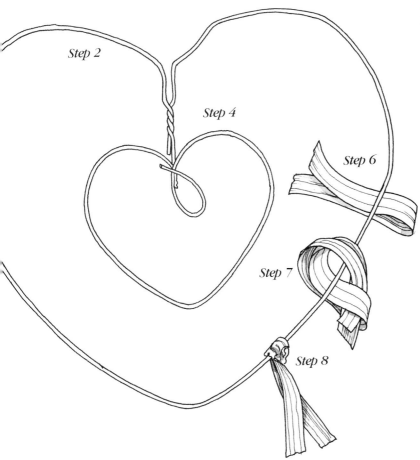

Step 2

Step 4

Step 6

Step 7

Step 8

# *Cornshuck Seat*

## MATERIALS

**Scissors**
**Cornshucks**
**Pan of warm water**
**Four-legged stool or chair**
**Screwdriver**

1. Use scissors to trim the coarse ends off cornshucks. Then tear the shucks lengthwise into 1½-inch-wide sections. Soak the shucks in the warm water.

2. Have someone help you hold the cord you'll form from the shucks tight as you begin. Overlap the ends of two shucks and, with a combination rolling and twisting motion, begin forming the cord. Before completely twisting both shucks, add a third and continue twisting and rolling. Continue adding a shuck by overlapping ends, then twisting and rolling. You can make a cord as long as you want.

3. After making a foot or so, start weaving the chair or stool seat as shown in the diagram, bringing the cord over and under the rungs of the chair or stool as illustrated. Add shucks to the cording as you work.

4. When you reach the middle of the seat, finish it off by pulling the cord tight and bringing it to the underside of the seat where it can be pushed into the woven seat with a screwdriver. Set in the sun to dry.

Woven chair or stool seats made from cornshuck cord have a homely beauty that is not a contradiction in terms. Seats made this way pair perfectly with the simple lines of Shaker furniture that marry so well with country, traditional, or contemporary design.

Cornshuck seats may be sprayed with clear polyurethane varnish once a year to keep them clean. But whether you do this or not, the seat will probably last a lifetime. An old discarded ladder-back chair can be readily restored to its original charm by the addition of a new shuck seat such as this.

# Miniature Indian Corn Starburst

Indian corn, with its calico hues, has become synonymous with autumn decorations, symbolizing as it does the harvest wealth. Displays of ornamental corn at Thanksgiving commemorate both the folklore and actual history of that first Pilgrim feast.

The easiest way to use ornamental corn is to tie three ears together, using floral wire, at the point where the cob and shuck meet. Add some tendrils of bittersweet and a bright bow to complement the white, red, blue, and yellow kernels.

In the last decade or so, a miniature ornamental corn has become readily available. Many of the mailorder seed catalogs now carry it. Like other ornamental corn, it should be planted in spring after the last frost and allowed to mature on the plant until after the first frost in autumn. Some varieties do double duty as popcorn.

This miniature Indian corn seems to me to be much easier to incorporate into fall arrangements with small gourds and mini-pumpkins than the larger ears. A starburst made from this corn looks unusual, but is very easy to construct.

## MATERIALS

**5 feet of #9-gauge wire**
**Side cutters**
**Pliers**
**About 25 additional cornshucks**
**Hot glue gun with clear glue sticks**
**8 ears of miniature Indian corn, with shucks attached**
**Scissors**
**Darning needle**

1. Make a circle of wire 10 inches in diameter; make another 3 inches in diameter. Use the side cutters to cut the wire and the pliers to twist the ends together.
2. Using the additional shucks, completely wrap the two wire circles. Secure the ends of the shucks with a glue gun.
3. Working on a flat surface, center the 3-inch circle inside the 10-inch circle.
4. Pull the shucks back from the ears of corn, but do not remove entirely.
5. Lay the ears of corn on top of the circles, spacing evenly like spokes of a wheel. Working one at a time, put some glue on the underside of an ear of corn at the points where it touches the circles and attach.
6. When the glue has completely hardened and corn ears are secure, cut the shucks so they are 2½ to 3 inches long. Use a darning needle to shred the shucks so they feather out by poking the needle through the shuck near the ear and splitting the entire length of the shuck. Make each about ¹⁄₁₆ to ⅛ inch wide.

*First Joint* ▷

# Wheat Straw Materials and Methods

Although few of us grow our own wheat, it obviously plays a significant role in our diet. And like corn, wheat has a long tradition for its use in crafts. As the world's most important grain crop, wheat covers more of the earth's surface than any other food crop. Products made from wheat are the main food of hundreds of millions of people. Wheat is grown everywhere on the planet with the exceptions of the coldest regions and the hot tropical zones.

Using wheat straw for crafts is an age-old custom linked both to religious ceremonies and to thrift, as people made use of the discarded parts of the harvest. Ornaments of wheat straw were considered to be a resting place for the grain spirit; keeping such ornaments in the home ensured a continuation of a crop the next year. Straw was also used for making such practical objects as thatched roofs, baskets, hats, bottle covers, and other objects.

The term "corn dolly" is often used for woven wheat ornaments, because in Europe all grain is called corn, and dolly refers to the shape of the first weavings. Wheat weaving is actually a more appropriate term.

## Procuring the Wheat

Perfectly dried stems of wheat straw with the beautiful bearded heads attached can be purchased from craft shops and supply companies (see Sources, page 169) for use in craft projects. You can also grow and harvest your own, or harvest wheat from a farmer's field. With either of these options, choose the bearded varieties of winter wheat over the beardless types. Also consider other grains such as oats, barley, rye, and spring wheat. If you choose to harvest farm-grown wheat, make arrangements with the farmer as to price, quantity, and where you can harvest.

Wheat for craft projects should be harvested in the "dough" stage, or about two weeks prior to the regular harvest. Harvest then because the heads are not likely to shatter, and the straw remains pliable and has good color.

The dough stage occurs just after the grain has changed color from green to gold, except for about 4 to 6 inches of stem right at the ground; the heads will still be standing straight. Pinch one of the grains with your thumbnail. If milky sap emerges, the wheat is still too green; if hard, the grain is too ripe. Instead, the grain should puncture easily, but no sap should appear.

Use a sickle or machete to cut the grain 4 to 6 inches above the soil. Collect the wheat in bundles 4 to 6 inches in diameter. Keeping all the heads at one end of the bundle, tie each bundle

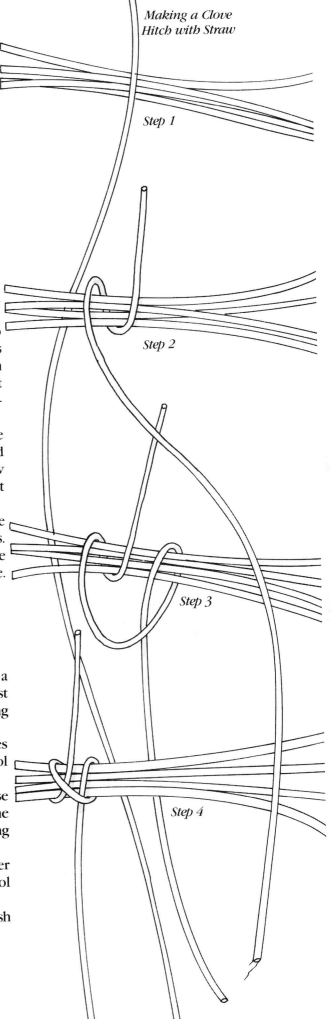

Step 1

Step 2

Step 3

Step 4

together one third of the way from the bottom with heavy cord or binder twine. Hang or loosely stack the bundles to air-dry for about two weeks. To make a variety of projects, 20 bundles should be enough.

## Cleaning the Wheat

Whether you purchase dried wheat from the craft shop, grow your own, or gather from a farmer's field, the wheat will need to be cleaned.

The part of the wheat you will want is the head and straw to the first joint. The head is the part at the tip of the stem that has 50 or so kernels of grain. The stem directly below this is smooth for 10 to 12 inches. Then, there is a small bump. This is the first joint. The straw below this point is called waste straw, or second-joint straw.

Take scissors and cut the wheat just above the first joint. Slide off the loose part around the straw, called the leaf sheaf, and discard it. Store the cleaned wheat in large boxes with a few mothballs to keep out insects and rodents. Save the second joint straw in a separate box.

When ready to make a weaving or other project, soak the clean wheat in a large pan of lukewarm water for 30 minutes. Drain the soaked wheat and wrap in a large, wet towel. Use the soaked wheat within several hours, or carefully redry for later use. Soaking and redrying can be done only once or twice.

## The Clove Hitch

When making straw ornaments, you will frequently need a knot that can be pulled very tight and will not slip. The best choice is a two-loop knot called the clove hitch. Practice making a clove hitch with carpet-and-button thread and a stick.

1. Hold the stick horizontally in your left hand. Put 2 inches of the end of the thread in front of and above the stick. The spool will be below the stick.

2. Holding the thread against the stick with your thumb, use your right hand to take the spool of thread under and behind the stick, then over the top on the left side of the 2-inch end. Bring the spool of thread down in front, leaving a large loop.

3. Next, bring the thread up from behind the stick, then over the stick to the right of the 2-inch lead. Now, put the spool through the large loop below the stick.

4. Pull on both ends until tight. Tie an overhand knot to finish the clove hitch.

# *Welsh Fan Wheat Weaving*

The unusual, angular design of the Welsh fan wheat weaving has a very modern look to it that belies its centuries-old origin. Make small fans of nine straws for Christmas tree ornaments, or make large ones with 25 straws and decorate them with dried flowers to give as gifts. Experiment with different sizes, always using an odd number of straws.

## MATERIALS

**Scissors**

**19 evenly matched wheat straws with heads (have a few extras available)**

**Large pan or wallpaper trough of warm water**

**Dampened, wrung-out bath towel**

**Beige-colored carpet-and-button thread**

**12 inches of ¼-inch-wide ribbon**

1. Prepare wheat by cutting off and discarding the second-joint straw, then removing the leaf sheaf. (See Wheat Straw Materials and Methods, page 142.) This leaves the first-joint straw with the head attached.

2. Soak the straws in the pan of warm water for 30 minutes. Drain and wrap in the bath towel.

3. Using a 12-inch piece of thread and the clove hitch (see Wheat Straw Materials and Methods, page 142), tie three straws together just below the heads. Put them flat on a table with the heads up. Form a V-shape with two straws on the right side and one on the left side.

4. Inserting the stem at an angle from right to left, place a new straw on the right side, going under the outer and over the inner straws on the right side. The stem of the new straw will lie parallel to the single straw on the left, making two straws on the left side now.

5. Inserting the stem at an angle from left to right, place a new straw

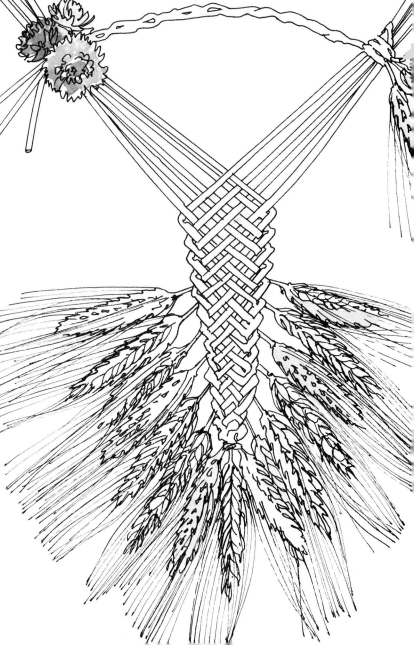

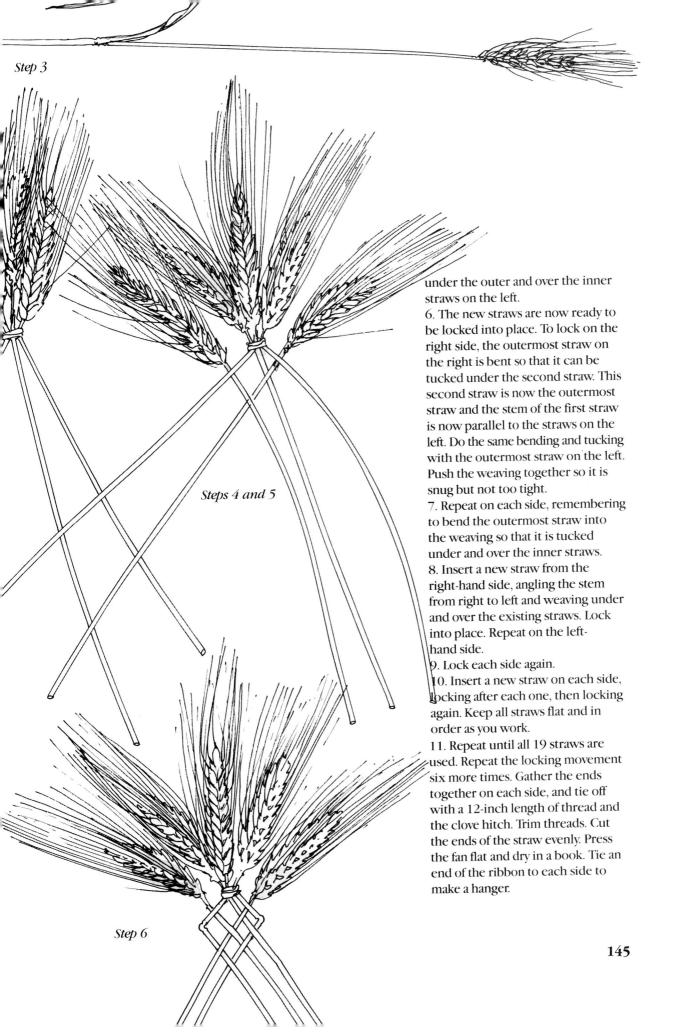

*Step 3*

*Steps 4 and 5*

*Step 6*

under the outer and over the inner straws on the left.

6. The new straws are now ready to be locked into place. To lock on the right side, the outermost straw on the right is bent so that it can be tucked under the second straw. This second straw is now the outermost straw and the stem of the first straw is now parallel to the straws on the left. Do the same bending and tucking with the outermost straw on the left. Push the weaving together so it is snug but not too tight.

7. Repeat on each side, remembering to bend the outermost straw into the weaving so that it is tucked under and over the inner straws.

8. Insert a new straw from the right-hand side, angling the stem from right to left and weaving under and over the existing straws. Lock into place. Repeat on the left-hand side.

9. Lock each side again.

10. Insert a new straw on each side, locking after each one, then locking again. Keep all straws flat and in order as you work.

11. Repeat until all 19 straws are used. Repeat the locking movement six more times. Gather the ends together on each side, and tie off with a 12-inch length of thread and the clove hitch. Trim threads. Cut the ends of the straw evenly. Press the fan flat and dry in a book. Tie an end of the ribbon to each side to make a hanger.

**145**

# *Mordiford Wheat Weaving*

## MATERIALS

**Scissors**
**About 50 to 60 wheat straws with heads**
**Large pan or wallpaper trough of warm water**
**Dampened, wrung-out bath towel**
**Beige-colored carpet-and-button thread**
**½-inch-wide ribbon made into an 8-loop florist's bow 4 inches across (see Tying the Perfect Bow, page 165), plus an 8-inch length of the same ribbon**

Different regions have become known for particular shapes in wheat weaving. The traditional heart-shaped "corn dolly" is associated with the Mordiford area in England. Originally intended to bring a good harvest, today a wheat weaving such as this is hung in the home to bring good luck.

1. Prepare wheat by cutting off and discarding the second-joint straw and removing the leaf sheaf (see Wheat Straw Materials and Methods, page 142). This leaves the first-joint straw with the head attached.
2. Soak the straws in the pan of warm water for 30 minutes. Drain and wrap in the bath towel to keep straws moist while working.
3. Count out 18 straws. Using the clove hitch knot (see Wheat Straw Materials and Methods, page 142) and 12 inches of carpet-and-button thread, tie the straws together just below the heads. Divide the straws into three groups of six, and braid as you would hair (right over center, left over center) for 5 inches. Tie at the end of the braided part with another 12-inch length of thread in a clove hitch knot. Set aside.
4. Repeat with another 18 straws, making sure this braid is the same length as the first.
5. Tie the two wheat braids together where the braids end, using a 12-inch length of thread and the clove hitch.
6. Lay the two braids in front of you with the unbraided straw at the bottom. Carefully bend the two braids inward, forming a heart shape.

**146**

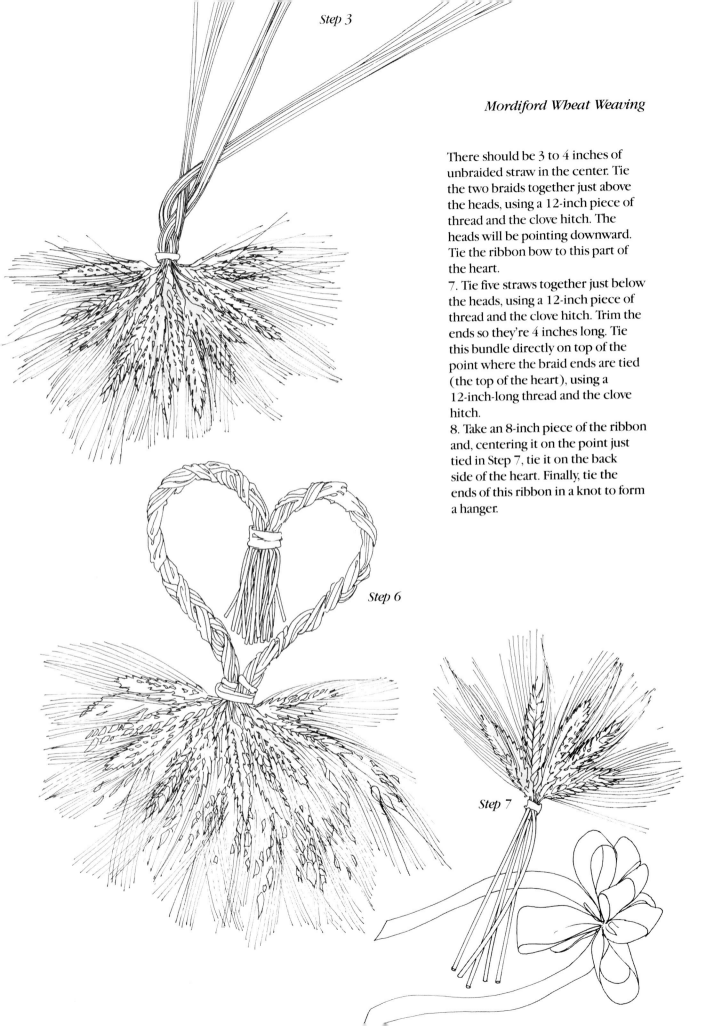

*Step 3*

*Mordiford Wheat Weaving*

There should be 3 to 4 inches of unbraided straw in the center. Tie the two braids together just above the heads, using a 12-inch piece of thread and the clove hitch. The heads will be pointing downward. Tie the ribbon bow to this part of the heart.

7. Tie five straws together just below the heads, using a 12-inch piece of thread and the clove hitch. Trim the ends so they're 4 inches long. Tie this bundle directly on top of the point where the braid ends are tied (the top of the heart), using a 12-inch-long thread and the clove hitch.

8. Take an 8-inch piece of the ribbon and, centering it on the point just tied in Step 7, tie it on the back side of the heart. Finally, tie the ends of this ribbon in a knot to form a hanger.

*Step 6*

*Step 7*

# Chapter 7
# Crafts from Fruit and Vegetables

I come from a family that lives to eat, and we enjoy all types of food, from the simple to the sublime. Vacation trips as a youngster introduced unusual foods to my life, but few can compare to the vegetables fresh from my mother's garden.

During haymaking season, Mother would cook for a crew of hungry teenage boys, and the table would be covered with corn on the cob, green beans, sliced tomatoes, slaw, mashed potatoes, tossed salad, fried okra, lima beans, and beets. There was, of course, always a contest to see who could eat the most corn. Dessert could be several berry or apple pies, cobblers, or dumplings. Life was good.

Crafts made from fruit and vegetables were of less interest to me at that point than jellies and casseroles. Even so, I made vegetable-printed gift wrap, dried apple dolls, and pomanders with some regularity.

Today, my fascination with food has intensified rather than abated, and so has my knowledge of the possibilities of crafts with fruit and vegetables. Well scrubbed and polished with a bit of vegetable oil, such mundane crops as beets, radishes, and carrots become a beautiful still life when artfully arranged with a basket or grapevine wreath. Pods of okra or bright red hot peppers can be added to dried swags or arrangements.

Dried apple rings and slices, or slices of other fruits and vegetables, can decorate wreaths or other projects. I always make plenty of grapevine wreaths for gifts, and find that a grapevine tree may be just the right touch of something different for Christmas. And those simple, childish vegetable prints can become elegant note cards and gift tags with a little practice.

A seed jar lamp adds a homey, rustic touch to an interior. Garlic braids, like pepper strings and wreaths, also bring a feeling of warmth to a kitchen.

Although you may need to till up a special area or build a strong trellis for gourds, as they are rampant growers, their fascinating shapes, forms, and colors make it worthwhile. Synonymous with fall decorating both indoors and out, gourds can also be painted, carved, or trimmed with dried flowers. Small gourds make grand Christmas ornaments, and larger ones are perfect for feeding and housing songbirds outside.

Making pomanders is as much a part of the Christmas ritual as trimming the tree, but why not get in the habit of creating some at other times of the year, perhaps using different fruits or spices? Their wonderful scent makes them welcome gifts at any time.

And those strange little unicorn plant "birds" still intrigue me as much as they did as a child. Learning to bleach them has given me new ideas of ways to use them. Their pristine look is a perfect accent for dried grasses and all-white or pastel arrangements.

Over the years, I have grown food crops in every possible way, from a tomato in a clay pot to a mammoth "traditional" row garden. I encourage you to grow the versatile vegetables featured in this chapter, and to think of them as raw materials for both food and crafts.

# Vegetable Printing

For versatility, few crafts can compete with block printing using vegetables. It can be done either simply or elaborately by just about anyone. With help on the carving by an adult, even toddlers can print their own T-shirts or wrapping paper for Grandma's present. At the opposite end of the spectrum are businesses based on clothing or other articles designed and printed by artists.

While potatoes and carrots are the vegetables most often used, any firm-fleshed vegetable or even fruit, such as a turnip, squash, or apple, can be carved with fanciful designs. Some food crops even have patterns already built in; for example, try cutting celery, peppers, green beans, or cabbage crosswise.

Different kinds of paints and inks can be used, depending on the project. Temperas are best for projects with children and paper. Stamp-pads, water-soluble printing ink, acrylic paint, and colorfast dyes are some of the more permanent possibilities for other surfaces. The equipment needed can be as simple as a kitchen paring knife or as elaborate as a set of linoleum block cutters.

The object decorated is up for grabs, too. Just skimming the surface turns up such ideas as sweatshirts and pants, T-shirts, camp shirts, skirts, shorts, beach coverups, chef's hats, aprons, pot holders, stencils around ceilings, windows, and doors, gift tags, wrapping paper, paper sacks for lunches or gifts, placemats, tablecloths, curtains, and dishtowels. The best fabrics to work with are cotton and cotton-polyester blends; the design will show up best on more tightly woven fabric.

Finally, the design can take any shape you desire, but it's best to keep it fairly simple. No matter what you choose to do, peeling potatoes will never be the same!

## MATERIALS

**Vegetable or fruit of your choice**
**Pocket or paring knife**
**Plastic garbage bag cut open, or other large piece of plastic**
**Newspapers**
**Paint or ink of your choice**
**Paper plates (for mixing paint or ink colors)**
**Knife or brush (for mixing paint or ink colors)**
**A 3- to 4-inch soft rubber roller, called an ink brayer, available from craft stores (optional)**
**Surface of your choice**

1. Cut the vegetable or fruit you choose and carve a design on the surface, removing everything you don't want in the design.
2. Spread out the plastic and the newspapers on your work surface.
3. Mix paint or ink, as desired, using a paper plate for each color. The ink brayer, if desired, can be used to spread the paint or ink evenly. (You'll get a more textured look if you don't use an ink brayer.)
4. Dip the cut vegetable into the paint, or ink it, and then apply it to your surface. Repeat, as desired. Allow to dry.

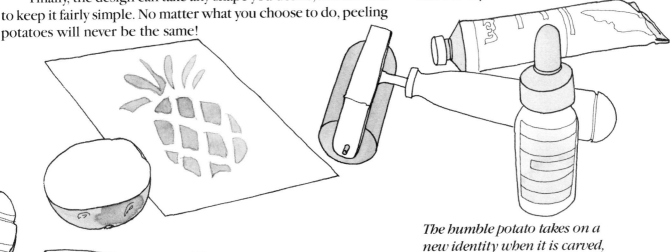

*The humble potato takes on a new identity when it is carved, inked, and used to print a design – here, a pineapple.*

# Seed Jar Lamp

## MATERIALS

**Quart jar**
**Assorted dried seeds**
**Lamp socket kit with lid**
**Lamp shade**

1. Clean the jar thoroughly, wiping until it shines.
2. Layer the seeds in a pattern that pleases you.
3. Attach lid with socket.
4. Attach a shade, perhaps one trimmed with dried flowers as on page 23.

Just as some plants have leaves, flowers, or stems that are more unique and colorful than others, the same can be said of seeds. Curiously, many of our most mundane plants have seeds with very interesting colors or combinations of colors. The panoply of color available among beans, peas, and corn, as well as other vegetables – especially in the older varieties – is truly amazing.

Obviously, your first priority is growing enough of these to eat, but if you happen to have a bumper crop (or conversely, not enough to make it worthwhile to cook), a seed jar lamp is a fitting trophy to commemorate your summer's efforts. If you also happen to have an unusual antique or flea-market-find quart jar that you have been saving but have put to no practical purpose, here is your chance to do so.

Although it is possible to do the wiring yourself, businesses that specialize in lamp parts usually have a prewired socket with a standard quart jar lid attached that is specifically made for projects like this.

**150**

# Garlic Braid

Pungent-scented garlic has a long history of magical powers, from curing ills to keeping werewolves and vampires at bay. As with so many plants, the early Chinese and Egyptian civilizations were probably the first to cultivate garlic. The Egyptians introduced it to the Romans, who fed it to their workers for strength and to their soldiers for courage.

Homer, Pliny, Aristophanes, Aristotle, Mohammed, and Culpeper have all praised garlic's qualities in their writings, and it is mentioned in the Bible. Garlic plays an essential role in many cuisines, including Chinese, Middle Eastern, Mediterranean, and Indian.

Garlic has become such a favorite flavoring in the United States that there are several books devoted solely to this aromatic subject (see Bibliography, page 172), including two cookbooks from the Gilroy (California) Garlic Festival with hundreds of recipes, some even for desserts!

Besides its culinary role, garlic is considered to have many beneficial medicinal qualities due to a crystalline amino acid called alliin in its oil. Garlic has been used to purge the liver and gall bladder, dispel intestinal worms, prevent growth of microorganisms, promote cardiovascular activity, and soothe the respiratory system. The juice of garlic also acts as an organic insect repellent.

To grow garlic, plant cloves in the fall and mulch in areas with severe winters, or set cloves out in early spring. Fall planting yields the largest bulbs. As the bulbs reach maturity, the tops will become weak and begin to fall over.

In hot, dry parts of the country, curing and drying garlic is relatively easy. In other areas, rot or sunscald can be a problem. One way to get around this is to break down the tops as they begin to weaken by walking on them. The stalk just above the bulb will be quite dry in a few days. Dig the bulbs at this point and leave them on top of the ground for a few hours so the soil can dry and be brushed off.

The garlic bulbs are now ready to be made into attractive traditional braids, or strings, for storage. Make the garlic braid even more special, whether for yourself or as a gift, by weaving in or gluing on dried flowers.

## MATERIALS

**Garlic bulbs, with the tops still attached**

**Baling twine or soft jute parcel-post string, cut into 4- to 6-foot lengths**

**Scissors**

1. Gather together three garlic bulbs. Tie the stems together securely with one end of twine. Begin braiding the stems like a three-section hair plait, working the twine as a unit with one of the stems.

2. After making several crosses, work in additional garlic bulbs, spacing them out evenly. You'll combine several stems into one section of the plait. No one stem will extend for the entire length of the braid.

3. Use the twine to make a loop at the end of the braid for hanging.

4. Hang the braid in an airy, dry, shaded place for about two weeks, or until the tops are completely dry.

## MATERIALS

**Large sewing needle**
**Heavy button or carpet thread**
**Red, ripe drying-type peppers,**
   **such as cayenne, Anaheim,**
   **Hungarian wax, or poblano**
**Scissors or pruning shears**
**Three-wire wreath form**
   **(diameter in proportion to**
   **size of peppers, but approxi-**
   **mately 8 to 14 inches across)**
**#22-gauge floral wire**
**Head of garlic**
**Ribbon bow**

1. Thread a needle with a long piece of thread, double, and knot the ends together.
2. Gather the peppers on a hot, sunny day when there is no surface moisture on them, using scissors or pruning shears to cut them from the plant with an inch or so of stem attached.
3. Run the needle and thread through the center of each pepper. Leave an inch or so of space between each pepper. When the string is full, attach each end to a nail or whatever is available in a dry, hot, well-ventilated place, such as between two poles outside or in an attic between rafters. In parts of the country where rain or dew are frequent, indoors is a better choice.
4. When dry, the peppers can be pushed close together and hung as a string or garland. To make a wreath, you will probably need to make several strings so that you have a total of at least 75 to 100 peppers.
5. To make a wreath, push the peppers close together and place on the wire wreath form. Using the floral wire, tie the strings securely to the form every 3 inches or so, twisting the wire on the back of the wreath form.
6. Wrap a piece of the wire around the neck of a bulb of garlic and attach in the center of the bow. Tie the bow to the wreath with a piece of wire.

152

# Pepper Wreath

Under the crystal blue skies and searing sun of the Southwest, the blazing red ristras, or strings, of hot peppers form a stark contrast to the adobe buildings. Hanging a string or wreath of dried red chilies by the door is said to bring good luck, and they are used extensively in decorations for Halloween, Thanksgiving, and Christmas throughout the Southwest.

Where growing seasons are shorter and humidity is higher, growing and drying the large red chiles is not so easy, but not impossible either. Whether you grow the authentic poblano (see Sources, page 170) or one of the more readily available types, such as long red cayenne, Hungarian wax, or Anaheim, with a little care, you'll have good luck, too!

Try growing some of the smaller-fruited ornamental peppers, too. Fiery hot, they can be used in cooking and make wonderful additions to dried decorations. Grow an assortment of these peppers that dry well because their brilliant color, smooth, shiny texture, and fascinating shapes lend an interesting effect to arrangements and wreaths. Or tie a ribbon or yarn loop to their stems for instant ornaments.

Step 5

Step 6

Step 3

# Dried Apple Doll

Dolls are loved the world around, by young and old, rich and poor, sophisticated and primitive. Dolls can cut across cultural lines like no human that they resemble. Within the imaginary world that so often surrounds them, all can be as we want it to be.

We Americans have inherited a tradition of dolls crafted from an assortment of plant materials, and among the most notable are the funny apple-headed dolls. Their wizened faces become darker, drier, and more wrinkled with time, taking on a distinct, evolving, lifelike personality all their own.

Made both by our native Americans and by European settlers, apple dolls may be considered crude by some standards. Still, no doubt, they were treasured friends to the person they entertained on the frontier. Without toy stores or hard cash, the dollmaker created a toy to be cherished.

There will be a great deal of variation in how the apple heads dry, so it's best to make several at once in order to have at least one you like.

Step 1

Step 2

## MATERIALS

**Paring knife**
**Medium-sized, hard, blemish-free fall apple, such as a McIntosh, Winesap, or Jonathan**
**Apple corer**
**#20-gauge floral wire**
**Equal parts vinegar or lemon juice and water**
**Bowl**
**Table salt**
**Powdered sulfur (available from a garden-supply store)**
**Hot glue gun with clear glue sticks, or white craft or household glue**
**Two brown or black beads ⅛ inch in diameter**
**Raw wool, cotton, or fur**
**Two 9-inch-long pipe cleaners**
**Cotton or polyester batting**
**Scissors**
**Old nylon hose, cut lengthwise into 2-inch-wide strips**
**Needle and thread**
**Calico**

1. Carefully peel an apple and remove a thin diameter of core. Shape the face by carving out two sockets for the eyes, with slits above for the eyebrows, and a broad nose; then cut a slit for the mouth. If you wish, carve away portions of the apple to represent prominent facial features, such as the nose, cheeks, and ears.
2. Insert a piece of floral wire into the apple. Start at the bottom ½ inch from the core on the side of the face, going up and out near the top hole, over the hole, down the other side of the apple, and out the bottom. Twist the two ends of the wire together directly under the apple.
3. Combine equal parts of vinegar or lemon juice and water in a bowl. Dip the carved apple in the mixture. This helps to keep the apple from darkening too much as it dries. Sprinkle the outside of the apple with table salt.
4. Fill the core with powdered

sulfur to disinfect it.

5. To dry the head, hang it in a cool, dry place for about a month, depending on the climate and weather. Or place it in an oven set at the lowest setting, leaving it for about four days. Check periodically and remove earlier, if necessary. Rub off the salt when the apple is thoroughly dry.

6. Glue a bead into each socket for the eyes. Glue on raw wool, cotton, or fur for hair.

7. Twist the center of one pipe cleaner around the floral wire just under the apple; this forms the arms. There should be about 4 inches of floral wire forming the torso. Bend a second pipe cleaner in half and wrap the ends of the floral wire around this bend to form the legs.

8. Wrap the wires with batting and strips of hose, sewing the ends.

9. Use the doll dress pattern (Apple Doll Dress Pattern, page 168) or one of your own choosing to clothe the doll.

*Steps 6 and 7*

# Dried Apple Wreath and Wall Hanging

When apples are abundant and inexpensive, dry center slices and wedges to use for decorating wreaths and wall plaques. The burgundy reds and gilded greens of the dried apples are particularly fitting for the Christmas holidays, but their harvest-home appearance makes them an attractive decoration year-round.

Select apples that are uniform in size and as free as possible of bruises and insect damage. Properly prepared, apples will last for a year or more in decorations, depending on the humidity. The dried apples last best in an environment where the humidity is controlled.

Experiment with using the dried apple slices and wedges in different craft projects. Attach them to small wreaths with multiflora rose hips and thin red ribbon for holiday ornaments or napkin rings. Include the dried pieces with other dried plant material in arrangements and wreaths.

By cutting both center slices and wedges from two dozen apples, you will have enough material to make a 12-inch wreath decorated with the wedges as well as a 12-inch wall hanging trimmed with the center slices. Why not keep one and give the other as a present?

## MATERIALS

Two large bowls
1-cup measuring cup
½-tablespoon measuring spoon
Reconstituted lemon juice
Salt
Paring knife
About a dozen fresh apples
Colander
Paper towels
Wire mesh drying racks
Oven or food dehydrator
12-inch polystyrene wreath form
Hot glue gun and clear glue sticks
Clear plastic craft spray or clear polyurethane spray
Dried flowers, herbs, or wheat, as desired
Ribbon (optional)
12-inch fiberboard half-circle or half-circle wooden basket top

1. In each of two bowls, combine 1 cup lemon juice with ½ tablespoon salt.
2. Making the slices ⅛ inch thick, cut three vertical center slices from each unpeeled apple. Place into one of the bowls with lemon juice and salt. Cut the remainder of each apple into ¼-inch-thick wedges and put into the other bowl. The lemon juice and salt keep the apples from darkening as they dry. Throw the solution away when the project is finished.
3. Drain apples in a colander and pat dry with paper towels.
4. Spread apples out in a single layer on drying racks. Dry at 140° F in a gas or electric oven or dehydrator until apples reach a stage between leathery and brittle (about five or six hours). Timing will vary greatly, so

*Wall Hanging*

155

check frequently after about four hours.

5. If not using immediately, store apples in an airtight container.

6. To make the apple wedge wreath, attach dried apple wedges in a random pattern to a polystyrene wreath form, using a hot glue gun. Cover the entire front surface. Spray the wreath thoroughly with two coats of clear plastic or polyurethane spray, following the manufacturer's directions for the time between coats. Decorate as desired.

7. To make the center-slice wall hanging, attach dried center slices to a fiberboard half-circle, using the hot glue gun. Start around the edge, extending the slices beyond the edge of the fiberboard. Overlap the following inside rows. Seal with the clear plastic or polyurethane spray. Decorate as desired.

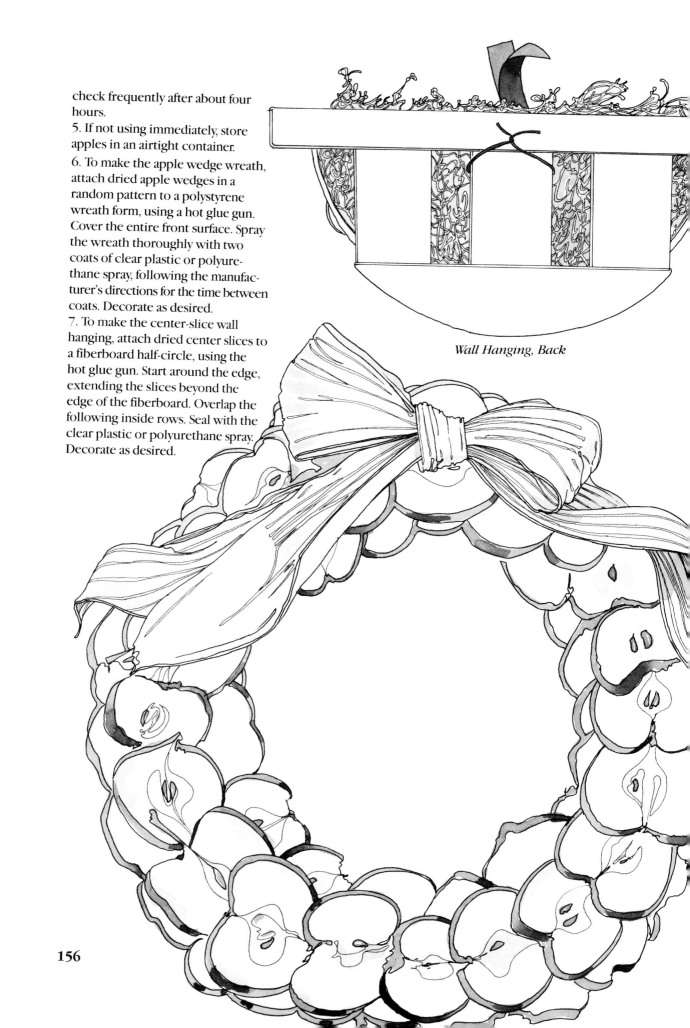

*Wall Hanging, Back*

# Okra Crafts

Okra has the dubious distinction of being the most maligned and misunderstood of vegetables. Curiously enough, it also has one of the longest histories as a food crop and a strong culinary tradition on five continents.

Native to that part of Africa which includes present-day Ethiopia, okra gradually spread throughout the continent, and from there to the Mediterranean countries, the Middle East, and India. A member of the mallow family, this "edible hibiscus" was brought to North America by slaves who also gave it two names by which it is known today: okra and gumbo.

A hot-weather plant, okra is generally best loved by Southerners, who also happen to know how to cook it. They know how to dip okra in cornmeal and deep-fry it, as well as how to cook it with tomatoes and serve it with spoonbread. The mixed heritage of French, Spanish, and African peoples in the Mississippi Delta have made okra an integral part of Creole cuisine, including all manner of soups and stews.

Nutritionally, okra is an excellent source of calcium and the B vitamins. In terms of the garden, okra is an easily grown plant that makes an attractive bush 3 to 5 feet tall with lovely yellow flowers centered with red. Plants start bearing pods two months after seeds germinate, and will continue until frost if the cylindrical, ridged pods are continually harvested.

Near the end of the growing season, anyone with an eye for dried plant material for craft projects will stop harvesting okra and let the pods mature on the plant. As frost becomes imminent, gather the stalks and hang upside down to dry in a dark, dry, well-ventilated place.

As the "lady's-fingers" dry, the pods will split slightly, giving a wonderful beige-and-brown striped effect. The vertical element that okra pods give to arrangements is unsurpassed. Use whole stems with several pods on each, or cut the pods off and wire and tape each one individually. (See Dried Flower Materials and Methods, page 1.) Prepared this way, okra can be added to dried-flower arrangements or wreaths, swags, and other projects.

Dried okra takes on a feathery appearance if the pods are split open at the seams with a knife before they dry. A different look is also achieved by growing and drying the burgundy variety of okra. Of course, the dried pods can be painted as well, if other colors are wanted.

No matter how you decide to use okra in craft projects, be sure to try some freshly cooked. Any way you look at it, okra is a vegetable that deserves more respect!

*Okra Plant with Flowers and Fruit*

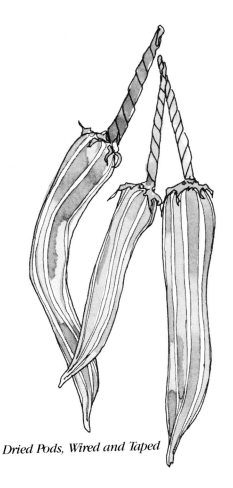

*Dried Pods, Wired and Taped*

# Pomanders

## MATERIALS

**Firm, unblemished, and ripe apples, quinces, oranges, or lemons**
**Ice or nut pick, knitting needle, or other pointed object**
**Whole cloves (about ½ ounce)**
**Bowl**
**Any or all of the following ground ingredients: cinnamon, allspice, nutmeg, coriander, and orris root (a fixative)**
**Ribbon, yarn, or netting (optional)**

1. Make a hole in the fruit with the ice pick or other pointed object.
2. Insert a clove in the hole, stem end in and round end out, so that the length of the stem is inside the fruit and the round head rests on the surface. If the hole you've made is too big, make the succeeding holes smaller.
3. Spacing the holes ⅛ to ¼ inch apart, cover the entire surface with the cloves.
4. In a bowl, mix together the spices you have chosen to use. Roll the clove-studded fruit in the mixture until completely covered.
5. Allow the pomander to dry at room temperature for several weeks. The pomander will shrink and harden as it dries. The process may be speeded up by placing the pomander in a gas oven with a pilot light, or in any oven set on low.
6. To hang in a closet, tie the pomander with ribbon or yarn; or, wrap in a square of netting and secure with ribbon or yarn.

From the French *pomme d'ambre,* meaning "apple or ambergris," pomanders originally were small pieces of ambergris (a strongly scented fixative from the sperm whale). These pieces were enclosed in elaborate cases and worn about the neck as a protection against illness and unpleasant odors. Later, they evolved into perforated china balls filled with a potpourri mixture, as well as the homemade pomanders of clove-studded fruit.

It is this last version of the pomander that has now become associated with the Christmas holidays, either for gift-giving, hanging on the Christmas tree, or mounded in a pretty bowl with greenery. Afterwards, they can be tied with ribbon, yarn, or netting, and hung in a closet where they'll keep clothes sweet-smelling and moth-free for years.

158

# Gourd Crafts

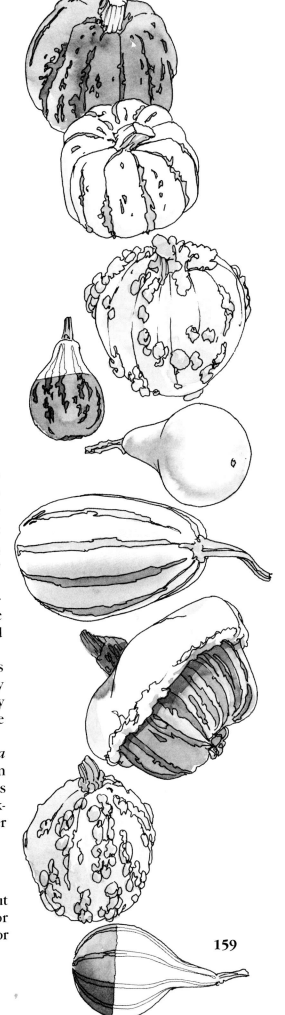

Bright colors and patterns combined with bizarre shapes make gourds among the most unusual plants in the garden. Although mature gourds are not edible, they do belong to the family Cucurbitaceae, which includes such commonly grown vegetables as squash, pumpkins, cucumbers, and many kinds of melon. In fact, some gourds can be eaten like summer squash when young and tender.

Native to tropical and subtropical regions of the world, the members of this family are frost-tender, vining plants that flourish in fertile, humus-rich soil, and grow readily in any temperate climate with about four to five months of frost-free days.

Among the oldest cultivated plants, gourds' remains have been found in Egyptian tombs dating to 2400 B.C. Hard-shelled and long-lasting, gourds have been used as dipping utensils, as containers for grain, water, and other items, and as musical instruments for centuries.

Although there are dozens of different gourds, all of the most commonly grown belong to two genera – *Cucurbita* and *Lagenaria.*

The *Cucurbita* types are the most colorful and naturally ornamental of the gourds. Surfaces may be smooth, warty, or ridged, and plain, patterned, or striped. This group includes our pumpkins and zucchini as well as gourds with such descriptive names as miniature bottle, nest egg, orange, pear, spoon, apple, bell, and crown-of-thorns. Fruit may be a single color, or multicolored in shades of yellow, orange, green, and cream.

*Cucurbita* varieties are native to the Americas and are distinguished when in bloom by their yellow flowers. The fruits are damaged by frost, and usually last only one season when used in projects.

*Lagenaria* varieties, on the other hand, are Old World natives with white flowers. Although immature fruits can be damaged by frost, the mature fruit is frost-proof. Drying to a thin, hard, extremely durable shell, these gourds last for several years. They provide the basis for much of gourd crafting and decorating.

Commonly called bottle or dipper gourds, the *Lagenaria* fruit may be smooth, ridged, or knobby, and range in size from only inches to well over 4 or 5 feet long. Shapes and names coincide: pipe, pear, globe, dish, club, dumbbell, dolphin, crookneck, powder horn, snake, swan, kettle, and, of course, dipper and bottle.

## Tips for Growing Gourds

Gourds, like squash, grow best with full sun in moist but well-drained soil, fed with a high-phosphorous fertilizer. For blemish-free fruit of uniform color, use an arbor or trellis for

**159**

*Gourd Birdhouse*

gourd vines to grow on. When the main, or central, vine is 8 to 10 feet long, remove the growing tip to stimulate side branches and more flowers that will develop into fruit.

## Harvesting Gourds

Although the *Lagenaria* gourds will withstand frost, it may be simpler to plan on harvesting all gourds just before the first frost. Use pruning shears or a sharp knife to sever the gourd with several inches of stem attached. Don't use the stem as a handle now; instead, gently lift the entire fruit from underneath.

## Curing Gourds

Right after harvest, the skin, or surface, of gourds is still very tender, so handle carefully to avoid scratches and bruises. If gourds are dirty, wash them in warm, soapy water and rinse in clean water with a household disinfectant added; dry with a soft cloth. For gourds that are not dirty, simply wipe the surface with a soft cloth dampened with rubbing alcohol.

To dry, spread the gourds out on newspapers on a rack or open shelves, or hang them individually in mesh bags in a warm, dry, well-ventilated place such as a garage, porch, or shed. Space the gourds so they don't touch. Turn the gourds daily to expose all sides to air. Change the newspapers if they become damp. During this time, throw away any gourds that begin to shrivel or develop mold or soft spots.

The drying time will vary with size and variety. Most of the *Lagenaria*, or hard-shelled, gourds will take from one to six months to cure. They will turn from pale green or yellow to beige or brown, the shell will harden, they will become lightweight, and the seeds will rattle. The *Cucurbita,* or ornamental, gourds will cure in about a month.

## Preserving Gourds

The longevity of both types of gourd can be extended by wiping the surface again with a cloth dampened with a non-bleaching household disinfectant, a solution of equal parts vinegar and water, or 2 tablespoons borax in a quart of water.

Wax gourds with a colorless paste wax, then buff to a shiny patina with a soft cloth. A hard, glossy appearance can be obtained by applying a coat of clear varnish.

## Decorating Gourds

Cured gourds are ready to be used in seasonal arrangements, decorated, and made into useful objects. Some of the ways to decorate gourds include carving with a knife or carving tools, or burning into the surface with an electric wood-burning tool. Carving exposes the pale inner surface of the gourd's skin. The carved areas may be left plain, stained with wood stain, or painted with felt-tip pens or oil or acrylic paints.

Before carving, some people prepare the surface by polishing it with a very fine grade of sandpaper or steel wool, then wiping with a soft cloth. After carving, rub with a very high grade of transparent furniture wax; renew this every few months.

Dye gourds all colors of the rainbow by immersing them in boiling water containing natural plant or commercial fabric dyes. The special dyes used for leather will give deeper colors. Gourds can also be painted with oil or acrylic paints. After dyeing or painting, apply a coat of the transparent furniture wax and buff.

## Using Gourds

The simplest and most obvious use for gourds is piling them about during the glorious fall season and holidays. Put big ones together on a porch or entrance hallway. The smaller ones look wonderful spilling out of baskets or mounded in arrangements on tables, mantels, and beside fireplaces. Combine them with chrysanthemums, autumn leaves, ivy, bittersweet, branches of sumac berries, seedpods, or polished apples and other fall fruit.

Wonderful ornaments for the Christmas holidays or year-round use are made by cutting a hole in the front or removing the top of the smaller gourds. To cut off the top, use a fine-toothed hacksaw. To cut a hole, start by tapping a depression in the side with a nail or awl, then drilling a small hole; insert a keyhole saw in this hole and cut an opening the size you want. To hang the ornament, use the nail or awl again to tap a depression, then drill a hole and attach a ribbon or cord. Fill the gourd with dried flowers, unicorn plant "birds," or teasel critters.

Round, bottle, and cylindrical gourds make ideal storage containers; just by cutting off the top with a hacksaw, you have a container and a lid. Use smaller ones for jewelry, straight pins, or coins. Larger ones can store yarn, scarves, hair ribbons, or toys.

Gourds are a natural for dried flower arrangements. Just cut off as much of the top as desired, using a hacksaw. If the gourd has a rounded bottom and isn't stable, glue it to a piece of wood.

Cut the long, narrow necks of club gourds into 1½-inch pieces for napkin rings.

Turn bottle gourds into birdhouses and birdfeeders by drilling a hole through the top for a hanging cord and cutting a hole in the side. The hole should be about 1¼ to 1½ inches in diameter for a wren or bluebird house. For a bird feeder, make the hole 3 or 4 inches across.

*Gourd Ornaments*

## MATERIALS

**Pruning shears**
**Grapevine trimmings**
**Large tub or sink of warm water**
**#22-gauge floral wire (optional)**

1. Soak the grapevines for at least 30 minutes in the warm water.
2. Make a circle with a vine, adding more pieces as necessary to get the thickness you want – about 12 times around is the average. If you have trouble making a perfect circle, wrap the vines around a bucket or other cylindrical object.
3. Tuck in the ends to secure or tie with floral wire. Decorate as desired.

## MATERIALS

**Pruning shears**
**Grapevine trimmings**
**Large tub or sink of warm water**
**Large wire tomato cage (about 3 feet tall)**
**Needle-nose pliers**

1. Soak the grapevines for at least 30 minutes in the warm water to make them pliable.
2. Turn a tomato cage upside down. With the pliers, turn under an inch or two of each of the stake wires, interlocking them so they hold together.
3. Begin wrapping a grapevine around the cage, tucking the ends under another piece in order to keep the tree from "unravelling." Use additional pieces as necessary until the tomato cage is completely covered.

# Grapevine Wreath

Whether you consider them ordinary or not, there's no denying the usefulness of grapevine wreaths. They are easy to make in a variety of sizes and are basically free. They can be a money-making project for a church or organization when sold plain or decorated.

A garden of perfectly trained grapevines is a sight to behold, and a passion of gardeners through the ages. Grapes are among the oldest of cultivated plants, having been grown by the Egyptians as long as 6,000 years ago. In many of the ancient religions, the origin of grapes is considered to be divine. They are mentioned in the Book of Genesis as well as other parts of the Bible.

Grapes must be carefully and completely pruned each year in order for the plants to bear a significant crop. This is ideally done in mid- to late winter before the sap begins to flow. Saving and using the trimmings of a plant with such an auspicious heritage would seem to be not only a logical way to ornament our homes, but also a means of insuring health, happiness, and a bountiful harvest.

# Grapevine Christmas Tree

Whether you're one of those people who has a different Christmas tree in every room of the house or the kind of person who's lucky to get a tree up at all, a grapevine Christmas tree is a clever alternative to the traditional conifer. And, of course, it's a far better option than artificial trees. Best of all, it will cost less than $2, since all you need are grapevines and a tomato cage.

Taking only about 18 inches of table or floor space, it's perfect for anyone with a limited area for living or storage. If you want to use lights, the little "twinkle" types are an ideal size; they'll look best if you push them through from inside the tree.

When gathering the grapevines, try to get vines with as many tendrils as possible because these add texture and interest. Although you obviously can use any small ornaments you want on your tree, handmade ornaments of dried flowers and other objects from the garden will make this an extra-special holiday decoration.

*Grapevine Christmas Tree*

# *Unicorn Plant Crafts*

*Unicorn Plant (Martynia) with Flowers and Fruit*

As a person who seldom throws anything away, my Christmas tree ornaments bear testimony to a lifetime of collecting. One of my favorites since childhood is a dried seedpod "bird" from a plant variously called unicorn plant, martynia, proboscis plant, devil's-claw, and ram's-horn. Then, as now, I found this pod tremendously fascinating.

As a garden plant, martynia may be used as an ornamental and as a vegetable. A heat-loving annual native to the southeastern and southwestern United States and Mexico, martynia has large, soft, hairy leaves and petunia-like flowers in shades of purple, pink, and yellow with contrasting speckles. The wide-spreading plants grow 2 to 3 feet tall.

As the flowers fade, soft, green seedpods form that are not unlike okra in appearance. These are traditionally pickled or used in soups. If they are left to ripen on the plant, the outer skin falls off and the curving seedpods become extremely hard, with bristles on one side, a long, arching, double-pronged "tail" or "horns," and a stem forming a "beak."

Let the pods dry on the plants or gather before frost and put in a warm, dark, dry, well-ventilated place. Use the pods as "birds" in arrangements, on wreaths and swags, as ornaments, or for mobiles. Glue in place, attach a thin cord for a hanger, or make a stem by wiring and taping the "beak." (See Dried Flower Materials and Methods, page 1.) Martynia pods can be left in their natural brown, bleached by soaking until the desired color is reached in a solution of 1 quart water and 1 tablespoon bleach, or painted.

To grow martynia, sow the seed directly into the garden, or start seedlings indoors and transplant them into the garden after all danger of frost is past. There are both "regular" and "giant" varieties (see Sources, page 169).

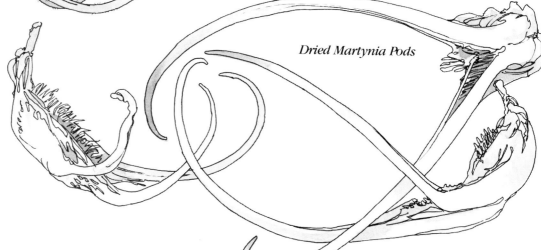

*Dried Martynia Pods*

# Appendix 1
# *Tying the Perfect Bow*

Often, the finishing touch to a wreath or other craft project is a lavish ribbon. Craft and florist shops will usually make these bows for you for a fee, but it is easy to learn to make them yourself. The same craft and florist shops usually sell ribbon by the yard, so you have gingham, satin, plaid, print, and many other choices at your disposal.

## MATERIALS

**2½ yards of ribbon**
**Chenille stem in a matching color**
**1 yard of the same ribbon for streamers (optional)**
**Scissors**

1. Holding the ribbon between your thumb and forefinger, have the right side of the ribbon facing you, with the end extending several inches above and beyond your fingers. Gather the ribbon tightly between your thumb and forefinger, as you would gather any fabric by hand.

2. Keeping the right side of the ribbon on the outside and making all loops the same size, form the first lower loop. As the ribbon is brought under your thumb again, hold it against the first gathering and make a second gathering.

3. Next, for the first upper loop, bring the ribbon under your thumb again and continue to gather it as you make the loop. Make three upper and lower loops, keeping each firmly gathered between your thumb and forefinger.

4. Giving the ribbon a twist to keep the right side out, form a loop over your thumb the same size as the previous loops and gather as before. Repeat two more times.

5. Run a chenille stem through all the loops made over the thumb. Pull the ends of the stem around to the back of the bow, twisting tightly.

6. If desired, fold an extra piece of ribbon (optional 1 yard) in half and attach it to the back of the bow by twisting the chenille stem around it.

7. Pull at the loops to spread them out and open them up so the bow takes on an attractive appearance.

8. Trim ends at an angle with scissors.

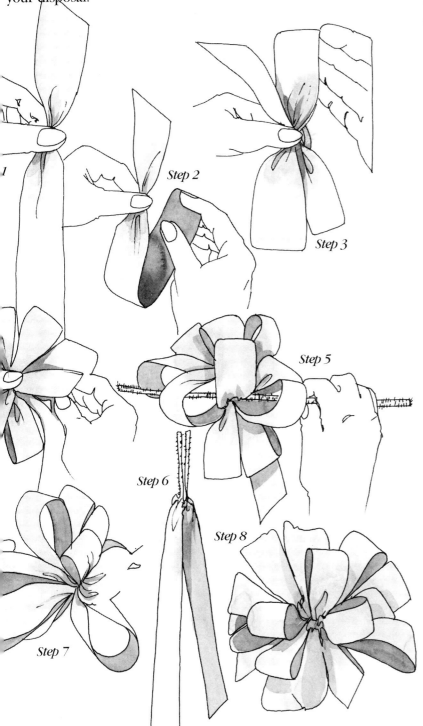

1

Step 2

Step 3

Step 5

Step 6

Step 8

Step 7

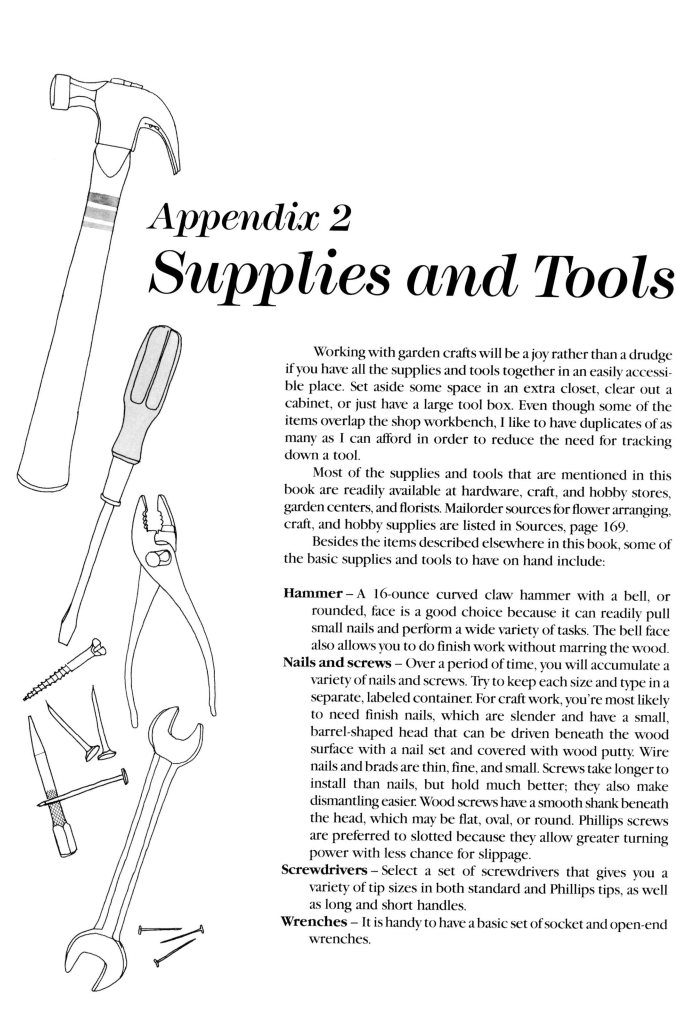

# Appendix 2
# Supplies and Tools

Working with garden crafts will be a joy rather than a drudge if you have all the supplies and tools together in an easily accessible place. Set aside some space in an extra closet, clear out a cabinet, or just have a large tool box. Even though some of the items overlap the shop workbench, I like to have duplicates of as many as I can afford in order to reduce the need for tracking down a tool.

Most of the supplies and tools that are mentioned in this book are readily available at hardware, craft, and hobby stores, garden centers, and florists. Mailorder sources for flower arranging, craft, and hobby supplies are listed in Sources, page 169.

Besides the items described elsewhere in this book, some of the basic supplies and tools to have on hand include:

**Hammer** – A 16-ounce curved claw hammer with a bell, or rounded, face is a good choice because it can readily pull small nails and perform a wide variety of tasks. The bell face also allows you to do finish work without marring the wood.

**Nails and screws** – Over a period of time, you will accumulate a variety of nails and screws. Try to keep each size and type in a separate, labeled container. For craft work, you're most likely to need finish nails, which are slender and have a small, barrel-shaped head that can be driven beneath the wood surface with a nail set and covered with wood putty. Wire nails and brads are thin, fine, and small. Screws take longer to install than nails, but hold much better; they also make dismantling easier. Wood screws have a smooth shank beneath the head, which may be flat, oval, or round. Phillips screws are preferred to slotted because they allow greater turning power with less chance for slippage.

**Screwdrivers** – Select a set of screwdrivers that gives you a variety of tip sizes in both standard and Phillips tips, as well as long and short handles.

**Wrenches** – It is handy to have a basic set of socket and open-end wrenches.

**Pliers** – An assortment of pliers is wonderfully advantageous for all sorts of expected and unexpected uses. You should have at least one pair each of slip-joint, needle-nose, channel-lock, and locking pliers.

**Wire cutters** – Also known as side cutters, these resemble pliers but have two sharp edges that readily cut wire. Some pliers also serve as wire cutters; to save money, you might consider getting this type of pliers.

**Rasps and chisels** – There are thousands of kinds of files, rasps, chisels, and gouges, but a simple solution is to buy a four-in-hand rasp and a 1-inch butt chisel.

**Nail set** – This spikelike object is used in conjunction with a hammer to drive a finishing nail below the surface of the wood. These come in various sizes; most craft work will require one with a fairly fine point.

**Power drill** – This is one of the most versatile and indispensable of tools. A ⅜-inch drill with reverse gears, variable speed, and a set of twist bits is a good choice.

**Hacksaw** – A very useful tool, the hacksaw has interchangeable blades of various degrees of coarseness for a variety of woods as well as various metals.

**Coping saw** – This saw has very thin interchangeable blades and is designed for cutting circles and patterns with tight curves.

**Bow saw** – A versatile saw that will do everything from pruning trees to sawing boards.

**Adhesives** – A hot glue gun (preferably one with a trigger-feed and clear glue sticks) opens up amazing vistas in craft work. Just be careful not to burn your fingers. Besides a hot glue gun, you will want to have white household or craft glue, a clear household cement, and rubber cement. If you plan to work with heavy pods and cones, select a brown, asphalt-free linoleum paste.

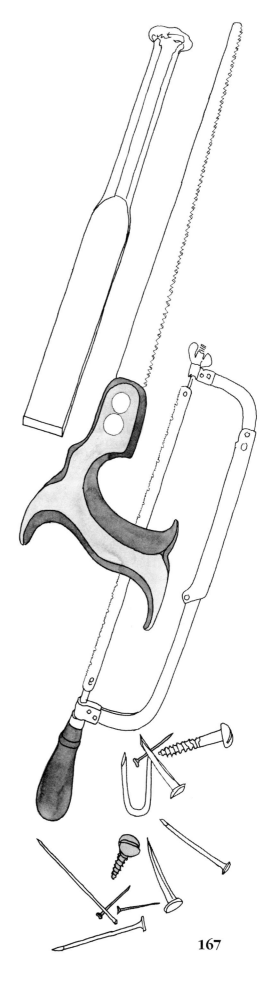

167

# Appendix 3
# Apple Doll Dress Pattern

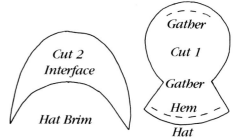

*Cut 2*
*Interface*

*Hat Brim*

*Gather*

*Cut 1*

*Gather*

*Hem*

*Hat*

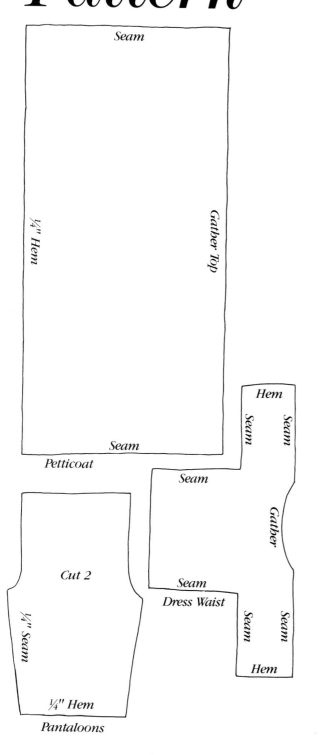

*Seam*

*¼" Hem*

*Gather Top*

*Seam*

*Petticoat*

*Hem*

*Seam*

*Seam*

*Seam*

*Gather*

*Seam*

*Seam*

*Dress Waist*

*Seam*

*Hem*

*Cut 2*

*¼" Seam*

*¼" Hem*

*Pantaloons*

*Seam*

*Turn Under ¼" For Hem*

*⅜" Gather For Top Of Skirt*

*Seam*

*Dress Skirt*

# Appendix 4
# Sources

I've found almost all of the supplies and materials mentioned in this book locally in craft, art, or hobby stores, discount department stores, hardware stores, or garden centers. If you do not have these available, or have difficulty finding a particular item, contact the appropriate supplier from the following list.

## Craft Supplies for Flower Arranging, Dried and Pressed Flowers, and Potpourri

Attar
Playground Road
New Ipswich, NH 03071
Catalog 25¢
Dried herbs, spices, oils, and
    potpourri supplies

Dorothy Biddle Service
U.S. Route 6
Greeley, PA 18425-9799
Wide selection of supplies and
    tools for fresh and dried
    flower arranging; books

Caswell-Massey
111 8th Avenue
New York, NY 10011
(212) 620-0900
Potpourri, oils, cosmetics,
    and toiletries

Cottage Gardens
9120 Blowing Tree Rd.
Louisville, KY 40220
(502) 491-6305
Dried flowers and herbs, many
    unusual colors; decorated
    wreaths, baskets, and
    arrangements

The Herb Greenhouse
Box 22061
Louisville, KY 40222
(502) 893-5198
Dried herbs, potpourri and
    supplies, oils, books,
    seasonings, seeds, and plants

The Keth Company
Box 645
Corona del Mar, CA 92625
Floral foam, pinholders,
    containers, candlestick
    cups, shears, pebbles, raffia,
    floral wire, tape, clay, pins,
    silica gel, and books

Roberta Moffitt
Box 3597
Wilmington, DE 19807
Silica gel, floral foam, tape,
    wire, pins and clay, dried
    flowers and leaves, books,
    preservative spray, candle
    adapter, and butterflies

Nature's Florist Supplies
Route 4, Nesco
Hammonton, NJ 08037
(609) 561-4678
Dried wild plants, cones, pods,
    cattails, grasses, grains, and
    flowers

On the Wind
Rte. 1, Box 188E
Mountain View, MO 65548
(417) 469-2616
Dried flowers, herbs, and
    garlic braids; decorated
    wreaths, baskets, and garlic
    braids

Penn Herb Company
603 North Second Street
Philadelphia, PA 19123
(215) 925-3336
Dried herbs and spices,
    extracts, oils, incense, gums,
    waxes, books, toiletries, and
    vitamins

Tom Thumb Workshops
Box 332
Chincoteague, VA 23336
(804) 824-3507
Dried flowers, herbs, spices,
    pods, cones, oils, fixatives,
    potpourri, books, silica gel,
    wreath forms, moss, and
    floral wire

Lee Wards Creative Crafts
1200 St. Charles Street
Elgin, IL 60120
Wide selection of craft
    supplies

Curtis Woodard
4150 Boulevard Place
Mercer Island, WA 98040
Dried materials, cones, exotic
   pods, grains, and fillers from
   United States, Africa, and
   Australia

# Sources of Plants and Seeds

### 'Cecile Brunner' Rose Plants
The Antique Rose Emporium
Route 5, Box 143
Brenham, TX 77833
(409) 836-9051
Catalog $2

Heritage Rose Gardens
16831 Mitchell Creek Drive
Fort Bragg, CA 95437
(707) 984-6959
Catalog $1

Keener Classics
205 East Edgewood
Friendswood, TX 77546
(713) 482-7400

Rose Acres
6641 Crystal Boulevard
Diamond Springs, CA 95619
(916) 626-1722
Business-size SASE

Thomasville Nurseries
1842 Smith Avenue, Box 7
Thomasville, GA 31792
(912) 226-5568

Wayside Gardens
Hodges, SC 29695-0001
(803) 374-3387
Catalog $1

### 'Bonica' Rose Plants
Donovan's Roses
P.O. Box 37800
Shreveport, LA 71133-7800
Business-size SASE

Roses by Fred Edmunds
6235 Southwest Kahle Road
Wilsonville, OR 97070
(503) 638-4671

Ferbert Garden Center
806 South Belt Highway
St. Joseph, MO 64507
(816) 279-7434

J. W. Jung Seed Company
335 South High Street
Randolph, WI 53957-0001
(414) 326-3121

Thomasville Nurseries
1842 Smith Avenue, Box 7
Thomasville, GA 31792-0007
(912) 226-5568

Wayside Gardens
Hodges, SC 29695
(803) 374-3387
Catalog $1

### Hot Pepper Seeds
Alston Seed Growers
Littleton, NC 27850

Horticultural Enterprises
Box 810082
Dallas, TX 75381-0082

The Pepper Gal
10536 119th Avenue North
Largo, FL 33543

Peter Pepper Seeds
Box 415
Knoxville, TN 37901
(615) 524-5965

Plants of the Southwest
1812 Second Street
Santa Fe, NM 87501
(505) 983-1548

Santa Barbara Seeds
Box 6520
Santa Barbara, CA 93160-6520
(805) 967-9679
Business-size SASE

Winders
Box 396
Midlothian, TX 76065

### Martynia (Unicorn Plant) Seeds
George W. Park Seed Company
Highway 254 North, Box 31
Greenwood, SC 29647
(803) 374-3741

Plants of the Southwest
1812 Second Street
Santa Fe, NM 87501
(505) 983-1548

### Red-Shucked Corn Seeds
Gurney Seed and Nursery
   Company
Yankton, SD 57079
(605) 665-4451

Johnny's Selected Seeds
Foss Hill Road, Box 2580
Albion, ME 04910
(207) 437-9294

### Gourds
American Gourd Society
John Stevens
Box 274
Mt. Gilead, OH 43338-0274
Dues $3/year

### Ornamental Grass Plants and Seeds
Kurt Bluemel, Inc.
2740 Greene Lane
Baldwin, MD 21013
(301) 557-7229
Catalog $1

Carroll Gardens
444 East Main Street, Box 310
Westminster, MD 21157
(301) 848-5422
Catalog $2

Garden Place
Box 388
Mentor, OH 44061-0388
(216) 255-3705
Catalog $1

Andre Viette Farm and Nursery
Route 1, Box 16
Fishersville, VA 22939
(703) 943-2315
Catalog $1.50

Wayside Gardens
Hodges, SC 29695
(803) 374-3387
Catalog $1

## Herb Plants and Seeds
Berkshire Garden Center
Routes 102 and 183
Stockbridge, MA 01262
(413) 298-3926

Capriland's Herb Farm
Silver Street
North Coventry, CT 06238
(203) 742-7244

The Country Garden
Route 2, Box 455A
Crivitz, WI 54114
(715) 757-2045
Catalog $2

Heirloom Gardens
Box 138
Guerneville, CA 95446

The Herb Cottage
Washington Cathedral
Mount Saint Alban
Washington, DC 20016
(202) 537-8982

Logee's Greenhouses
55 North Street
Danielson, CT 06239
(203) 774-8038

Merry Gardens
Camden, ME 04843
(207) 236-9064

Sandy Mush Herb Nursery
Route 2, Surrett Cove Road
Leicester, NC 28748
(704) 683-2014

Shady Hill Garden
821 Walnut Street
Batavia, IL 60510
(312) 879-5665

Taylor's Garden
1535 Lone Oak Road
Vista, CA 92083
(619) 727-3485

Well-Sweep Herb Farm
317 Mount Bethel Road
Port Murray, NJ 07865
(201) 852-5390

## Perennial Plants
Blackthorne Gardens
48 Quincy Street
Holbrook, MA 02343-1898
(617) 767-0308

Kurt Bluemel, Inc.
2740 Greene Lane
Baldwin, MD 21013
(301) 557-7229
Catalog $1

Bluestone Perennials
7211 Middle Ridge Road
Madison, OH 44057
(216) 428-7535

Carroll Gardens
444 East Main Street, Box 310
Westminster, MD 21157
(301) 848-5422
Catalog $2

Holbrook Farms and Nursery
Route 2, Box 223
Fletcher, NC 28732
(704) 981-7790

Inter-State Nurseries
Box 208
Hamburg, IA 51644
1-800-325-4180

Rockknoll Nursery
9210 U.S. 50
Hillsboro, OH 45133
(513) 393-1278
Catalog for 2 first-class stamps

Andre Viette Farm and Nursery
State Route 608
Route 1, Box 16
Fisherville, VA 22939
(703) 943-2315
Catalog $1.50

Wayside Gardens
Hodges, SC 29695
(803) 374-3387
Catalog $1

White Flower Farm
Route 63
Litchfield, CT 06759-0050
(203) 567-0801
Catalog $5

## Everlasting Flower Seeds
W. Atlee Burpee Company
300 Park Avenue
Warminster, PA 18974
(215) 674-4915

The Country Garden
Route 2, Box 455A
Crivitz, WI 54114
(715) 757-2045
Catalog $2

Johnny's Selected Seeds
Foss Hill Road, Box 2580
Albion, ME 04910
(207) 437-9294

Nichols Garden Nursery
1190 North Pacific Highway
Albany, OR 97321
(503) 928-9280

George W. Park Seed Company
Highway 254 North, Box 31
Greenwood, SC 29647
(803) 374-3741

# Bibliography

There are many excellent books that expand more fully on gardening as well as the various cra[...] included in this book. If your imagination has been kindled, and you would like to learn more, t[...] following books may be of interest to you. This list is not meant to be comprehensive, rather they a[...] books that I have found useful. Check your local book and craft stores as well as garden centers for the[...] and other books.

**Basketmaking**

Cary, Mara. *Basic Baskets*. Boston: Houghton Mifflin, 1975.

Hart, Carol and Dan. *Natural Baskets*. New York: Watson-Guptill Publications, 1976.

Meilach, Dona Z., and Menagh, Dee. *Basketry Today with Materials from Nature*. New York: Crown Publishers, 1979.

Porter, Liz, and Fons, Marianne. *Classic Basket Patterns*. Westminster, Calif.: Yours Truly, 1984.

**Birds**

Harrison, George H. *The Backyard Bird Watcher*. New York: Simon and Schuster, 1979.

Proctor, Dr. Noble. *Garden Birds*. Emmaus, Pa.: Rodale Press, 1985.

Robbins, Chandler S.; Bruun, Bertel; and Zim, Herbert S. *Birds of North America*. Rev. ed. New York: Golden Press, 1983.

**Dried and Pressed Flowers**

Bauzen, Peter and Susanne. *Flower Pressing*. New York: Sterling Publishing Company, 1972.

Black, Penny. *The Book of Pressed Flowers*. New York: Simon and Schuster, 1988.

Hillier, Malcolm, and Hilton, Colin. *The Book of Dried Flowers*. New York: Simon and Schuster, 1986.

Laking, Barbara, Guest Editor. *Dried Flower Designs*. Brooklyn, N.Y.: Brooklyn Botanic Garden, 1974.

Moffitt, Roberta. *The Step-by-Step Book of Dried Bouquets*. Wilmington, Del.: Roberta Moffitt Designs, 1981.

————. *The Step-by-Step Book of Preserved Flowers*. Wilmington, Del.: Roberta Moffitt Designs, 1982.

Scott, Margaret Kennedy, and Beazley, Mary. *Making Pressed Flower Pictures*. New York: Dover Publications, 1982.

Thorpe, Patricia. *Everlastings – The Complete Book of Dried Flowers*. New York: Facts on File Publications, 1985.

Wiita, Betty Smith. *Dried Flowers for All Seasons*. New York: Van Nostrand Reinhold Company, 1982.

## Flower Arranging
Ascher, Amalie Adler. *The Complete Flower Arranger*. New York: Simon and Schuster, 1976.

Dale, John, and Gunnell, Kevin. *The Flower Arranger's Handbook*. New York: E. P. Dutton, 1986.

Horton, Alvin. *Arranging Cut Flowers*. San Francisco: Ortho Books, 1985.

Nehrling, Arno and Irene. *Gardening for Flower Arrangement*. New York: Dover Publications, 1976.

## Flowers (Annuals, Perennials, Bulbs) and Grasses
Cox, Jeff and Marilyn. *The Perennial Garden*. Emmaus, Pa.: Rodale Press, 1985.

Fell, Derek. *Annuals – How to Select, Grow, and Enjoy*. Tucson, Ariz.: HP Books, 1983.

Harper, Pamela, and McGourty, Frederick. *Perennials – How to Select, Grow, and Enjoy*. Tucson, Ariz.: HP Books, 1985.

Hebb, Robert S. *Low Maintenance Perennials*. New York: Quadrangle/The New York Times Book Company, 1975.

Hudak, Joseph. *Gardening with Perennials Month by Month*. New York: Quadrangle/The New York Times Book Company, 1976.

Meyer, Mary Hockenberry. *Ornamental Grasses*. New York: Charles Scribner's Sons, 1975.

Scheider, Alfred F. *Park's Success with Bulbs*. Greenwood, S.C.: Geo. W. Park Seed Company, 1981.

Scott, George Harmon. *Bulbs – How to Select, Grow, and Enjoy*. Tucson, Ariz.: HP Books, 1982.

## Fragrant Flowers
Coon, Nelson. *Gardening for Fragrance*. New York: Hearthside Press, 1967.

Taylor, Norman. *Fragrance in the Garden*. New York: D. Van Nostrand Company, 1953.

Verey, Rosemary. *The Scented Garden*. New York: Van Nostrand Reinhold Company, 1981.

Wilder, Louise Beebe. *The Fragrant Garden*. New York: Dover Publications, 1974.

Wilson, Helen Van Pelt, and Bell, Leonie. *The Fragrant Year*. New York: Crown Publishers, 1967.

## Gourds
American Gourd Society. *Gourds, Their Culture and Craft*. Mt. Gilead, Ohio: The American Gourd Society, n.d.

Hamel, Esther, and Sparkman, M. *Creativity with Gourds*. St. Ignatius, Mont.: Ponderosa Publishers, 1977.

Heiser, Charles. *The Gourd Book*. Norman, Okla.: University of Oklahoma Press, 1979.

**Herbs**

Boxer, Arabella, and Back, Philippa. *The Herb Book*. London: Octopus Books, 1980.

Foster, Gertrude B., and Louden, Rosemary F. *Park's Success with Herbs*. Greenwood, S.C.: Geo. W. Park Seed Company, 1980.

Jacobs, Betty E. M. *Growing and Using Herbs Successfully*. Pownal, Vt.: Storey Communications, 1981.

Kowalchik, Claire, and Hylton, William H., Editors. *Rodale's Illustrated Encyclopedia of Herbs*. Emmaus, Pa.: Rodale Press, 1987.

Lathrop, Norma Jean. *Herbs – How to Select, Grow, and Enjoy*. Tucson, Ariz.: HP Books, 1981.

O'Connor, Audrey H., and Hirshfeld, Mary. *An Herb Garden Companion*. Ithaca, N.Y.: Cornell University Press, 1984.

Shaudys, Phyllis. *The Pleasure of Herbs*. Pownal, Vt.: Storey Communications, 1986.

Simmons, Adelma Grenier. *Herb Gardens of Delight*. New York: E. P. Dutton, 1979.

————. *Herbs through the Seasons at Caprilands*. Emmaus, Pa.: Rodale Press, 1987.

Swanson, Faith, and Rady, Virginia. *Herb Garden Design*. Hanover, N.H.: University of New Hampshire Press, 1984.

Vanderhoff, Barbara. *An Atlanta Herb Sampler*. Powder Springs, Ga.: The Chattahoochee Unit of the Herb Society of America, 1985.

**The Meaning of Flowers**

Greenaway, Kate. *Kate Greenaway's Language of Flowers*. New York: Gramercy Publishing Company, 1978 reprint of 1884 edition.

Powell, Claire. *The Meaning of Flowers*. Boulder, Colo.: Shambhala Publications, 1979.

**Soap**

Bramson, Ann. *Soap – Making It, Enjoying It*. New York: Workman Publishing Company, 1975.

**Trees, Shrubs, and Vines**

Cox, Jeff and Marilyn. *Flowers for All Seasons – A Guide to Colorful Trees, Shrubs and Vines*. Emmaus, Pa.: Rodale Press, 1988.

Davis, Brian. *The Gardener's Illustrated Encyclopedia of Trees and Shrubs*. Emmaus, Pa.: Rodale Press, 1987.

Wolf, Rex, and McNair, James. *All About Roses*. San Francisco: Ortho Books, 1983.

Wyman, Donald. *Wyman's Gardening Encyclopedia*. New York: Macmillan Company, 1985.

## Vegetables and Fruits

Andrews, Jean. *Peppers – The Domesticated Capsicums*. Austin, Tex.: The University of Texas Press, 1984.

Cox, Jeff, and the Editors of *Rodale's Organic Gardening* Magazine. *How to Grow Vegetables Organically*. Emmaus, Pa.: Rodale Press, 1988.

Fell, Derek. *Vegetables – How to Select, Grow, and Enjoy*. Tucson, Ariz.: HP Books, 1982.

Gilroy Garlic Festival Association. *The Garlic Lovers' Cookbook, Volumes 1 and 2*. Berkeley, Calif.: Celestial Arts, 1982 and 1985.

Halpin, Ann, Editor. *The Organic Gardener's Complete Guide to Vegetables and Fruits*. Emmaus, Pa.: Rodale Press, 1982.

Harris, Lloyd J. *The Book of Garlic*. Berkeley, Calif.: Aris Book, Harris Publishing Company, 1979.

———. *The Official Garlic Lover's Handbook*. Berkeley, Calif.: Aris Books, Harris Publishing Company, 1986.

Hill, Lewis. *Fruits and Berries for the Home Garden*. New York: Alfred A. Knopf, 1977.

Owen, Millie, Editor. *Lois Burpee's Gardener's Companion and Cookbook*. New York: Harper & Row, Publishers, 1983.

## Wildflowers

Art, Henry W. *The Wildflower Gardener's Guide*. Pownal, Vt.: Storey Communications, 1987.

Bruce, Hal. *How to Grow Wildflowers & Wild Shrubs & Trees in Your Own Garden*. New York: Van Nostrand Reinhold Company, 1982.

Comstock, Anna Botsford. *Handbook of Nature Study*. Ithaca, N.Y.: Cornell University Press, 1939.

Michael, Pamela. *All Good Things Around Us*. New York: Holt, Rinehart and Winston, 1980.

Stokes, Donald and Lillian. *A Guide to Enjoying Wildflowers*. Boston: Little, Brown and Company, 1985.

# Index

Page numbers in italics indicate photos; page numbers in boldface indicate illustrations.

**A** *Achillea* wreaths, 52-53
Aftershave lotion, 101, 102
Aging jar, 84
Air-drying method, 2-3
Air fresheners, 95
Allspice potpourris, 89
Apple(s)
    dolls, 153-54
        dress pattern for, 168
    in wreaths and wall hangings, *37*, 155-56
Aromatic rubbing lotions, 103
Aromatic water, 100
Arrowroot, 106
Artemisia
    Christmas tree, *42*, **43**
    dried flower wreath, *36*
    in moth bags, 96
Astringents, 101-2

**B** Bacon balls, 113
Balance, 9
Basket(s)
    with dried flowers and herbs, *33*
    with dried flowers and vegetables, *40*
    fireside, 131
    folklore of, 129
    herb-woven, 61-62
    potpourri-covered, 86
    round market, 129-30
    towel holder, 133-34
    trimmed with dried flowers and herbs, 24, *28-29*
Basketweaving, 129-31
Bath bags, 111
Bath salts, 111
Beauty products, plants used in, 97-99
Beauty-spa bath, 111

Beauty vinegars, 103
Bells-of-Ireland wreath, *49*
Bergamot, 97
Bird cakes, 113, 114
Bird feeders, 161
Birdhouse, gourd, 160-61
Birds, 113-14
    unicorn plant, 148, 164
Bird treat cup, 113
Bittersweet, 16
Body powders, 106
'Bonica' rose, 58
Bookends, pressed flower, 79
Bookmark, pressed flower, 72
Borage, 97
Bottles, decorative, *38, 39*
Bouquets, 20, *26, 35*
Bows, 165
Burdock, 109

**C** Calendula, 97, 109
Candle holder, cone-and-nut, 122
Candlemaking equipment, 93
Candles
    scented, 93-94
    trimmed with pressed flowers, 76
Castile soap, 107
Catnip
    in hair care, 109
    mice, 91
'Cecile Brunner' rose, 58
Cedarwood shavings, 96
Chamomile, 97, 109
Chervil, 98
Christmas corsage, 118
Christmas ornaments. *See also* Holiday ornaments
    dried apple, 155-56
    evergreen, 115-16

gourd, 148, 161
    pinecone, 119
    potpourri-filled, 87
    pressed flower, 74, 78
    pressed flower eggshell, 80
Christmas tree
    for birds, 113-14
    dried artemisia, 42, *43*
    dried flower- and herb-trimmed,
        *30*
    grapevine, 162-63
Cinnamon potpourris, 89
Classic toilet water, 102
Cleansing herbs, 95
Cleansing products
    for face, 108
    for hair, 109-10
    such as soaps, 107
Clocks, pressed flower, 79
Clove hitch, 143
Clove pink, 98
Coasters, pressed flower, 79
Cockscomb wreath, 49
Cologne, 102
Color, in flower arrangements, 10
Colored-fire pinecones, 122
Comfrey, 98, 109
Cone-and-nut candle holder, 122
Cookie-cutter vine wreaths, 132
Corn, 135
    craft items from, 138-41
    dolly, 142, 146
    ornamental displays of, 141
    starburst, Indian, 141
    wreaths, *32*
Cornshuck
    doll, *28-29,* 136-37
    materials and methods for, 135-36
    seat, 140
    wreaths, 138-39
Cornstarch powder, 106
Corsage, Christmas, 118
Cosmetics, herb and flower, 104
Costmary, 98

Crafts
    from corn and wheat, 135-47
    from dried flowers, herbs, grasses
        artemisia Christmas tree,
            42-43
        basket trimming, 24
        dried flower and herb
            swags, 55
        dried flower lapel pin, 46
        dried flower standard, 44-45
        dried flowers under glass,
            59-60
        dried grass arrangements, 64
        flower and herb arrange-
            ments, 18-19
        flower arrangements, 12-17
        hat trimmings, 22
        herb-woven basket, 61-62
        lamp shade, 23
        lavender sticks, 56-57
        materials and methods of, 1-12
        nosegays, 20-21, 63
        rosebud-covered ornament,
            58
        silver spoon wall hanging, 41
        wreaths, 47-54, 58, 66-67
    from fruit and vegetables, 148-64
    from the landscape, 112-34
    potpourri, 81-96
    from pressed flowers, 68-80
Creams, facial, 108
Crescent flower arrangement, 14
Crimson leaf wreaths, 78

D  Dandelion, 98
    Dandruff control, 98, 109
    *Deck the Halls with Artemisia,* 74
    Decoctions, 100
    Decorations. *See* Christmas
        ornaments; Ornaments; Wall
        hangings
    Desiccant drying method, 4-6

Dolls
  cornshuck, 136-37
  dress pattern for, 168
  dried apple, 153-54
Dried apple wreath, *37,* 155-56
Dried artemisia Christmas tree, 42, *43*
Dried flower and herb arrangement,
  18-19
Dried flower and herb swag, 55
Dried flower arrangements, 7. *See
  also* Flower arrangements; *specific
  types of*
  containers for, 8, 18, 41
  equipment for, 8
  mechanics of, 8-9
  samples of, 12-19
  shape of, 10, 18
  styling principles of, 9-10
Dried flower lapel pins, *27, 46*
Dried flower standard, 44-45
Dried flower(s). *See also* Dried flower
  arrangements
  bouquets, 20, *26, 35*
  crafts from, 1-67
  miniature nosegays, 63
  storage of, 3, 6
  supply sources for, 169-70
  under glass, 59-60
*Dried Flowers for All Seasons,* 49
Dried grass arrangements, 64. *See also*
  Grasses
Dried okra, 157
Drying racks, **11**
Dry potpourri. *See* Potpourri(s), dry

E Egg ornaments, pressed flower, 80
Elder, 98, 109
Embroidery hoop hanging, potpourri-
  filled, 87
English cologne, 102
English lavender, 56
*Erianthus ravennae,* 64
Essential oils, 82, 104

Eulalia grass
  variants of, 66
  wreath, 66-67
Evergreen
  ball, 115
  garland, 116
  wreath, 115
Everlastings
  drying of, 3
  microwave drying of, 7
  in wreath, 49-50
Extractions, 101-2

F Facial moisturizers, 108
Fennel, 21
Ferns, pressed, 69
Feverfew, 98
Fireside basket, 131
Fire starters, 121
Fixatives, 82
Floral clay, 8
Floral dictionaries, 20
Floral foam, 9, 13, 14
Floral tape, 9
Floral wire, 9
Flower-and-herb incense pastilles, 95
Flower arrangements. *See also* Dried
  flower arrangements; Flower(s)
  beauty of, 10
  containers for, 12, 13, 14, 15
  supply sources for, 169-70
Flower-arranging devices, 8-9
Flower(s). *See also* Dried flowers;
  Pressed flowers
  in aromatic water, 100
  in beauty products, 97
  in body powder, 106
  collection of, 1
  drying methods for, 1
    air drying, 2-3
    desiccant drying, 4-6
    microwave drying, 7
  drying racks for, **11**
  egg cream, 108

meanings of, 21
pressing of
    materials for, 68-69
    methods of, 69
    varieties for, 68-69
styling principles of, 9-10
Flower-trimmed hat, 22, *28-29, 33*
Foliage. *See also* Leaves; Plants
gathering of, 1
glycerinized, 126-27
imprints, 123
skeletonized, 124-25
spiky, 13
Fragrances, 81. *See also* Potpourris
essential oil, 104
plants used for, 97-99
in rubbing lotions, 103
in vinegars, 103
Fragrant oils, 82, 104
Fruit(s), 148. *See also* Apple(s);
  Grapevine(s)
crafts made from, 153-63
and nut cups, 113
Garlands
for birds, 113
evergreen, 116
pressed flower and leaf, 78
Garlic
braids, 148, 151
  and herbs, *34*
for dandruff control, 98, 109
Geranium, scented, 98
Glass-domed dried flowers, 59-60
Glass hanging, pressed flower, 74-75
Glycerine, 101
hand-care products, 105
soaps, 107
Glycerinized leaves, 7, 126-27
Gourd(s), 148
birdhouse, 160-61
crafts using, 161
curing of, 160
decoration of, 160-61
growing tips for, 159-60

harvesting of, 160
preservation of, 160
Grapevine
Christmas tree, 162-63
wreaths, 78, 162
Grasses
annual, 64-65
with decorative flowers, 64, 65
dried, 64
perennial, 64-65
in swags, 55
varieties for pressing, 68-69
in wreath, 66-67
Gravel, 9
Greenaway, Kate, 20
Greens, for holiday decorations, 115-16
Greeting card, potpourri-filled, 89
Gum resins, 82

**H** Hairbrush/mirror sets, pressed flower,
  79
Hair-care products, 109-10
Hair rinses, 109-10
Hand-care products, 105
Hand cream, 105
Hand jelly, 105
Hand lotion, 105
Hand rinse, 105
Hanging ornaments
potpourri-filled embroidery
  hoop, 87
pressed flower, 74-75
Harvest basket, *40*
Harvest grapevine wreath, *37*
Hats, trimmed with dried flowers and
  herbs, 22, *28-29, 33*
Hemlock cone corsage, 118
Henna, 109
Herb(s)
air fresheners, 95
amulets, 88
antiseptic properties of, 95
in aromatic water, 100
in beauty products, 97

Herb(s) *(continued)*
   egg cream, 108
   meanings of, 21
   moth-repellent, 90, 96
   in nosegays, 20
   pressing, 68-69
   scent of, 61
   and spice body powder, 106
   wreaths, 51
Herb-woven basket, 61-62
Hills-of-snow hydrangea, 54
Hogarth flower arrangement, 16
Holiday greens, 115-16
Holiday ornaments, *31. See also*
   Christmas ornaments
     trimmed with dried flowers and
      herbs, *30*
Honeysuckle, 78
   vine wreaths, 132
Hops potpourri, 88
Horizontal flower arrangement, 14
Horsetail, 98, 109
Hydrangea wreath, 54
Hyssop, 98

**I** Imprints, leaf, 123
Incense, 95
Indian corn starburst, miniature, 141
Infusions, 100

**J** Jars, decorative, *38, 39*
Jewelry
   potpourri-filled, 88
   pressed flower, 79
Jewelry boxes, pressed flower, 79

**K** Knife, long-bladed, 8

**L** Lady's mantle, 98
*Lagenaria,* 159, 160
Lamp, seed jar, 150
Lamp shades, trimmed with dried
   flowers and herbs, 23
Landscaping, 112

*Language of Flowers,* 20
Lapel pins, dried flower, *27, 46*
*Lavandula angustifolia,* 56
Lavender
   sachets, 88
   in skin products, 98
   sticks, 56-57
Leaves
   glycerinized, 126-27
   imprints, 123
   printing, 124-25
   skeletonized, 128
   varieties for pressing, 69
Lemon balm, 88, 98
Lemon verbena, 98
   in potpourris, 89
Linden, 98, 109
Looped cornshuck wreaths, 138
L-shaped arrangement, 13
Lye-based soaps, 107

**M** Maiden grass, 64
Marjoram, 99, 109
Marsh mallow, 99
Martynia pods, dried, 164
Mechanics of flower arranging,
   8-9, 14, 15
Mice, catnip, 91
Microwave drying method, 7
Mint, in skin products, 99
*Miscanthus sinensis,* 64, 66
Mixed flower wreath, 47-48
Moist potpourri, 85
Moisturizers, 108
Mordiford wheat weaving, *34,* 146-47
Moth bags, 96
Mullein, 99, 109

**N** Napkin holders, pressed flower, 79
Nasturtium, 109
*Nepeta cataria,* 91
Nettle, 99, 109
Nosegays, 20
   meanings of, 21
   miniature dried flower, 63

Notecards, pressed flower, 72
Nutmeg potpourris, 89

Oak moss, 82
Oil(s)
 essential, 82, 104
 hair conditioners, 109
 in soaps, 107
Okra crafts, 157
Onions, in hair care, 109
Ornamental grasses
 with decorative flowers, 65
 perennials and annuals, 64-65
 popularity of, 64
 wreaths, 66-67
Ornaments. *See also* Christmas
 ornaments; Hanging ornaments
 eggshell, 80
 pinecone, 113, 114, 119
 pressed flower and leaf, 78
 pressed flower glass, 74-75
 rosebud-covered, 58
 scented wax, 92
Orris root, 82, 88
 in body powder, 106
 in moth bags, 96

Padded hangers, potpourri, moth-
 repellent, 90, 96
Parsley, 99, 109
Peanut butter pinecone ornaments, 114
Pebbles, 9
Peegee hydrangea, 54
Pendants, pressed flower, 79
Pennyroyal, 99
Pepper strings, 148
Pepper wreath, 152
Perfumes, 97
Phantom bouquets, 128
Pictures, pressed flower, 70-71
Pillows, potpourri-filled, 88-89
Pine and lavender potpourris, 89
Pinecone(s)
 for Christmas, 119
 colored-fire, 122

 as fire starters, 121
 as ornaments, 113, 114
 wreath, *31,* 120
Pine trees, 112
Pinholders, 9
Pins, pressed flower, 79
Placemats, pressed flower, 73
Plant press, 68-69
Plants. *See also* Foliage; Grasses; Herb(s)
 beauty products from, 97, 98-99
 drying, 83
  methods for, 1-7
 gathering of, 1
 for hair care, 109
 for potpourri, 82-84
 sources for, 170-71
 storage of, 83
 varieties for pressing, 68-69
Plaques, pressed flower, 79
Plume grass, 64
Pomander(s), *25,* 148, 158
 beeswax with herbs and spices,
  92
Posey bouquet, 20
Potpourri-covered forms, 86
*Potpourri . . . Easy as One, Two, Three!,*
 82
Potpourri-filled objects, 88-89
 embroidery hoop hanging, 87
 sachet, *27*
Potpourris, *25, 28*
 body powder, 106
 in catnip mice, 91
 crafts using, 81-96
 crushing or grinding of, 88
 definition of, 81
 dry, 81, 82
  basic recipe for, 84
 equipment for making, 84
 fixatives for, 82
 materials and methods for
  making, 81-84
 moist, 81, 85
  materials for, 85

Potpourris *(continued)*
  moth-repellent, 96
  in padded hangers, 90
  in scented candles, 93, 94
  scents of, 82
  supply sources for, 169-70
Powders, body, 106
Pressed flower(s). *See also* Flower(s),
  pressing of
  bookmark, 72
  candles trimmed with, 76
  crafts using, 68-80
  decorations, *26*
  egg ornaments, 80
  glass hanging, 74-75
  and leaf Christmas decorations, 78
  pictures, *25,* 70-71
  placemats, 73
  serving tray, 77
  stationery, 72
  supply sources, 169-70
  on wooden objects, 79
Printing
  leaf, 124-25
  vegetable, 149
Pruning shears, 8

**Q** Queen Anne's lace, 78

**R** Rhubarb, 109
Rhythm, 9
Rose(s), 13
  in beauty products, 99
  dried, 58
  in potpourri, 83
  rugosa, 83
  sachets, 88
Rosebud(s)
  ornament, 58
  wreath, *27,* 58
Rosemary, 99
  in hair care, 109
  sachets, 88

Round flower arrangement, 12
Round market basket, 129-30
Rubbing lotions, 103

**S** Sachets
  moth-repellent, 96
  potpourri-filled, 88-89
Sage, 99, 109
Salad burnet, 99
Sand, 9
  in drying plants, 4
Sandalwood potpourris, 89
Saponins, 107
Sassafras leaves, 78
Scale, principle of, 9
Scented candles, 93-94
Scented wax ornaments, 92
Scissors, 8
Seat, cornshuck, 140
Seed jar lamp, 148, 150
Seed sources, 170-71
Serving tray, pressed flower, 77
Shampoo, 109
  plants used in, 97-99
Shape, of flower arrangements, 10,
  12-16, 18
Shredded cornshuck wreath, 139
Shrubs, 112
Silica gel, in drying plants, 4, 6
  with microwave, 7
Silver spoon wall hanging, 41
Skeletonized leaves, 128
Skin-care products, 101-2
  for hands, 105
  plants used in, 97-99, 105
Small herb wreaths, 51
Snowflakes, pressed flower, 78
Soaps, 107
Soapwort, 107, 109
Sources
  for craft supplies, 169-70
  for plants and seeds, 170-71
Southernwood, 99, 109

Spices
    in aftershave lotion, 102
    for potpourri, 83
Squash, 159
Standard, dried flower, 44-45
Starburst, miniature Indian corn, 141
Statice wreath, 49-50
Stationery, pressed flower, 72
Strawflower wreath, 49
Suet bags, 113-14
Supplies, 166-67
    sources for, 169-70
Swags, dried flower and herb, 55
Sweet bags, 88-89

Tables, pressed flower, 79
Talcum, 106
Thyme, 99
Toiletries, 101-2
Toilet water, 102
Tools, 166-67
Towel holder, wall basket, 133-34
Trays, pressed flower, 77
Trees, 112
Triangular flower arrangement, 12-13
Tussy-mussy, 20
    miniature, 63
Twig basket, 12

Unicorn plant birds, 148, 164
Unicorn plant crafts, 164

Valentine's Day wreath, 139
Vases, 8
    tall, 15
Vegetable(s), 148
    crafts using, 148-52, 157
    printing, 149
    soaps, 107
Vertical flower arrangements, 15
Vinegars, 103
Vines, 112, 132. *See also* Grapevine(s)

Vine wreaths, 132
Violet(s)
    in beauty products, 99
    sachets, 88

**W** Wall basket towel holder, 133-34
Wall hangings
    dried apple, 155-56
    silver spoon filled with dried
      flowers, 41
Walnuts, 109
Wastebaskets, pressed flower, 79
Waterproof floral clay, 8
Waterproof floral tape, 9
Wax ornaments, scented, 92
Welsh fan wheat weaving, 144-45
Wheat
    cleaning of, 143
    clove hitch knotting of, 143
    craft items from, 144-47
    cutting of, 142-43
    dollies, 113, 114
    materials and methods for crafts
      with, 142
    procuring of, 142-43
Wheat weaving, 142
    Mordiford, 146-47
    Welsh fan, 144-45
Wire cutters, 8
Wire netting, 8-9
Witch hazel, 109
Wooden objects, pressed-flower
    trimmed, 79
Wood-framed screens, *11*
Wreaths
    cookie-cutter vine, 132
    crimson leaf, 78
    dried apple, *37,* 155-56
    dried corn, *32*
    dried flowers, on green artemisia,
      *36*
    eulalia grass, 66-67
    evergreen, 115

Wreaths *(continued)*
    everlasting, 49-50
    grapevine, 78, 162
    harvest, *37*
    hydrangea, 54
    looped cornshuck, 138
    mixed flower, 47-48
    pepper, 152
    pinecone, *31,* 120
    potpourri, 86

    rosebud-covered, 58
    shredded cornshuck, 139
    small herb, 51
    Valentine's Day, 139
    yarrow, *37,* 52-53

**Y** Yarrow
    in beauty products, 99
    wreath, *37,* 52-53
Yule log, *31,* 117